MODERN JAPANESE
A Basic Reader

HOWARD HIBBETT and GEN ITASAKA

VOLUME I

Vocabularies and Notes

Second Edition

HARVARD UNIVERSITY PRESS

CAMBRIDGE, MASSACHUSETTS

Second Edition, 1967
Fifth Printing, 1974

The research reported herein was performed
pursuant to a contract with the
United States Office of Education,
Department of Health, Education, and Welfare.

Library of Congress Catalog Card Number 67-22864
ISBN 0-674-58000-1
Printed in the United States of America

PREFACE

This textbook in two volumes is designed to offer a rapid but thorough introduction to modern Japanese. After finishing it, a student armed with a few dictionaries should be able to make his own way safely through the jungle of print--the books, magazines, and newspapers which flourish so luxuriantly in Japan. Those whose interests lie in reading within a specialized field may be able to fend for themselves even earlier.

It is assumed, however, that the student will not begin this book until he has acquired a sound grasp of the fundamentals of the spoken language, possibly by completing the extensive materials in Eleanor Harz Jorden, Beginning Japanese (New Haven, Yale, 1962-63, 2 vols.), the more concise introduction in Samuel E. Martin, Essential Japanese (Tokyo, Tuttle, 3rd rev. ed., 1962), a new and useful work by Tamako Niwa and Mayako Matsuda, Basic Japanese for College Students (Seattle, University of Washington, 1964), or one of the other elementary Japanese language texts in romanization. Also, he will need to provide himself with Florence Sakade, ed., A Guide to Reading and Writing Japanese (Tuttle, 1961), both for its convenient lists of the characters now commonly used in Japan and its charts which show how to write them. Sooner or later he will find it worthwhile to have at hand two important dictionaries: Senkichiro Katsumata, ed., New Japanese-English Dictionary (Tokyo, Kenkyūsha, 1954), and Andrew Nathaniel Nelson, The Modern Reader's Japanese-English Character Dictionary (Tuttle, 1962).

The statistically minded may be interested to know that this text book contains 1,333 Chinese characters, apart from variant forms and characters which are not expected to be memorized, in addition to the two Japanese syllabaries. As far as possible the choice of characters has been guided by the practical needs of the student: to this end, the authors have attempted to include all the characters of higher frequency as listed in the study Sōgō zasshi no yōji (The Use of Written Forms in Japanese Cultural Reviews), published by the Kokuritsu kokugo kenkyūjo (The National Language Research Institute) of Tokyo in 1960. According to this study, some 1,400 characters of higher frequency constitute about 97% of all those encountered in the periodicals examined--that is, in the kind of writing which most advanced students should be prepared to read. Vocabulary selection has also been coordinated with the frequency tables of 4,200 words in Sōgō zasshi no yōgo (Research

PREFACE

on Vocabulary in Cultural Reviews), published by the Kokuritsu kokugo kenkyūjo in 1957.

However, the chief concern of the authors--beyond any statistical considerations--has been to prepare texts which are representative of good modern Japanese usage. After an introductory lesson on the <u>hiragana</u> phonetic syllabary (the other syllabary is taken up in Lesson 7), the text is divided into a graded series of sixty lessons, about two-thirds of which have been edited from the writings of leading scholars and men of letters. The beginning lessons are in easy informal styles; there are a number of lessons concerned with the Japanese language itself, as well as with other aspects of Japanese culture; readings in history, political thought, and economics are centered on Japan; later lessons include selections from the works of several modern novelists, and introduce the traditional orthography which still survives the language reforms of 1946; and Lesson 60 is a symposium (<u>zadankai</u>) of the kind which is such a prominent feature of Japanese intellectual life. Lessons 1 through 25 are supplemented by shorter texts which, while introducing no new characters, give further practice in using the characters, vocabulary, and structures of each of these lessons. All of the Japanese texts are written by hand, in what is thought to be an acceptable model script; the student is urged to write Japanese as much as possible, in order to ensure mastery of the characters. He will find that reading the usual somewhat squared printed forms offers no real difficulty.

The annotation has been kept concise and sparing, both on the principle that finer points of usage are best explained orally in Japanese by the teacher or informant and for the practical reason that this tentative edition of the reader will eventually be revised to link it to a textbook of spoken Japanese in romanization. Meanwhile, the authors will be grateful to anyone who is kind enough to draw their attention to errors, omissions, or inadequacies in this work.

The authors wish to express appreciation to their former colleague Edwin O. Reischauer, co-author with Serge Elisséeff and Takehiko Yoshihashi of <u>Elementary</u> <u>Japanese</u> <u>for</u> <u>College</u> <u>Students</u> (Cambridge, Harvard, 1944), for help in planning this reader. Much of the work has been done by past or present members of the teaching staff of the Department of Far Eastern Languages at Harvard University: Mrs. Teruko Craig, Mr. Teruhiro Hayata, Mrs. Yasuko Horioka, Dr. Cornelius J. Kiley, Mrs. Michiko Kwok, Mr. Yoshinori Morita, and Dr. Tamako Niwa. Miss Aiko Okada and Mr. Larry Wendell are others to whom special thanks is due for their

PREFACE

research assistance.

We should like also to make grateful acknowledgment to the
Charles E. Tuttle Company for permitting us to add references to
Sakade and Nelson to our own character lists in Part Two, and to all
the Japanese authors and publishers (listed under the source and
author notes which follow most of the lessons) who have granted us
permission to use materials on which they hold copyright.

Howard Hibbett

Gen Itasaka

Cambridge, Massachusetts

CONTENTS

INTRODUCTION   1

Lesson I. KAIWA   13

Lesson II. TŌKYŌ NO MACHI   17

Lesson III. NIKKI   22

Lesson IV. CHICHI NO TEGAMI   28

Lesson V. ON   33

Lesson VI. KAIWA   37

Lesson VII. NIHON NO MOJI   42

Lesson VIII. KANJI NO HANASHI (SONO ICHI)   46

Lesson IX. KANJI NO HANASHI (SONO NI)   48

Lesson X. NIKKI   50

Lesson XI. BENRI NA MOJI   54

Lesson XII. OBASUTEYAMA   57

Lesson XIII. TEGAMI   61

Lesson XIV. JISHO NI TSUITE   64

Lesson XV. JITEN NO HIKIKATA   68

Lesson XVI. NIHON NO CHIRI   71

Lesson XVII. NIHON NO REKISHI   75

Lesson XVIII. KAKEKOMIDERA   79

Lesson XIX. YUMEDONO   82

Lesson XX. KUBUNDEN   86

CONTENTS

Lesson XXI. DEJIMA   89

Lesson XXII. NIHON NO HŌKEN SEIDO   92

Lesson XXIII. DENPŌ NI TSUITE   95

Lesson XXIV. AME NI MO MAKEZU   100

Lesson XXV. KYŌSEI SARETA DOKUSHO   103

Lesson XXVI. ARU OSORE   107

Lesson XXVII. GENJITSU TO IMĒJI   110

Lesson XXVIII. BOKU   113

Lesson XXIX. NIHONJIN NO YOMIKAKI NŌRYOKU   116

Lesson XXX. HEIWARON NI TSUITE   120

Lesson XXXI. KENPŌ TO HEIWA   123

Lesson XXXII. MORI ŌGAI TO JUNSHI   126

Lesson XXXIII. ISHO (SONO ICHI)   130

Lesson XXXIV. ISHO (SONO NI)   133

Lesson XXXV. NIHON KEIZAI NO TOKUSHOKU   136

Lesson XXXVI. PĀMANENTO ENPUROIMENTO   139

Lesson XXXVII. DEKASEGIGATA RŌDŌ   142

Lesson XXXVIII. TSUBOUCHI SHŌYŌ   145

Lesson XXXIX. NIHON NO SHIZENSHUGI   149

Lesson XL. WATAKUSHI NO KOJINSHUGI (I)   154

Lesson XLI. WATAKUSHI NO KOJINSHUGI (II)   160

Lesson XLII. "SOREKARA" YORI (I)   164

Lesson XLIII. "SOREKARA" YORI (II)   169

Lesson XLIV. HANABI   173

Lesson XLV. KOKUGO MONDAI TO MINZOKU NO SHŌRAI   179

CONTENTS

Lesson XLVI. GENGO SEISAKU NI TSUITE (I)   184

Lesson XLVII. GENGO SEISAKU NI TSUITE (II)   188

Lesson XLVIII. NIHONJIN NO NINGEN KANKEI (I)   192

Lesson XLIX. NIHONJIN NO NINGEN KANKEI (II)   196

Lesson L. NIHON NO SHINJŌ   199

Lesson LI. NIHONJIN NO SHŪKYŌ SEIKATSU   202

Lesson LII. YŪBINKYOKU NO MADOGUCHI DE   209

Lesson LIII. BUNKAZAI HOGO   211

Lesson LIV. KOBAYASHI TAKIJI E NO TEGAMI   214

Lesson LV. KAMIGATAGO   217

Lesson LVI. YUME NO UKIHASHI (I)   221

Lesson LVII. YUME NO UKIHASHI (II)   227

Lesson LVIII. WATAKUSHI NO SAKUHIN   236

Lesson LIX. YAMA NO OTO   239

Lesson LX. ZADANKÁI   243

INDEX   251

The Japanese Writing System

The modern Japanese writing system is the product of more than
a millenium of adaptation of the beautiful and sophisticated writing
system of the Chinese. The use of Chinese characters, natural under
the circumstance that the ancient Japanese had no means of writing
of their own, has continued in spite of the early development of
phonetic symbols (kana) derived from the characters, recent attempts
to supplement if not supplant the kana by roman letters (rōmaji),
and the fact that the Chinese writing system was at first wholly
unsuited to the orthographical needs of the Japanese language.

Although Japanese is not a member of the Sinitic family of
languages, it has adopted an enormous number of loan words from the
Chinese, writing them in characters and trying to imitate their
native pronunciations, and has also created an extensive lexicon of
words coined on the analogy of the borrowed ones. At times this
complex process has resulted in the use of many thousands of
Chinese characters (kanji), along with hundreds of kana. A further
complexity (discussed in Lesson 7) is that almost all kanji have
been given at least two or three "readings," some of them native
Japanese words and others more or less modified from the
monosyllabic Chinese pronunciations of the characters.

Happily, the beginning student of today will find that most
publications follow a comparatively easy standardized system of
using kanji and kana. In 1946 the Japanese government began to
put into effect a vigorous program of simplifying and limiting the
number of kanji in ordinary use, simplifying the kana orthography,
and reducing the number of multiple readings of the kanji (see
Lessons 45 to 47). Anomalies still abound; a great many writers
cling to the "old" orthography (Lesson 40); and the more advanced
student will wish to be able to recognize the older forms in order
not to be cut off from everything printed before, or in defiance of,
the language reforms.

Kanji

Many Chinese written characters are indeed pictographs or

ideographs (such as 木 "tree" and 一 "one"), but the vast majority
are made up of two components: a "radical," or "classifier," which
indicates the general category of meaning to which the character
belongs, and a "phonetic," an element which indicates very roughly
the original Chinese pronunciation of the word represented by this
composite character. Thus, 木 is the radical for a large number of
characters representing words of varied pronunciation which are
related to the idea of "tree" (柳 "willow," 楓 "maple," etc.) or
"wood" (梁 "beam," 楫 "oar") as well as for some characters which
elude ready categorization by meaning. There are 214 radicals,
ranging from one (一) to seventeen (龠) strokes. Lessons 8 and
9 discuss this system in more detail, and Lessons 14 and 15 explain
how to cope with Japanese dictionaries, including dictionaries of
kanji.

The readings of the kanji are of two kinds: the on readings,
those based on the sound of Chinese words, and the kun readings,
which are native Japanese words corresponding semantically to the
Chinese characters with which they are associated. If the on may
be called the Sino-Japanese pronunciation of a character, the kun
is in effect a Japanese translation of its meaning, or one of its
meanings. Thus, the character 柳 has the on reading ryū, remotely
derived from a Chinese word meaning "willow," and the kun reading
yanagi, the native Japanese word for "willow"; similarly, 楓 (maple)
is read fū or kaede. Most kanji have two or more on (the two major
classes of on readings are called kan'on and goon), since these
reflect the Chinese of different ages and different dialects; some
have an even larger number of kun, each corresponding to one of the
possible meanings of the character.

In practice, these formidable ambiguities are usually resolved
by the aid of context and supplementary kana. As a broad rule,
admitting many exceptions, it may be said that on readings are
preferred when two or more characters are combined to form a single
word. We would therefore follow the kun readings hana for 花
(flower) and yanagi for 柳 (willow) when these two words are used
independently, but karyū 花柳 (based on their on readings) when they
are joined in the compound meaning "flowers and willows." However,
there are a great many kun compounds as well, and even a few
compounds with mixed readings--hybrids of on and kun, that is.
There are also a few characters (apart from the kana) which were
invented in Japan, and these of course have only kun readings.

Kana

By the eighth century the Japanese were making extensive use

2

of Chinese characters as phonetic symbols, because of the problems
imposed by the desire to record native poetry, prayers, and legends.
In the ninth century this cumbrous method of transcribing
polysyllabic Japanese words began to give way to a fairly regular
system of using certain abbreviated characters--the origin of the
modern kana--to represent the five vowels (a, i, u, e, o) and
syllables composed of the nine consonants (k, s, t, n, h, m, y, r,
w) and these vowels. Eventually the kana symbols were standardized
in two parallel syllabaries of "50 sounds" (47 in fact, and 45 in
modern Japanese), together with a syllabic nasal (n). The two
kinds of kana are known as hiragana (smooth kana), which are cursive
forms of whole kanji, and katakana (side kana), abbreviated forms
made by taking parts of single kanji. The derivation of kana from
kanji is illustrated in a table in Lesson 7. Both hiragana and
katakana are widely used, but the latter, which is introduced in
Lesson 7, is chiefly restricted to writing foreign words, words
singled out for clarity or special emphasis, telegrams, and official
notices. (Before Lesson 7, words normally written in katakana will
be "underlined" by a vertical line in the Japanese text.) Both kana
syllabaries are augmented by adding two dots (nigori or dakuten) to
symbols of the k, s, t, and h columns of the table to indicate
voiced consonants (=g, z, d, b), or by adding a small circle (han-
dakuten) to indicate the "half-voiced" consonant of the h column
(=p). The few orthographical irregularities of the romanized
transcription of these syllables, and of the sounds indicated by
combining a syllable ending in -i with another beginning in y-,
are pointed out in the accompanying tables.

The introductory hiragana lesson (pp. i-vi of Part Two) begins
with the kana in their standard order, followed by a series of
Japanese words written with two or more kana. Although tabular
matter is set off at the top of the page, all texts are written
vertically from top to bottom and right to left, as Japanese is
ordinarily written. (Words or phrases are sometimes spaced in kana
writing, but the spacing in Lessons 1 to 10 of this book is purely
for the convenience of the student, since normal Japanese writing
relies on the segmentation afforded by the mixed use of kana and
kanji.) Note that the signs i わ and e ゑ of the "wa column" are
found only in the old orthography (Lesson 40). The next section
(2) gives the voiced consonants, written with the nigori, and then
the syllables which can take the han-dakuten. It should be pointed
out that the sounds ji and zu are written じ and ず except when they
follow chi or tsu respectively (chijimu ちぢむ , tsuzuku つづく)
or occur in a compound word (hanaji はなぢ , from hana + chi) of
which the second element originally began with an unvoiced chi ち
or tsu つ.

3

P	b	d	z	g		w	r	y	m	h	n	t	s	K	-	
ぱ	ば	だ	ざ	が	ん (n)	わ	ら	や	ま	は	な	た	さ	か	あ	a
ぴ	び	ぢ (ji)	じ (ji)	ぎ		(ゐ) (i)	り		み	ひ	に	ち (chi)	し (shi)	き	い	i
ぷ	ぶ	づ (zu)	ず	ぐ			る	ゆ	む	ふ (fu)	ぬ	つ (tsu)	す	く	う	u
ぺ	べ	で	ぜ	げ		(ゑ) (e)	れ		め	へ	ね	て	せ	け	え	e
ぽ	ぼ	ど	ぞ	ご		を (°)	ろ	よ	も	ほ	の	と	そ	こ	お	o

P	b	d	z	g	r	m	h	n	t	s	K	
ぴゃ	びゃ	ぢゃ (ja)	じゃ (ja)	ぎゃ	りゃ	みゃ	ひゃ	にゃ	ちゃ (cha)	しゃ (sha)	きゃ	-ya
ぴゅ	びゅ	ぢゅ (ju)	じゅ (ju)	ぎゅ	りゅ	みゅ	ひゅ	にゅ	ちゅ (chu)	しゅ (shu)	きゅ	-yu
ぴょ	びょ	ぢょ (jo)	じょ (jo)	ぎょ	りょ	みょ	ひょ	にょ	ちょ (cho)	しょ (sho)	きょ	-yo

KATAKANA

p	b	d	z	g		w	r	y	m	h	n	t	s	K	-	
パ	バ	ダ	ザ	ガ	ン n	ワ	ラ	ヤ	マ	ハ	ナ	タ	サ	カ	ア	a
ピ	ビ	ヂ ji	ジ ji	ギ	(ヰ) i	リ		ミ	ヒ	ニ	チ	シ	キ	イ		i
プ	ブ	ヅ zu	ズ	グ		ル	ユ	ム	フ	ヌ	ツ	ス	ク	ウ		u
ペ	ベ	デ	ゼ	ゲ	(ヱ) e	レ		メ	ヘ	ネ	テ	セ	ケ	エ		e
ポ	ボ	ド	ゾ	ゴ		ヲ	ロ	ヨ	モ	ホ	ノ	ト	ソ	コ	オ	o

p	b	d	z	g		r	m	h	n	t	s	K	
ピャ	ビャ	ヂャ ja	ジャ ja	ギャ		リャ	ミャ	ヒャ	ニャ	チャ cha	シャ sha	キャ	-ya
ピュ	ビュ	ヂュ ju	ジュ ju	ギュ		リュ	ミュ	ヒュ	ニュ	チュ chu	シュ shu	キュ	-yu
ピョ	ビョ	ヂョ jo	ジョ jo	ギョ		リョ	ミョ	ヒョ	ニョ	チョ cho	ショ sho	キョ	-yo

The long vowels (3) are usually written by adding the sign for the same vowel, and indicated in romanization by the macron (thus, sā さあ , sū すう , etc.); however, in most cases the ō sounds are written by adding う (kō こう , sō そう , etc., except for ōi おおい "many," ōkii おおきい "big," and a few other such words). The combinations formed by adding syllables of the ya column (や, ゆ, or よ) to other syllables (4) may similarly be lengthened (ryū りゅう , byō びょう). In the katakana transcriptions of foreign words, vowels are lengthened by adding a short vertical bar (horizontal in horizontal writing) to the kana syllable (chīzu チーズ "cheese"); otherwise, all the kana orthographical principles discussed here apply alike to hiragana and to katakana. The double consonants (5) are now uniformly indicated by writing the symbol tsu つ (somewhat smaller and a little to the right, as with the ya や , yu ゆ , and yo よ in 4) before the consonant to be doubled: thus, sukkari すっかり , nikki にっき , katta かった , etc. (But note the use of the syllabic n, as in onna おんな, and the slightly irregular romanization of itchi いっち and isshō いっしょう , for example). The next section (6) gives a few examples of phrases including the particles wa, e, and o, which are written irregularly with the kana signs for ha は , he へ , and (w)o を respectively. (In the new orthography を is used only for writing the particle o.)

The next-to-last section (7) shows the more important marks of punctuation and miscellaneous signs: the comma 、 and period 。 (a), quotation marks「 」and ゛ 』(b), and the optional repeat signs (c) for a single kana ゝ and for more than one kana 〱 , the latter being used only in vertical writing, and taking the nigori when the first of the repeated syllables begins with a newly voiced consonant. There is also a repeat sign for kanji 々 , which is itself repeated when two or more characters are to be reduplicated, as in 一日々々 (= 一日 一日).

The hiragana lesson ends with a brief connected text (8).

Under the influence of the postwar language reforms many words once written in kanji are now written entirely in kana. However, the practice of adding kana "endings" (okurigana) to kanji adjectives and verbs remains in vigor. The complicated official rules tend to prefer a fuller, less ambiguous use of okurigana: thus, sukunai is to be written 少ない instead of 少い and okonau is 行なう rather than 行う . But usage still varies widely, subject to the taste of the writer. In this book the first twenty lessons are written in accordance with current rules, while the later lessons follow the usage of the original author.

A further tendency is to add small kana (called furigana) alongside difficult kanji--those not included in the approved list

of kanji, or difficult because of their unusual readings--to
indicate their pronunciation. In this book all characters which
students are not yet expected to memorize are accompanied by
furigana.

Romanization

This book uses the Hepburn system of romanization, as found in
Kenkyūsha's New Japanese-English Dictionary (1954 edition). The same
system, with minor variations, is used in most of the other reference
works which the student will need to consult.

Vocabularies and Notes

Each lesson is provided with a vocabulary and brief notes, the
notes being interpolated in the vocabulary so that the student will
find all the necessary information in a single sequence. Lengthier
notes, such as those on the various styles (Lessons 1, 3, and 16),
will be found after the source and author notes which follow the
vocabularies.

All new words and words written with new kanji are included in
the vocabularies, with the exception of ordinary functional words
and a small number of "basic words"--the first 240 words of the
frequency list in Sōgō zasshi no yōgo, pp. 96-98. In addition,
some well-established phrases are entered as such, rather than in
the usual dictionary form. New words in the supplementary texts of
Lessons 1 through 25 (these texts have no new kanji) are given in
short supplementary vocabularies but repeated if they recur in later
lessons.

It should be remembered that the English equivalents by no
means cover the same broad lexical ground as those given in a
dictionary entry. Instead, words are listed more than once, when
used in new "meanings" such as are discriminated in dictionary
listings. (Within the same lesson, however, discriminated meanings
will be grouped together, separated by semicolons.) As a rule, the
first English word given is the one considered more appropriate to
the context of the lesson, while the second is either more generally
applicable or helpful in focusing on the particular meaning of the
word as used in this context. For example, in each of the following
entries taken from page 150 of this volume, with reference to the
text of Lesson 39 as given on pages 207 and 208 of Part Two, the
first English expression is considered suitable as a translation of

the Japanese word in its present context:

page 207
line 11 引く   hiku   attract, draw

      12 凡人   bonjin   ordinary person, plebeian
page 208
line 2 排する   haisuru   reject, push aside

     4 背景   haikei   background, setting

None of the English words supplied here would lead the student far
astray, but "draw" is closer to the literal meaning of hiku,
"plebeian" has English connotations which are not as appropriate as
those of "ordinary person" in this context (though quite suitable in
other Japanese contexts), "push aside" in the literal sense is an
acceptable related use of haisuru, and "setting" occurs as a meaning
of haikei which Kenkyūsha discriminates when used for an actual
stage setting. However, the student is advised not to generalize
freely on the basis of these limited (and inevitably inconsistent)
entries: it will be enough if he can gradually increase his powers
of understanding by concentrating on the Japanese texts themselves,
seeking to grasp the sense of the words in their living contexts
rather than in isolation.

     The notes provided within these vocabularies may seem meager,
but they are intended only to give assistance at points of particular
difficulty, as concisely as possible. These notes are of two kinds:
(1) English translations or simple romanized Japanese equivalents
(augmented, if necessary, by translations, literal versions,
explanatory words or phrases, and the like), and (2) structural
notes which will help to clarify syntactical relationships. Entries
of the first kind are keyed to the Japanese texts by romanizing the
phrase concerned, as in the following examples:

page 3
line 9   hanashite ita tokoro = "was (in the midst of) talking"
page 11
line 2   to no koto deshita = to iu koto o kikimashita ("I was
page 69   told that")
line 9   ari wa shimai ka = aru no de wa nai darō ka
page 209
line 10   sore dake ni = "in so far as (it was an intellectual
             phenomenon)"

line 13   taru = to aru ("as," literary)

Notes of the second kind are given in Japanese orthography (kanji

and kana) exactly as found in the text, except for omissions to
save space and symbols to indicate the syntactical relationships.
Their basic forms are as follows:

(A)→ B   means that "A modifies B"

A ‖ B   means that "A is parallel to (or correlative
with) B"

In either case, of course, A or B may be phrases of some length.
Here are a few examples of these notes, with added explanations:

page 10
line 2   (国木田独歩という ...... と言った)→ の
means that the clause modifying the の in line 3 begins
with 国木田独歩 in line 2 and ends with と言った

page 57
line 7   目で見ることの出来るもの ‖ つまり形を持ったもの
means that these two phrases on lines 7 and 8 are
"parallel"--that is, in this case, in apposition--
and are both objects of the same verb (画く)

page 209
line 8   (科学を ...... 組織だてる)→ コントやテーヌ の努力
means that the clause modifying "the efforts of Conte
and Taine" is the one which might be translated "who
systematized thought on a scientific basis"

VOCABULARIES AND NOTES

Lesson I. KAIWA

1	会話	kaiwa	conversation
2	今日は	konnichi wa	Hello. (from late morning to late afternoon)
	よくいらっしゃいました	yoku irasshaimashita	Welcome.
	どうぞお入り下さい	dōzo o-hairi kudasai	Please come in.
3	今日	kyō	today
	お一人ですか	o-hitori desu ka	Are you alone?
4	二人で	futari de	together (of a couple)
	つごうがわるい	tsugō ga warui	be inconvenient (tsugō = opportunity; circumstances)
5	上がる	agaru	pay a call (humble)
6	十二三人	jūnisan nin	twelve or thirteen people
9	ご存じの方	go-zonji no kata	people you know (honorific)
10	お目にかゝる	o-me ni kakaru	meet (someone) (humble)
11	人	hito	person
13	白い	shiroi	white
	せーたー	sētā	sweater (sleeved pull-over)
	田中	Tanaka	(surname)

1	となりの	tonari no	next to, beside
	はじめて	hajimete	(for) the first time
3	ほわいと	Howaito	White (surname)
4	存じる	zonjiru	know (humble)

p2

4	入口	iriguchi	entrance
5	近い	chikai	near
6	今田	Imada	(surname)
	ぶらっく	Burakku	Black (surname)
7	十日	tōka	ten days
	あめりか	Amerika	America (United States)
9	日下	Kusaka	(surname)
	申す	mōsu	be called, say (humble)
	どうぞよろしく	dōzo yoroshiku	I am pleased to meet you. (I request your kind favor.)
11	はじめまして	hajimemashite	How do you do? (I am meeting you for the first time.)
	こちらこそ	kochira koso	It is I who ...
12	名前	namae	name
	字	ji	character
13	やさしい	yasashii	easy
	日の下と書く	hi no shita to kaku	write "hi no shita (under the sun)"

p3

1	読む	yomu	read, pronounce
5	漢字	kanji	Chinese character
6	おぼえる	oboeru	learn, memorize
7	今月の十日	kongetsu no tōka	the 10th of this month
	勉強する	benkyō suru	study
9	話す	hanasu	talk

hanashite ita tokoro = "was (in the midst of) talking"

11	目上	meue	superior

14

p3			
11	目下	meshita	inferior
13	むずかしい	muzukashii	difficult
	一々	ichiichi	one by one
	二つ	futatsu	two
p4			
1	三つ	mittsu	three
2	自由に	jiyū ni	freely
3	ところで	tokoro de	by the way
4	分る	wakaru	understand
5	つける	tsukeru	attach
8	そうすると	sō suru to	then, if so
	上下	jōge	superior and inferior, upper and lower
10	君	-kun	(familiar suffix to personal name, chiefly used by men and boys)
13	自分	jibun	self, oneself
p5			
1	かんがえる	kangaeru	think, consider
2	入る	hairu	fit in, enter
5	一口に言う	hitokuchi ni iu	say (explain) in a word
6	ことにしている	koto ni shite iru	make it a rule to
9	ですけれども	desukeredomo	however
	とても	totemo	very
11	まちがいはありません	machigai wa arimasen	it is safe (there is no mistake)
12	みんな	minna	all, every person
p6			
1	えい語	eigo	English (language)
	語	-go	language
2	日本語	nihongo	Japanese (language)

15

p6

6	八月	hachigatsu	August
	できれば	dekireba	if possible
	十月	jūgatsu	October
7	二月	futatsuki	two months
8	一日	ichinichi	a day
	一日中	ichinichijū	all day long
9	中	-jū	throughout (space or time)
10	その中	sono uchi	soon, before long

kikasete kudasai = "please tell me (inform, cause to hear)"

Supplement

p7

2	下田	Shimoda	(surname)
	日本人	Nihonjin	a Japanese, the Japanese

p8

3	八つ	yattsu	eight (years of age)
	下	shita	younger
6	分ける	wakeru	divide, classify
10	由である	yoshi de aru	I am told that

This lesson is in the polite conversational style, standard for educated people. On more formal occasions, or to express special respect, such honorific verbs as gozaimasu (=aru), asobasu (=suru), and meshiagaru (=taberu, nomu) would be used.

Lesson II. TŌKYŌ NO MACHI

1	東京	Tōkyō	Tokyo
	町	machi	city, town, district
2	今年	kotoshi	this year
	二月三日	nigatsu mikka	February 3rd
	四五人	shigo nin	four or five (people)
	友達	tomodachi	friend
	方々	hōbō	here and there, various places
3	見る	miru	look at, see
	歩く	aruku	walk
	見て歩く	mite aruku	walk around looking at
	六七時間	rokushichi jikan	six or seven hours
4	大変	taihen	very much, very
	勉強になる	benkyō ni naru	be beneficial (in knowledge, experience)
	家	uchi	home, house
5	帰る	kaeru	return, go back
	いろいろと	iroiro to	various(ly)
6	百年	hyakunen	a hundred years
	まったく	mattaku	completely
	変わる	kawaru	change, be altered
8	江戸	Edo	(former name of Tokyo)
	言う	iu	be called

17

p9

8	頃	koro	time, period
	山	yama	hill, mountain
9	川	kawa	stream, river
	しずかな	shizuka na	quiet, calm
	明治	Meiji	Meiji era (1868-1912)
10	年々	nennen	year by year
	人口	jinkō	population
	多くなる	ōku naru	increase, grow (in number)
	一千万	issenman	ten million
	大きな	ōkina	large
11	九千万	kyūsenman	ninety million
12	日本人	Nihonjin	Japanese (person)
	人	-jin	people (members of a nation, etc.)
	十分の一	jūbun no ichi	one-tenth (one of ten parts)
	ことになる	koto ni naru	amount to, come about that
13	そのため	sono tame	consequently, for that reason

p10

1	木	ki	tree
	本	-hon	(counter for long cylindrical objects such as trees and pencils)
2	少ない	sukunai	few, little
	(国木田独歩という……と言った)→ の		
	国木田独歩	Kunikida Doppo	(novelist, 1871-1908)
	山林	sanrin	woodlands
	自由	jiyū	freedom
4	大木	taiboku	large tree

18

p10			
5	武蔵野	Musashino	<u>Musashino</u> (1901) (a plain on the outskirts of Tokyo)
	本	hon	book
6	美しい	utsukushii	beautiful
	林	hayashi	wood, grove
	渋谷駅	Shibuya-eki	Shibuya Station
7	十分	jippun, juppun	ten minutes
	もちろん	mochiron	of course
9	まいる	mairu	mile
	富士山	Fujisan	Mt. Fuji
10	下町	shitamachi	downtown
11	ほとんど…ない	hotondo...nai	hardly (<u>hotondo</u> = almost)
	ことが出来る	koto ga dekiru	can
12	隅田川	Sumidagawa	Sumida River
13	水	mizu	water
	きれい	kirei	clean
	白魚	shirauo	whitebait
	とれる	toreru	be able to catch
	この間	konoaida	the other day, recently
p11			
1	きたない	kitanai	dirty

2   to no koto deshita = to iu koto o kikimashita ("I was told that")

(この川をせーぬ川のように……つくった)→人

| 3 | せーぬ川 | Sēnugawa | River Seine |
| | ぷらん | puran | plan |

p11

4	つくる	tsukuru	make
6	えどわーどもーす	Edowādo Mōsu	Edward Morse (American naturalist, 1838-1925)
7	日本その日その日	Nihon sonohi sonohi	Japan <u>Day</u> by <u>Day</u> (Boston, 1917)
	はじめ	hajime	beginning
8	くわしく	kuwashiku	in detail

10　(「日本その日……新しかった)→ 人力車

	いちばん	ichiban	the most (superlative)
	新らしい	atarashii	new
11	人力車	jinrikisha	jinrikisha (rickshaw)
	多少	tashō	some
13	七月	shichigatsu	July
	もう一度	mō ichido	once more

Supplement

p13

2	木曜日	mokuyōbi	Thursday
	東京たわー	Tōkyō tawā	The Tokyo Tower
	上る	noboru	go up, climb
9	大分	daibu	considerably

p14

5	四つ	yottsu	four (years of age)
	五つ	itsutsu	five (years of age)
8	九つ	kokonotsu	nine (years of age)
10	下水	gesui	sewerage (system)

p15

11	六つ目	muttsu-me	the sixth
	七つ目	nanatsu-me	the seventh
	田町	Tamachi	(district in Tokyo)

20

p15
11 下りる   oriru   get off, get down

12 二町   ni-chō   two chō (a cho is about
p16   119 yards)
2 申し上げる   mōshiageru   say, mention (humble)

Lesson III. NIKKI

1	日記	nikki	diary
2	土曜日	doyōbi	Saturday
3	いゝ	ii	good
	えいが	eiga	movie
	ごご	gogo	afternoon, p.m.
	行く	iku	go
4	お金	o-kane	money
	どる	doru	dollar
	止める	yameru	give up (an idea)
5	土田	Tsuchida	(surname)
	あそびに行く	asobi ni iku	go to visit (informally)
6	ちょうど	chōdo	just (at that time)
	来る	kuru	come
7	面白い	omoshiroi	interesting
8	(日本のことに…… もっている)→人		
	きょうみをもつ	kyōmi o motsu	be interested, have an interest (in)
10	円	en	yen (Japanese monetary unit)
	何円	nan'en	how many yen
11	かゝる	kakaru	take, require (time, money)
	あれこれ	are kore	this and that
	しつもんする	shitsumon suru	ask (a question)

22

Lesson III

13	はっきり	hakkiri	exactly, clearly
	おぼえる	oboeru	remember
	たしか	tashika	I think, if I am right

1	こたえる	kotaeru	answer
	ひこうき	hikōki	airplane
2	早い	hayai	quick; early
	私	watakushi	I
3	とけい	tokei	watch, clock
	とけいをすすめる	tokei o susumeru	set a watch ahead
4	じっさいに	jissai ni	actually
5	ふね	fune	ship, boat
7	年	toshi	age, years of age
	かぞえ方	kazoekata	way of counting
	方法	hōhō	method
8	誕生日	tanjōbi	birthday
	才	-sai	(counter for years of age)
9	同じ	onaji	the same
	一日	tsuitachi	first (day of the month)
10	たとえば	tatoeba	for example
11	来月	raigetsu	next month
12	説明する	setsumei suru	explain
	困る	komaru	be at a loss, be in trouble

1	やはり	yahari	still, all the same
	二回	nikai	twice

23

p19

3	夕方	yūgata	twilight, early evening
	明り	akari	light(s)
	つく	tsuku	be lit
	頃	koro	time, period
4	川下 (の)	kawashimo (no)	downstream
	少し	sukoshi	a little
	さんぽする	sanpo suru	take a walk
	このへん	kono hen	this area
	みち	michi	road
	そばに	soba ni	beside
5	小さな	chiisa na	small
	たくさん	takusan	large number, amount
6	頁	pēji	page
7	一行一行	ichigyō ichigyō	line by line
	ていねいに	teinei ni	carefully, thoroughly
	時間	jikan	time
8	四日	yokka	fourth (day of the month)
	日曜日	nichiyōbi	Sunday
9	火曜日	kayōbi	Tuesday
	しけん	shiken	examination
10	の中で	no uchi de	among

ikken nan demo nai yō na bun demo = "even passages which seem easy at first glance"

一見	ikken	apparently, at first glance

24

p19
11 文　　　　　　　　bun　　　　　　　passage, sentence

yoku yonde miru to = "when (I) read carefully"

12 上中下　　　　　jō chū ge　　　　vols. 1,2, and 3 (when
　　　　　　　　　　　　　　　　　　　　three volumes only)
　 冊　　　　　　　　-satsu　　　　　　(counter for books)

13　taihen da = "it's quite a job (terrific! awful!)"

　 今晩中に　　　　konbanjū ni　　　before the night is over
p20
　1 のこす　　　　　nokosu　　　　　　leave

　 中止する　　　　chūshi suru　　　stop, discontinue

　 へや　　　　　　heya　　　　　　　room

　2 少々　　　　　　shōshō　　　　　　a little (=sukoshi)

　 つかれる　　　　tsukareru　　　　become tired, fatigued

　3 五日　　　　　　itsuka　　　　　　fifth day (of the month)

　 月曜日　　　　　getsuyōbi　　　　Monday

　4 昼すぎ　　　　　hirusugi　　　　　early afternoon

　 ずぼん　　　　　zubon　　　　　　　trousers (from French
　　　　　　　　　　　　　　　　　　　　"jupon")
　 大中小　　　　　dai chū shō　　　large, medium, and small

　5 ちょうどいゝ　chōdo ii　　　　　just right

　 帰りみちで　　　kaerimichi de　　on the way home

　 小川　　　　　　Ogawa　　　　　　　(surname)

　6 方言　　　　　　hōgen　　　　　　　dialect

　 同君　　　　　　dōkun　　　　　　　that person, he

　 同　　　　　　　dō-　　　　　　　　the same

　 あくせんと　　　akusento　　　　　(syllabic) accent

　7 研究　　　　　　kenkyū　　　　　　research, study

　 上　　　　　　　-jō　　　　　　　　from the viewpoint of

25

Lesson III

p20

7	時	-ji	o'clock
	小山	Koyama	(surname)
8	でんわがかかる	denwa ga kakaru	have (receive) a telephone call
	由である	yoshi de aru	I understand that, I hear that
9	水曜日	suiyōbi	Wednesday
	昼	hiru	noon
	明日	ashita, asu	tomorrow
10	今夜	kon'ya	tonight
	なるべく	narubeku	as ... as possible
	ねる	neru	go to bed, lie down

Supplement

p21

2	金曜日	kin'yōbi	Friday
5	旅行	ryokō	travel, trip
10	同時に	dōji ni	at the same time
p22 1	時々	tokidoki	sometimes, at times
6	車	kuruma	car
	止める	tomeru	park, stop
10	たばこ	tabako	cigarette
	火	hi	light, fire
	まっち	matchi	matches
11	持って来る	motte kuru	bring
12	来月早々	raigetsu sōsō	early next month
p23 1	回る	mawaru	go round, go (home) via
3	昨日	kinō	yesterday

3 夜   yoru   night, evening

     In contrast with the polite conversational style of Lessons 1 and 2, this lesson is written in a "plain style" characterized by the brief forms of familiar speech. The plain style is used in writing diaries, familiar letters, and other kinds of informal prose, but may be almost as impersonal as the <u>de aru</u> style (see Lesson 16), which is used only in writing or in formal lectures, announcements, and the like.

     The following chart shows some examples of these differences. There are differences in vocabulary as well.

Polite conversational style	Plain style	Impersonal style
ikimashita	itta	itta no de aru
hazu desu ga	hazu da ga	hazu de aru ga
wakarimasen	wakaranai	wakaranai no de aru
muzukashii desu	muzukashii	muzukashii no de aru
taihen desu	taihen da	taihen de aru

Lesson IV. CHICHI NO TEGAMI

1	父	chichi	father
	手紙	tegami	letter
2	十一月六日	jūichigatsu muika	November 6th
	うけとる	uketoru	receive
	犬	inu	dog
3	子	ko	child, offspring
	犬の子	inu no ko	puppy
	生まれる	umareru	be born
	日本犬	Nihonken	Japanese dog (indigenous breed)
	犬の手	inu no te	dog's foreleg, paw (<u>te</u> = hand, arm)
4	太い	futoi	large, thick (cylindrical objects)
	お父さん	otōsan	father (honorific)
	きっと	kitto	surely, undoubtedly
5	力	chikara	strength
	つよい	tsuyoi	strong
	思う	omou	think, feel
6	心	kokoro	heart, mind
	大事にする	daiji ni suru	take good care of, treasure
8	とまる	tomaru	stay (at)
	ほてる	hoteru	hotel (Western-style)
	窓	mado	window
	通り	tōri	street

28

Lesson IV

8	向こう側	mukōgawa	the other side
9	家	ie	house
	さっき	sakki	a little while ago
	かわいらしい	kawairashii	cute
	白人	hakujin	white (person)
10	女の子	onna no ko	girl
	出る	deru	come out, go out
	あそぶ	asobu	amuse oneself, play
11	よし子	Yoshiko	(woman's first name)
	思い出す	omoidasu	recall, remember
13	(お父さんが小さい頃……はやった)→ よーよー		

1	はやる	hayaru	be popular (be wide spread)
	よーよー	yōyō	yoyo
2	又	mata	again
3	竹山	Takeyama	(surname)
	中心	chūshin	center, heart
	大学	daigaku	university, college
4	門	mon	gate
	めーとる	mētoru	meter
5	立つ	tatsu	stand; set out, leave
	便利(な)	benri (na)	convenient (physical thing or place)
6	先に	saki ni	earlier
7	さんふらんしすこ	Sanfuranshisuko	San Francisco
	いっしょに	issho ni	together

p25
8 ずっと   zutto   throughout, all the way through

  旅行する   ryokō suru   travel, take a trip

9 上手に   jōzu ni   skillfully

  話す   hanasu   speak

  下手な   heta na   unskillful

  あまり…ない   amari ... nai   not very, not so

10 (あめりかで生まれて……話している)→人

11 eigo no hō ga jōzu na kurai desu = "his English seems (almost) better than his Japanese"

13 私立(の)   shiritsu (no)   private (institution)

  学生   gakusei   (university, college) student

p26
1 女子学生   joshi gakusei   female student, coed

  外の   hoka no   other

2 先ず   mazu   first of all

3 先生   sensei   teacher

  先生をしている   sensei o shite iru be a teacher, teach (at a university, etc.)

  すみす氏   Sumisu-shi   Mr. Smith

  見せる   miseru   show, display

4 会う   au   meet, see

5 手紙を出す   tegami o dasu   send a letter

6 大分   daibu   rather, considerably

  さむい   samui   cold (atmospheric temperature)

7 雪   yuki   snow, snowfall

  すっかり   sukkari   entirely, thoroughly

8 自動車   jidōsha   automobile

30

p26

8	けむり	kemuri	smoke
9	はしる	hashiru	run
	今度	kondo	next time; this time
10	anmari = amari		
	字	ji	character
	目	me	eye
	いたい	itai	painful
12	しゃしん	shashin	photograph
	おくる	okuru	send
13	しゃしんをとる	shashin o toru	take a picture

p27

1	ちょっと	chotto	a little, a bit
	外出する	gaishutsu suru	go out
2	どうしても	dōshitemo	(not) possibly, by any means
3	お母さん	okāsan	mother
	しっかり	shikkari	hard, steadily
4	にゅーよーく	Nyūyōku	New York (city)
5	学会	gakkai	(academic) conference
6	十二月七日	jūnigatsu nanuka	December 7th
8	様	sama	(politer form of <u>san</u>)

Supplement

p28

10	会場	kaijō	place of meeting
11	おどろく	odoroku	be surprised

p29

6	母	haha	mother
	学力てすと	gakuryoku tesuto	achievement test

31

7	小学校	shōgakkō	elementary school, grade school
8	中学校	chūgakkō	junior high school, middle school
9	いそがしい	isogashii	busy
10	太郎	Tarō	(man's first name)
12	外	soto	outside, outdoors
13	立てる	tateru	can stand

This is an example of the polite conversational style as used in a letter from a father to his little daughter. The colloquial inversion of a subordinate clause so that it stands alone after the main clause (see 26. 10-11: anmari ... kara) helps to soften the tone.

p31

1	恩	on	(kindness or favor of a superior and the resulting debt of gratitude of an inferior)
2	父母	fubo	father and mother, parents
	海	umi	sea
	深い	fukai	deep
	高い	takai	high, tall
3	思想	shisō	idea, thought
	大事な	daiji na	important
	長い間	nagai aida	a long time
	人々	hitobito	people
4	持つ	motsu	have, possess
	むかし	mukashi	the old days, ancient times
	学校	gakkō	school
5	町人	chōnin	merchant, townsman
	百姓	hyakushō	farmer, peasant
	寺	tera	Buddhist temple
6	寺子屋	terakoya	temple school

（この寺子屋に入った……教えられる）→ 本

7	時間	jikan	(class) hour
	教える	oshieru	teach
	第一行目	dai ichigyōme	the first line

33

p31

9	言葉	kotoba	saying, word
10	子供	kodomo	child
11	習う	narau	learn, study (with a teacher)
12	一生	isshō	lifetime
	人間	ningen	human being
13	生活	seikatsu	life, living
	信じる	shinjiru	believe

p32

1	ちがう	chigau	differ
	侍	samurai	samurai
3	明治維新	Meiji Ishin	Meiji Restoration
	西洋	Seiyō	West, Occident
	国	kuni	country, nation
5	問題にする	mondai ni suru	call into question
	天	ten	heaven
7	福沢諭吉	Fukuzawa Yukichi	(journalist, educator, 1834-1901)

（「人間には上下の区別がない」という……教えた）→もの

	区別	kubetsu	distinction

8　（それまで男性と……信じられていた）→上下の区別

	男性	dansei	man, male
	女性	josei	woman, female
10	人間性	ningensei	human nature
	反する	hansuru	run counter to, be inconsistent with

11　（人間には上下の……生まれた）→もの

	もとづく	motozuku	be based on

34

Lesson V

1	若い	wakai	young
	自ら	mizukara	oneself (by oneself)
2	たすける	tasukeru	help
	者	mono	man, person
3	口にする	kuchi ni suru	mention, talk about
	反対する	hantai suru	oppose
4	こういう風に	kō iu fū ni	in this manner
	古い	furui	old
8	残る	nokoru	remain
10	男	otoko	man
11	(女の人がどの国立の……ようになった)→の		
	国立の	kokuritsu no	national (established by the government)
12	入学	nyūgaku	entry into a school
	大戦	taisen	great war
	今度の大戦	kondo no taisen	World War II (recent great war)
	すむ	sumu	end, be finished
13	選挙	senkyo	election, vote

1	後	ato	after

Supplement

5	入学	nyūgaku	entering school, matriculation
8	姓	sei	surname
12	中津	Nakatsu	(place name)

3	翻訳する	hon'yaku suru	translate
8	神	kami	god

p37
4 僕ら   bokura   we (familiar)

文字   moji   character, letter

お前   omae   you (familiar)

8 海中   kaichū   in the sea

Lesson VI. KAIWA

2	女中	jochū	maid
	もしもし	moshi-moshi	hello (on the telephone)
3	寺田	Terada	(surname)
	川口	Kawaguchi	(surname)
	お宅	o-taku	house (honorific)
	京都	Kyōto	Kyoto
4	者	mono	person (humble)

6   de irasshaimasu ka = desu ka (honorific, used for people)

	待つ	matsu	wait
9	何時	itsu	when
10	見える	mieru	come, appear (=<u>kuru</u>) (honorific)
11	先週	senshū	last week
13	ああ	ā	ah, oh
	心理学	shinrigaku	psychology
	新聞	shinbun	newspaper

2	ぜひ	zehi	by all means
5	午前	gozen	morning, a.m.
	九時	kuji	nine o'clock
	半	-han	half (a suffix adding half a unit to the preceding term of measure)
	せみなー	seminā	seminar

37

6   sore de o-shimai desu = "that's all (that's the end)"

7	じゃあ	jā	well, then (=de wa) (familiar)
	午後	gogo	afternoon, p.m.
8	そうですね	sō desu ne	well, let me see
10	時間	jikan	(free) time
	御都合	gotsugō	(your) convenience (honorific)
12	結構です	kekkō desu	all right, fine

    doko ni shimashō ka = "Where shall we make it?"

13	東大	Tōdai	University of Tokyo (=Tōkyō Daigaku)
	近所	kinjo	neighborhood, vicinity
	その後	sono ato	after that

1	近く	chikaku	neighborhood; near; around
2	所	tokoro	place
4	それじゃあ	sorejā	well, then (=sore de wa)
	本郷	Hongō	(district in Tokyo)
	丁目	-chōme	(numbered sub-division of a district)
	田村	Tamura	(name of a restaurant)
6	知る	shiru	be acquainted with, know
	さよなら	sayonara	good-bye

9   shibaraku deshita = "Nice to see you again. (It has been a long time.)"

10	元気（な）	genki (na)	well, healthy
11	お蔭様で	o-kage-sama de	Thanks (to you).

    nan da ka isogashii bakari de = "Somehow I've been so busy..."

38

p40
11	何だか	nandaka	somehow
	忙しい	isogashii	busy
12	如何	ikaga	how (=dō) (literary)
13	全国	zenkoku	the entire country
	学者	gakusha	scholar
	集まる	atsumaru	gather, congregate
	外国	gaikoku	foreign country

p41
1	有名な	yūmei na	famous
	なかなか	nakanaka	quite, considerably
2	大体	daitai	mainly, on the whole
	米国	Beikoku	America (United States)
4	全体で	zentai de	in all
5	近年	kinnen	recent years
7	近頃	chikagoro	recently
	本を出す	hon o dasu	publish a book
8	仕事	shigoto	business, work

shigoto mo o-ari da = shigoto mo aru (honorific)

	ずっと	zutto	far more
10	何でもない	nan de mo nai	it is nothing
11	新しく	atarashiku	newly

13 hito ni atte kita tokoro desu = "I have just come from meeting someone."

p42
1	この前	konomae	before this, previously
5	書き上げる	kakiageru	finish writing
	半年	hantoshi	half a year

6	日中	nitchū	during the day
	休日	kyūjitsu	holiday
7	全く	mattaku	really, completely
8	無理をする	muri o suru	overwork, do (something) to excess
9	体を休める	karada o yasumeru	rest (one's body)
10	休む	yasumu	rest (oneself)
	大事(な)	daiji (na)	important
11	それはそうと	sore wa sō to	by the way, be that as it may
12	聞く	kiku	hear
13	先月	sengetsu	last month
	二十日	hatsuka	the twentieth (day)
	男の子	otoko no ko	boy

1	お目出度う	o-medetō	congratulations
2	有り難う	arigatō	thank you
3	名前をつける	namae o tsukeru	name
4	一男	Kazuo	(man's first name)
6	長男	chōnan	eldest son
	君	-kun	(familiar suffix to personal name, chiefly used by men and boys)
7	幾つ	ikutsu	how many (years of age)
8	八つ	yattsu	eight (years of age)
	小学校	shōgakkō	primary school
	三年生	sannensei	third-grader
9	来年	rainen	next year
	学校に上がる	gakkō ni agaru	enter a school

40

Lesson VI

p44
1   hitotsu ima kara bīru demo nomimasen ka = "How about having a beer or something?" (<u>hitotsu</u> = <u>chotto</u>)

2	飲む	nomu	drink
3	ゆっくり	yukkuri	(in a) leisurely (manner)

Supplement

p45
2	しばらく	shibaraku	for a while
3	後に	ushiro ni	behind
	月	tsuki	the moon
12	東	higashi	east

p46
6	知人	chijin	acquaintance

p47
1	半ば	nakaba	halfway
	新たに	arata ni	anew, again
3	聞こえる	kikoeru	be heard, can hear

1	文字	moji (monji)	character, letter
2	昔	mukashi	ancient times, the old days
	種類	shurui	kind, type
	使う	tsukau	use
	すなわち	sunawachi	namely
3	漢字	kanji	Chinese character
	平仮名	hiragana	(the cursive Japanese syllabary)
	片仮名	katakana	(the square Japanese syllabary)
	主に	omo ni	mainly
4	世紀	seiki	century
	中国	Chūgoku	China
5	輸入する	yunyū suru	introduce, import
	もとにする	moto ni suru	take as a basis
7	日本語	Nihongo	Japanese (language)
	語	-go	language

mattaku to itte ii hodo = "almost completely (to the degree that one may say "completely")"

9	書き表わす	kakiarawasu	express in writing
	困難な	konnan na	difficult
10	方法	hōhō	method
	発明する	hatsumei suru	invent

42

p48
11	音	on	(a modified Chinese reading for a Chinese character); sound
	訓	kun	(a native Japanese reading for a Chinese character)
	読み方	yomikata	pronunciation, (way of) reading
13	説明する	setsumei suru	explain
	発音	hatsuon	pronunciation
	の通りに	no tōri ni	in the (same) manner

p49
1	フォネティック・システム	fonetikku shisutemu	phonetic system
2	非常に	hijō ni	extremely
4	たしか(な)	tashika (na)	certain, sure
5	(漢字をそれと同じ……読む)→ 方法		
	意味	imi	meaning
6	例えば	tatoeba	for instance
	書く	kaku	write
8	関係	kankei	relation(ship)
	英語で言う	eigo de iu	say (give an example) in English
10	十分に	jūbun ni	sufficiently
	言い表わす	iiarawasu	express (in words), describe
12	あたる	ataru	correspond to
	ところが	tokoro ga	however

p50
| 4 | 表わす | arawasu | express, indicate |

5 'ku' to iu on o motte sae ireba ii wake desu = "all you need is a character with (it is all right as long as the character has) the sound 'ku'"

| 11 | 同時に | dōji ni | at the same time |

43

p50			
11	簡単な	kantan na	simple
12	つぎに	tsugi ni	next, following
	例をあげる	rei o ageru	give an example
p51 8	部分	bubun	part
	草書	sōsho	cursive writing
9	出来上がる	dekiagaru	be created, come into being
12	普通	futsū	usually
13	中学校	chūgakkō	junior high school, middle school
p52 1	読本	tokuhon	reader, (language) text book
	教える	oshieru	teach
2	雑誌	zasshi	magazine
	読書	dokusho	reading (of books, etc.)
5	難しい	muzukashii	difficult
7	ヨーロッパ	Yōroppa	Europe
	ガラス	garasu	glass (material)
	コップ	koppu	(drinking) glass
8	主として	shu to shite	chiefly (=omo ni) (literary)
	外来語	gairaigo	word of foreign origin, loan word
9	電報	denpō	telegram

denpō kurai no mono desu = "only such things as telegrams (and other special kinds of texts)"

Supplement

| p53 8 | 教育漢字 | kyōiku kanji | characters for education (881 characters designated by the Ministry of Education as the basic |

p53
  8 | | | requirement for the 6 years of elementary school)

9 当用漢字   tōyō kanji   characters for practical use (the 1850 characters currently prescribed by the Ministry of Education)

p54
  4 振仮名   furigana   (<u>kana</u> attached to characters to indicate the reading)

8 新字体   shinjitai   new (simplified) form of Chinese character (used since 1946)

10 スペリング   superingu   spelling

13 味ノアル文   aji no aru bun   pregnant writing, a flavorful style

p56

1	話	hanashi	story
2	歴史	rekishi	history
3	作る	tsukuru	create, make
	御存じのはずです	go-zonji no hazu desu	you should know, I suppose you know
4	大変	taihen	very, very much
5	第一図	daiichi zu	Figure I.
	ごらんになる	goran ni naru	look (=miru) (honorific)
7	絵に近い	e ni chikai	akin (close) to a picture
	一目で	hitome de	at a glance
8	物	mono	thing, object
	形	katachi	shape
	を絵に画く	...o e ni kaku	draw a picture of (something)
9	こういう風に	kō iu fū ni	in this way
	象形文字	shōkeimoji	pictograph
11	想・像する	sōzō suru	guess, imagine

p57

7	歯	ha	tooth
	鳥	tori	bird
	草	kusa	grass

8 目で見ることの出来るもの‖つまり形を持ったもの

	つまり	tsumari	in other words
10	動き	ugoki	movement

46

p57
11　言葉　　　　　　　kotoba　　　　　　　word

作字する　　　　　sakuji suru　　　　create a character

13　指事文字　　　　　shijimoji　　　　　ideograph (diagrammatic character)

考え出す　　　　　kangaedasu　　　　devise, think of

p58
3　(今 私達が使っている)⟶ 上．下の字

4　イ は木の下の方にしるしをつけて……を‖ロは反対に……という意味を

5　しるし　　　　　　shirushi　　　　　mark

反対に　　　　　　hantai ni　　　　on the contrary

6　末　　　　　　　　sue　　　　　　　end

7　示す　　　　　　　shimesu　　　　　indicate

手を広げる　　　　te o hirogeru　　extend the arms

11　(いろいろとちがった)⟶ 形

12　だんだんと　　　　dandan to　　　　gradually

13　図示する　　　　　zushi suru　　　　show in a graph

変り方　　　　　　kawarikata　　　　manner of change

Supplement

p60
2　四谷第七小学校　　Yotsuya dai-shichi shōgakkō　　the Seventh School of Yotsuya District

p62　石井　　　　　　　Ishii　　　　　　(surname)

3　話題　　　　　　　wadai　　　　　　topic (of conversation)

Lesson IX. KANJI NO HANASHI (SONO NI)

2	合わせる	awaseru	combine
4	右	migi	right, right-hand
5	左	hidari	left, left-hand
6	好	kō	(good)
7	後に	nochi ni	afterwards
	好き	suki	liking, fondness
	好い	ii, yoi	good, desirable
8	もともと	motomoto	originally
	子供	kodomo	child
	育てる	sodateru	rear, raise
11	日	hi	sun
	月	tsuki	moon
	明るい	akarui	bright
12	会意文字	kaiimoji	ideograph (composite character)
13	面白い	omoshiroi	interesting
	お目にかける	o-me ni kakeru	show (humble)

2	屋根	yane	roof
4	氷	kōri	ice
	割れ目	wareme	crack, fissure
	家	ie	house
6	寒	kan	(cold)

48

p64			
6	寒い	samui	cold (atmospheric temperature)
7	ベッド	beddo	bed (Western-style)
	画く	kaku	sketch, draw
9	形声文字	keiseimoji	phonetic character
10	パーセント	pāsento	per cent
11	グループ	gurūpu	group
p65			
6	それぞれ	sorezore	respectively
7	カテゴリー	kategorī	category
8	虫	mushi	insect, worm
10	魚	sakana	fish
13	すぐ	sugu	immediately
p66			
1	左右	sayū	left and right
	分ける	wakeru	divide
2	勉強	benkyō	study
	都合がいい	tsugō ga ii	beneficial, convenient
3	時には	toki ni wa	from time to time
4	一つ一つの	hitotsu-hitotsu no	each
	面	men	aspect, face

Supplement

p67			
11	場合	baai	occasion, case

49

Lesson X. NIKKI

1	課	-ka	lesson
2	九日	kokonoka	the ninth day (of the month)
3	雨	ame	rain
	当分	tōbun	for some time
4	天気	tenki	weather
	ツヅク	tsuzuku	continue
	日本史	Nihonshi	Japanese history
	講義ニ出ル	kōgi ni deru	attend a lecture (class)
5	アジア	Ajia	Asia
	国々	kuniguni	countries
6	タダ一ツ	tada hitotsu	alone
	中世	chūsei	medieval age
	西洋	seiyō	West, Occident

8 （中世ト名ヅケテモヨイヨウナ）→ 時代

	名ヅケル	nazukeru	call, name
	時代	jidai	period, era
9	近代化	kindaika	modernization
	化	-ka	-ization, -ification, etc.
	関係	kankei	relation(ship)

ari wa shimai ka = aru no de wa nai darō ka

10	図書館	toshokan	library

mattaku   quite, entirely, completely, simply

p69
11	返ス	kaesu	return
	文化	bunka	culture
	関スル	kansuru	concern
12	借リル	kariru	borrow
	行ク途中デ	iku tochū de	on the way
	長町	Nagamachi	(surname)
13	出会ウ	deau	run into, happen to meet
	今学期	kongakki	this (school) term

p70
1	考古学	kōkogaku	archeology
2	代リ	kawari	exchange, compensation

omoshiroi kawari ni = "although (at the same time that) it is interesting"

	沢山	takusan	large number, amount
4	買物	kaimono	shopping
	ノート	nōto	notebook
	ボールペン	bōrupen	ballpoint pen
5	カード・ボックス	kādo bokkusu	card box
	タイプライター用紙	taipuraitā yōshi	typing paper
	クリスマス	kurisumasu	Christmas
	カラー・フィルム	karā firumu	color film
	キー・ホールダー	kī hōrudā	key holder
7	オ金ヲ使ウ	o-kane o tsukau	spend money
8	木曜	mokuyō	Thursday
	大雪	ōyuki	heavy snow
9	昨日	kinō	yesterday

51

p70 9	一晩中	hitobanjū	throughout the night
	一米以上	ichimētoru ijō	more than a meter
10	自動車	jidōsha	automobile
	ノロノロト	noronoro to	slowly, sluggishly
	歩道	hodō	sidewalk
	歩ク	aruku	walk
11	アパート	apāto	apartment house
p71 2	中食	chūshoku	lunch, noon meal
	食堂	shokudō	dining hall, restaurant
	シバラク	shibaraku	for a while
3	日本近代史	Nihon kindaishi	modern Japanese history (i.e., since 1868)
4	明治	Meiji	Meiji era (1868-1912)
	英国	Eikoku	United Kingdom
	フランス	Furansu	France
	問題	mondai	question, problem
5	話題	wadai	topic, subject
6	明晩	myōban	tomorrow night
	君	kimi	you (familiar form used by men and boys)
	車	kuruma	automobile, vehicle
	スキー	sukī	ski
	高村	Takamura	(surname)
7	パーティー	pātī	party
8	今度	kondo	this time
	休ミ	yasumi	vacation, holiday (yasumu = rest)
10	今晩	konban	this evening

hotondo

almost, nearly, all but practically

52

p71
10 アーネスト・サトウ   Ānesuto Satō   Sir Ernest Mason Satow (British scholar and diplomat, 1843-1929)

11 一外交官ノ見タ明治維新   Ichi gaikōkan no mita Meiji Ishin   <u>A Diplomat in Japan</u> (London, 1921) (The Meiji Restoration as Seen by One Diplomat)

外交官   <u>gaikōkan</u>   diplomat

12 カードヲトル   <u>kādo o toru</u>   take notes on cards

西沢   Nishizawa   (surname)

手紙   tegami   letter

Supplement

p72
4 動カス   <u>ugokasu</u>   move, put in motion

8 語学   gogaku   language study

p73
6 西   nishi   west

Lesson XI. BENRI NA MOJI

1	便利な	benri na	handy, convenient
2	位	gurai, kurai	about, approximately
	南太平洋	Minami Taiheiyō	South Pacific
	トンガ島	Tongatō	Tonga Island
3	ウィリヤム・マリイナー	Uiriyamu Mariinā	William Mariner (1791-1853)
	のる	noru	be on board, get on board, ride in
	船	fune	boat, ship
	難破する	nanpa suru	be shipwrecked
4	船員	sen'in	crew, crewman
	島	shima	island
	上がる	agaru	land, go up
	たすけを求める	tasuke o motomeru	seek (ask for) help
5	土人	dojin	native, aborigine
	わたす	watasu	hand over, deliver
6	着く	tsuku	arrive
	船長	senchō	(ship) captain
7	たのむ	tanomu	ask, request
	あやしい	ayashii	suspicious, dubious
	しゅう長	shūchō	tribal chief
	持って行く	motte iku	take (something)
9	彼	kare	he, that man

54

Lesson XI

9   呼ぶ   yobu   call, send for

10   setsumei shite kikaseta = "explained (to him)"

12 声の聞こえる所	koe no kikoeru tokoro	where the voice can be heard
通じる	tsūjiru	reach, get through, be understood
13 とおい	tōi	far, distant
ぜんぜん	zenzen	completely, (not) at all

1 こちらの考え	kochira no kangae	our (my) idea
2 伝える	tsutaeru	convey, pass on

（どんなに大きな……ような）→ 所

3 声を出す	koe o dasu	raise one's voice
4 命令を出す	meirei o dasu	give an order
5 むこう	mukō	over there
6 動作	dōsa	action
7 感心する	kanshin suru	be impressed
翌日	yokujitsu	the following day
8 老人	rōjin	old man
やって来る	yatte kuru	come along, turn up
9 自分達	jibuntachi	ourselves, us, we
10 つけ加える	tsukekuwaeru	add
11 せっかくの	sekkaku no	precious, hard-earned

sekkaku no moji = "the writing system which men have gone to such trouble to create"

役に立たない	yaku ni tatanai	be useless, serve no purpose
12 覚える	oboeru	learn, memorize
13 やりはじめる	yarihajimeru	start to do

p76			
13	地位	chii	position, rank
	あぶない	abunai	insecure, dangerous
p77			
2	もっとも	mottomo	however
3	そっと	sotto	stealthily, secretly
	呼びよせる	yobiyoseru	call, send for (an inferior)

Supplement

p78			
2	山本有三	Yamamoto Yūzō	(novelist, 1887-)
6	ニユース	nyūsu	news
13	路傍の石	Robō no Ishi	Robō no Ishi (1937) (A
p79			Stone by the Roadside)
2	テキスト	tekisuto	text(book)

Based on Yamamoto Yūzō 山本有三 , "Moji to kokumin" 文字と国民 (Writing and the people), Sekai 世界, April, 1946, pp. 80-81.

Yamamoto Yūzō (1887-   ) is a novelist and playwright.

Yamamoto's works are pervaded by sympathy for the poor and indignation against social evils. Toward 1935 he began to show a deep interest in simplifying the Japanese writing system, and he played a leading role in the language reforms carried out after World War II. In his own writings, Yamamoto cultivates simplicity of style and avoids difficult kanji.

For a different version of this anecdote, based on more trustworthy sources, see James A. Michener and A. Grove Day, Rascals in Paradise (New York, 1957), pp. 275-305, especially p. 294.

Lesson XII. OBASUTEYAMA

1	姥捨山	obasuteyama	(mountain where aged women were abandoned)
2	親	oya	parent
3	連れて行く	tsurete iku	take (someone) along
	捨てる	suteru	abandon
	習慣	shūkan	custom
	有る	aru	be, exist
	誰	dare	who
4	孝行な	kōkō na	filial
5	若者	wakamono	youth, young man
	年をとる	toshi o toru	grow old, age
	母親	hahaoya	mother
	暮す	kurasu	live, lead a life
7	村	mura	village
8	悲しい	kanashii	sad
9	しかたがない	shikata ga nai	it cannot be helped
	背負う	seou	carry (hold) on one's back
	上る	noboru	climb, ascend
10	夜	yoru	night
	泣く	naku	cry, weep
11	山道	yamamichi	mountain path
	道中	dōchū	en route

p80
11 （背中の母親が……くり返している）→こと

	背中	senaka	(one's) back
12	何度も（何度も）	nando mo (nando mo)	again and again
	くり返す	kurikaesu	repeat
	気がつく	ki ga tsuku	notice, become aware of
	気をつける	ki o tsukeru	pay attention
13	生える	haeru	grow (of hair, plants)
	枝を折る	eda o oru	break a branch

p81
3	たずねる	tazuneru	ask, inquire
	お前	o-mae	you (familiar)
	慣れない	narenai	unfamiliar
4	帰る	kaeru	return, go home
	迷う	mayou	lose one's way, be confused
5	答える	kotaeru	answer
	返事	henji	reply
6	（する）気になる	(suru) ki ni naru	feel like (doing), be inclined to (do)

ki ni wa dōshitemo narezu = "utterly unable to bring himself to
(abandon his mother)" (narezu=negative potential of naru)

8	かくす	kakusu	hide
9	いつの間にか	itsu no ma ni ka	before one knows, before one is aware
	知れ渡る	shirewataru	become widely known
12	説話	setsuwa	traditional tale, legend
	内容	naiyō	content, story
13	北	kita	north
	南	minami	south

p81
13 残る　　　　　　　nokoru　　　　　remain
p82
1 有名　　　　　　　yūmei　　　　　famous

長野県　　　　　　Nagano-ken　　　Nagano prefecture

更科　　　　　　　Sarashina　　　(place name)

4 世紀　　　　　　　seiki　　　　　century

以来　　　　　　　irai　　　　　since

文学　　　　　　　bungaku　　　literature

5 以前は　　　　　　izen wa　　　formerly, in former times

大きくなる　　　　ōkiku naru　　grow up

かならず　　　　　kanarazu　　　definitely, without fail

6 終り　　　　　　　owari　　　　　end

両親　　　　　　　ryōshin　　　(both) parents

7 普通(な)　　　　　futsū (na)　　usual, ordinary

Supplement

p83
2 北海道　　　　　　Hokkaidō　　　(northernmost island of Japan)

帰京する　　　　　kikyō suru　　return to Tokyo

残金　　　　　　　zankin　　　　money left (over)

3 連中　　　　　　　renchū, renjū　company, group

4 南村　　　　　　　Minamimura　　(surname)

5 東北　　　　　　　tōhoku　　　　the Northeast, the northeastern section of Japan

8 しし　　　　　　　shishi　　　　lion

すし　　　　　　　sushi　　　　rice flavored with vinegar and combined with fish, seaweed, etc.

すす　　　　　　　susu　　　　　soot

p83

9	動物	dōbutsu	animal
10	食べる	taberu	eat
	天井	tenjō	ceiling
13	シンデレラ	Shinderera	Cinderella

p84

| 3 | 感じ | kanji | feeling |
| 4 | の背後に | no haigo ni | behind |

It has not been proved that the custom described in this story actually existed in Japan. Seki Keigo 関敬吾, an ethnologist, points out that the custom of fūsō 風葬 (exposure of corpses), which still exists in some southwestern islands of Japan, may be the origin of the traditional tale of Obasuteyama.

Narayamabushi-kō 楢山節考 (The songs of Oak Mountain), a 1956 readaptation of this tale by Fukasawa Shichirō 深沢七郎, revived public attention to the old legend.

Lesson XIII. TEGAMI

2	有り難うございました	arigatō gozaimashita	thank you (for something already done)
	御元気に	o-genki ni	happily, pleasantly (honorific)
	旅行	ryokō	trip
	なさる	nasaru	do (=suru) (honorific)
3	安心する	anshin suru	feel relieved
	いたす	itasu	do (=suru) (humble)
4	一同	ichidō	all (of us)
	過す	sugosu	pass time, live
5	毛	ke	fur, hair
	毎日	mainichi	every day
	庭	niwa	garden, yard
	走り廻る	hashirimawaru	run around
6	一緒 (に)	issho (ni)	together
	本当に	hontō ni	truly
	家	uchi	home, house
7	一人旅	hitoritabi	traveling alone
	言葉	kotoba	word, expression
9	疲れる	tsukareru	become tired, fatigued
13	冬休み	fuyuyasumi	winter vacation

1	セール	sēru	sale
	はじまる	hajimaru	begin

61

p86			
1	今週	konshū	this week
	土曜日	doyōbi	Saturday
2	買物	kaimono	shopping
	ついて行く	tsuite iku	accompany, follow
	去年	kyonen	last year
	人形	ningyō	doll
3	スケート靴	sukētogutsu	(shoe) skates
	欲しい	hoshii	want; desirous (of)
4	高過ぎる	takasugiru	too expensive
	安い	yasui	inexpensive, cheap
5	自転車	jitensha	bicycle
6	多分	tabun	perhaps
9	元より	moto yori	than before
	太る	futoru	gain weight
10	きれい	kirei	pretty, beautiful
11	是非	zehi	without fail
13	テレビ	terebi	television
	ロックフェラー・センター	Rokkuferā sentā	Rockefeller Center
p87			
1	クリスマス・ツリー	kurisumasu tsurī	Christmas tree
4	例年	reinen	average year, ordinary year
5	朝	asa	morning
	冷たい	tsumetai	chilly, cold (of water, wind, an object)
	雨	ame	rain
	降る	furu	fall (rain, snow)
	雪	yuki	snow

p87
8   nashi no = no nai (literary)

本物	honmono	genuine thing
11 お祈り申し上げる	o-inori mōshiageru	pray, wish (epistolary form)
プレゼント	purezento	present, gift
12 送る	okuru	send

Supplement

p89

3 年末	nenmatsu	the year-end, the end of the year
4 日毎	higoto	day after day, every day
5 早朝	sōchō	early morning
7 降りる	oriru	get off, alight from
ジングルベル	jinguruberu	Jingle Bells
8 ショーウィンドウ	shōwindō	show window, display window
9 サンタクロース	santakurōsu	Santa Claus
11 過ぎる	sugiru	pass (by), go past

p90

5 発送する	hassō suru	send, dispatch
6 七時過ぎ	shichiji-sugi	(a little) after 7 o'clock
8 クリスチャン	kurisuchan	Christian
過去	kako	past
13 夕食	yūshoku	supper

63

Lesson XIV. JISHO NI TSUITE

1	辞書	jisho	dictionary
5	二三	nisan	two or three, a few
6	国語辞典	kokugo jiten	Japanese language dictionary
	漢和字典	kanwa jiten	(Chinese-)Japanese character dictionary
	必要 (な)	hitsuyō (na)	necessary
7	最近	saikin	recently
	始める	hajimeru	begin
9	ただ	tada	however
	漢英辞典	kan'ei jiten	Japanese-English character dictionary
10	旧漢字	kyūkanji	old form of Chinese character (used before 1946)
11	間に合う	ma ni au	(that) will do, serve the purpose
13	現在	genzai	at present
	最も	mottomo	the most (superlative)
	新村	Shinmura	(surname)
	広辞苑	Kōjien	(name of a dictionary)

1　人名地名など ‖ 百科事典にあるような言葉

	人名	jinmei	name of person
	地名	chimei	name of place
	百科事典	hyakka jiten	encyclopedia
3	金田一	Kindaichi	(surname)
	辞海	Jikai	(name of a dictionary)

64

p92

3	良い	yoi, ii	good, desirable
4	当用漢字	tōyō kanji	characters for practical use (the 1850 characters currently prescribed by the Ministry of Education)
5	始終	shijū	continually
7	博士	hakushi, hakase	doctor (of philosophy)
	言語学者	gengogakusha	linguist
	者	-sha	(suffix indicating person involved in a given activity)
8	平仮名で引く	hiragana de hiku	consult, look up in <u>hiragana</u>
9	五十音順	gojūon jun	AIUEO order ("the 50 sounds" = the <u>kana</u> syllabary)
	ならぶ	narabu	be arranged, be lined up
10	順序	junjo	order
11	全部	zenbu	wholly, all
12	だから	dakara	therefore, so
13	和英辞典	waei jiten	Japanese-English dictionary
	用いる	mochiiru	use, make use of

p93

1	研究社	Kenkyūsha	(name of a publishing company)
	新和英辞典	Shin Waei Jiten	(name of a dictionary)
2	将来	shōrai	future
	必らず	kanarazu	definitely, without fail
3	それ以外に	sore igai ni	other than that
	アルファベット	arufabetto	alphabet
4	出る	deru	be published
	国語新辞典	Kokugo Shin Jiten	(name of a dictionary)

p93

5 見出し   midashi   (vocabulary) entry,
                                    heading

   ローマ字   rōmaji   Roman letter(s)

6 終り   owari   end

7 現代の   gendai no   modern, contemporary

   以上の   ijō no   above (mentioned)

9 o-isogashii tokoro o hontō ni arigatō gozaimashita = "Thank
   you very much (for helping me) when you are so busy."

   忙しい   isogashii   busy

   早速   sassoku   at once

   本屋   hon'ya   bookstore

10 注文する   chūmon suru   order (something)

Supplement

p94

2 ブーム   būmu   a boom

3 ベスト・セラー   besuto serā   best-seller

7 利用する   riyō suru   use, utilize

8 売る   uru   sell

p95

1 使用する   shiyō suru   use, employ

2 ペーパーバック   pēpābakku   paperback

   非常に   hijō ni   very, extremely

4 戦後   sengo   after the war

5 スタイル   sutairu   style (manner of writing)

   用語   yōgo   vocabulary, wording

   戦前   senzen   before (and during) the war

6 教科書   kyōkasho   (school) textbook

p95
10 現象   genshō   phenomenon

11 多忙   tabō   busy

Lesson XV.   JITEN NO HIKIKATA

2   質問   shitsumon   question, inquiry

お暇ですか   o-hima desu ka   Do you have time?

4   おかけなさい   o-kake nasai   Please sit down.

(shitsumon) te = (shitsumon) to iu no wa (colloq.)

5   実は   jitsu wa   actually

休暇   kyūka   vacation

6   調べる   shiraberu   investigate

見つける   mitsukeru   find

8   部首   bushu   radical (of a character)

見つかる   mitsukaru   be found

9   偏   hen   left side of a character

旁   bō   right side of a character

冠   kan, kanmuri   crown, upper part of a
                                         character

脚   kyaku   lower part of a character

12   (hen) te no wa = (hen) to iu no wa

側   -gawa   side

1   表   hyō   chart

2   お願いします   o-negai shimasu   yes, please; please do

13   大字典   Daijiten   (name of a dictionary)

索引   sakuin   index

1   名   na   name

p98			
1	覚えて置く	oboete oku	memorize (for future use)
3	場合	baai	case
6	すべて	subete	all
7	つくり	tsukuri	right side of a character (=bō)
p99			
1	原則として	gensoku to shite	as a rule
	次に	tsugi ni	next, following
p100			
8	似る	niru	resemble
	頭	kashira	head, upper part of a character
10	人頭	hitogashira	a top made of the character hito
	入頭	irigashira	a top made of the character iru
11	八頭	hachigashira	a top made of the character hachi
p101			
1	クロス・レファレンス	kurosu refarensu	cross reference
4	構	kamae	enclosure radical
5	前者	zensha	former
	門構	mongamae	radical for "gate"
	後者	kōsha	latter
	国構	kunigamae	radical for "country"
6	垂	tare	radical enclosing character from top to lower left
7	にょう	nyō (nyū)	radical enclosing character from top left to lower right
	かける	kakeru	stretch (extend) across
12	簡単な	kantan na	simple, easy
13	後に	ushiro ni	at the back
p102			
1	片仮名	katakana	square Japanese syllabary

p102

4	時々	tokidoki	sometimes
5	総画	sōkaku	total number of strokes
	画数	kakusū	number of strokes
6	数	kazu	number, figure
7	たいてい	taitei	generally, usually

Supplement

p103

4	地図	chizu	map
8	変った	kawatta	peculiar
13	大阪	Ōsaka	Osaka
	土偏	tsuchi-hen	earth radical

p104

2	肇国	chōkoku	founding of an empire
9	ニックネーム	nikkunēmu	nickname
11	難訓字典	nankun jiten	(dictionary of difficult readings, without definitions, of Chinese characters and compounds)
12	名刺	meishi	calling card

Lesson XVI. NIHON NO CHIRI

p105

1	地理	chiri	geography
2	島国	shimaguni	insular country
	北海道	Hokkaidō	(northernmost island of Japan)
	本州	Honshū	(main island of Japan)
	四国	Shikoku	(island off southern Honshū)
	九州	Kyūshū	(southernmost island of Japan)
3	北東	hokutō	northeast
	南西	nansei	southwest
	大陸	tairiku	continent
	東海岸	higashi kaigan	east coast
	平行する	heikō suru	parallel
	細長い	hosonagai	long and narrow
	一列に	ichiretsu ni	in a line
5	メイン	Mein	Maine
	州	-shū	state
	フロリダ	Furorida	Florida
	マイアミ	Maiami	Miami
6	まわりに	mawari ni	around, surrounding
	西	nishi	west
	東支那海	Higashi Shina Kai	East China Sea
7	日本海	Nihon Kai	Sea of Japan
	太平洋	Taiheiyō	Pacific Ocean
		narande iru	arranged

71

p105

7	オホーツク海	Ohōtsuku Kai	Sea of Okhotsk
8	地図	chizu	map, atlas
	狭い	semai	small, narrow
	しかも	shikamo	moreover
9	非常に	hijō ni	extremely
	大部分	daibubun	the major part
10	国土	kokudo	land, national territory
	農業	nōgyō	agriculture
11	利用する	riyō suru	use, utilize
	何所	doko	where
12	畑	hatake	(cultivated dry) field
	見受ける	miukeru	see, come across
	入れる	ireru	include
13	そうかといって	sō ka to itte	even so

p106

1	カナダ	Kanada	Canada
2	比べる	kuraberu	compare (with)
	面積	menseki	area (of a surface)
3	火山	kazan	volcano
	特長	tokuchō	characteristic, (special) feature
	歴史時代	rekishi jidai	the period of recorded history
	(歴史時代に……ことのある)→ 火山		
4	活動する	katsudō suru	be active
	世界	sekai	world
5	十パーセント近く	juppāsento chikaku	nearly 10 per cent

72

p106
6 集まる　　atsumaru　　gather, congregate

点　　ten　　point, regard, respect

その点で　　sono ten de　　in that respect

国　　-koku　　country

8 河川　　kasen　　rivers

短い　　mijikai　　short

流れ　　nagare　　current, flow, stream

9 交通　　kōtsū　　transportation, traffic

水力発電　　suiryoku hatsuden　　hydroelectricity

10 湖　　mizuumi　　lake

11 平野　　heiya　　plain

そして　　soshite　　and, thus

都会　　tokai　　city

多く　　ōku　　most(ly)

12 京都　　Kyōto　　Kyoto

東京　　Tōkyō　　Tokyo

横浜　　Yokohama　　Yokohama

名古屋　　Nagoya　　Nagoya

大阪　　Ōsaka　　Osaka

13 神戸　　Kōbe　　Kobe

p107
3 調べ　　shirabe　　census, survey

約　　yaku　　approximately

以後　　igo　　after

半世紀　　hanseiki　　half a century

73

p107

4	二倍	nibai	two times, double
	毎年	mainen	every year
5	平方キロメートル	heihō kiromētoru	square kilometer
7	オランダ	Oranda	Holland, The Netherlands
	ベルギー	Berugī	Belgium
	共に	tomo ni	along with, together with
	密度	mitsudo	density

Supplement

p108

2	土地	tochi	land
	失う	ushinau	lose
	今日	konnichi	today, present
6	生活出来る平地	seikatsu dekiru heichi	habitable level land
10	農民	nōmin	farming population, farmer
p109			
2	作物をとる	sakumotsu o toru	gather in a crop
5	量	-ryō	amount, quantity
	第六位	dai-roku i	the sixth place

From this lesson on you will frequently meet the "impersonal style" --- that found in most books, articles, lectures, announcements, and the like. The impersonal style is chiefly characterized by the use of plain forms, of the <u>de aru</u> copula (see Lesson 3), and of the stem of the -<u>masu</u> form (e.g., <u>aruki</u> from <u>arukimasu</u>) in place of the -<u>te</u> form (as in <u>nari</u>, 107. 4, for <u>natte</u>).

Lesson XVII. NIHON NO REKISHI

2 特色　　　　　　tokushoku　　　　characteristic, feature

（非常に早くから……今日まで続いている）→ こと

3 民族　　　　　　minzoku　　　　　people, race

　　による　　　　ni yoru　　　　　by (agent)

　　統一国家　　　tōitsu kokka　　　unified nation

4 分れる　　　　　wakareru　　　　　separate, divide

　　今日　　　　　konnichi　　　　　present time, today

5 続く　　　　　　tsuzuku　　　　　continue

8 色々な　　　　　iroiro na　　　　various

10 （統一国家が……調べる）→ こと

11 逆に（言うと）　gyaku ni (iu to)　conversely, on the other hand

（それほど……統一されていた）→ こと

13 家　　　　　　　-ka　　　　　　　specialist (rekishika = historian)

　　政治　　　　　seiji　　　　　　government, politics

　　中心地　　　　chūshinchi　　　　center (location)

　　場所　　　　　basho　　　　　　place

1 奈良　　　　　　Nara　　　　　　　(city near Kyoto)

　　平安　　　　　Heian　　　　　　(abbreviation of Heiankyō, old name for Kyoto)

　　鎌倉　　　　　Kamakura　　　　(city near Tokyo)

　　室町　　　　　Muromachi　　　　(district in Kyoto)

4 常に　　　　　　tsune ni　　　　always

　　　　　　　　　mottomo　　　　　extremely

出来上がる　　　　dekiagaru　　　　be finished
　　　　　　　　　　　　　　　　　be ready for
　　　　　　　　　　　　　　　　　be made for
　　　　　　　　　　　　　　　　　be cut out for

75

motomoto　　originally
tashika　　for sure, for certain
ni shite mo　though, even if, and yet, granting

Lesson XVII

p111

4	天皇	tennō	emperor (of Japan)
7	戦う	tatakau	fight, make war
8	一時的な	ichijiteki na	temporary
9	(江戸時代の……一度もない)→ 強力な統一国家		
10	戦争	sensō	war
	強力な	kyōryoku na	powerful, strong
11	何故	naze	why
	原因	gen'in	cause
12	広い	hiroi	large, broad, wide

p112

2	持続する	jizoku suru	continue, endure
5	あるいは	aruiwa	or
9	条件	jōken	(limiting) condition
10	広狭	kōkyō	area (large or small)
11	遠い	tōi	far, distant
13	文明	bunmei	civilization
	言うまでもない	iu made mo nai	be needless to say

p113

1	影響	eikyō	influence, effect
	受ける	ukeru	receive, be exposed to
	続ける	tsuzukeru	continue
2	通して	tōshite	through (the agency of)
	インド	Indo	India
	西方	seihō	west
	輸入する	yunyū suru	introduce, import
3	元	Gen	Yüan (Mongol) dynasty (1279-1368)

76

p113
3 大軍　　　　　taigun　　　　　great force, large army

（大陸の方から……近づいた）→こと

4 近づく　　　　chikazuku　　　approach

5 （文明文化を輸入……作りあげることが出来た）→の

7 （近過ぎもせず……日本があったから）→だ

8 強過ぎる　　　tsuyosugiru　　be too strong

10 低い　　　　　hikui　　　　　low

12 及ぶ　　　　　oyobu　　　　　reach, extend to

（日本の場合には……良かった）→こと

p114
2 無理（な）　　muri (na)　　　unreasonable, impossible

4 述べる　　　　noberu　　　　state, relate

Supplement

p115
6 遠方　　　　　enpō　　　　　distant place, a very long distance

輸送　　　　　yusō　　　　　transport, carriage

9 豊臣秀吉　　　Toyotomi Hideyoshi　　general, statesman (1536-1595)

12 速い　　　　　hayai　　　　quick, fast

p116
3 遅い　　　　　osoi　　　　　slow

4 二週間　　　　ni-shūkan　　2 weeks

6 馬　　　　　　uma　　　　　horse

8 リレー　　　　rirē　　　　　relay

オールコック　Ōrukokku　　Sir Rutherford Alcock (British diplomat, 1809-1897)

9 長崎　　　　　Nagasaki　　（seaport on west coast of Kyūshū)

10 遅れる　　　　okureru　　　be delayed, late

p117

1	カミカゼ	kamikaze	divine wind
2	吹く	fuku	blow
4	大風	ōkaze	gale, violent wind
6	二度目	nidome	the second time
7	シーズン	shīzun	season

p118

1	駈込寺	kakekomidera	running-in temple (another name for Tōkeiji)
2	東京駅	Tōkyō-eki	Tokyo Station
	電車	densha	electric train, streetcar
	鎌倉	Kamakura	(city near Tokyo)
3	大仏	daibutsu	Great Buddha
	奈良	Nara	(city near Kyoto)
4	幕府	bakufu	shogunate government
	忘れる	wasureru	forget
7	東慶寺	Tōkeiji	(name of a temple)
	禅	Zen	Zen Buddhism
8	尼寺	amadera	convent (ama = nun)
9	江戸	Edo	(former name of Tokyo)
10	結婚する	kekkon suru	marry
	理由	riyū	reason, cause
11	夫	otto	husband
	分かれる	wakareru	be divorced, separate
12	法律	hōritsu	law
	許す	yurusu	permit
13	妻	tsuma	wife
	絶対に	zettai ni	absolutely

p119

2	けれども	keredomo	however
	当時	tōji	those days
3	逃げ込む	nigekomu	take refuge in, escape into
4	修行	shugyō	ascetism, spiritual discipline (training)
	歴史上	rekishijō	historically

79

p119			
4	生活を送る	seikatsu o okuru	lead a life
6	出す	dasu	expel
7	宣言	sengen	declaration
9	もっとも	mottomo	however, nevertheless
10	後半	kōhan	latter half
12	大した	taishita	considerable
p120			
3	ハムレット	Hamuretto	Hamlet
7	興味	kyōmi	interest
8	夏目漱石	Natsume Sōseki	(novelist, 1867-1916)
9	程	hodo	about
10	お坊さん	o-bōsan	Buddhist priest, monk
	移る	utsuru	move
11	経験	keiken	experience
	小説	shōsetsu	novel, fiction
	門	Mon	Mon (1910) (The Gate)
12	作品	sakuhin	(literary or artistic) work
	認める	mitomeru	notice, recognize
p121			
1	死ぬ	shinu	die

Supplement

p122			
4	円覚寺	Enkakuji	(Zen temple)
5	東京教育大学	Tōkyō Kyōiku Daigaku	Tokyo Education University
p123			
1	知人	chijin	acquaintance
3	結びつける	musubi-tsukeru	connect, tie (something) to
5	あける	akeru	open

p123
5 　門番　　　　　　　monban　　　　　　　gate-keeper

　　戸　　　　　　　　to　　　　　　　　　door

6 　遂に　　　　　　　tsui ni　　　　　　　in the end, at last

　　顔　　　　　　　　kao　　　　　　　　　face

7 　通る　　　　　　　tōru　　　　　　　　pass through

　　…ないですむ　　　… nai de sumu　　　can do without -ing...

8 　日が暮れる　　　　hi ga kureru　　　　(the sun) sets, days pass
　　　　　　　　　　　　　　　　　　　　　by
　　不幸な　　　　　　fukō na　　　　　　unfortunate

10 真理　　　　　　　shinri　　　　　　　truth

13 ある程度　　　　　aru teido　　　　　to a certain degree

p124
2 　表われる　　　　　arawareru　　　　　reveal, be expressed

4 　亡くなる　　　　　nakunaru　　　　　　die

　　禅宗　　　　　　　Zen-shū　　　　　　the Zen sect

　　葬儀　　　　　　　sōgi　　　　　　　　funeral (service)

7 　最後　　　　　　　saigo　　　　　　　the last (time)

p125

1	夢殿	Yumedono	Hall of Dreams (name of a building in Hōryūji)
2	或る	aru	a certain, one
	法隆寺	Hōryūji	(name of a temple in Nara)
	様子	yōsu	appearance
3	たずねる	tazuneru	visit
4	仏像	butsuzō	Buddhist statue
	目的	mokuteki	purpose
6	最初	saisho	(at) first
7	きれ	kire	cloth
	紙	kami	paper
	まきつける	makitsukeru	wind around, wrap around
9	断る	kotowaru	refuse, decline

(明治時代の……ことがある)→ という話

	雷がなる	kaminari ga naru	thunder (naru = sound, peal)
10	おどろく	odoroku	be startled, be frightened
	途中で	tochū de	in the middle, midway

11   miseyō to shimasen deshita = "didn't seem to want to show it"

12	我々	wareware	we (literary)
	政府	seifu	(central) government
	許し	yurushi	permission
13	主張する	shuchō suru	insist, claim

82

Lesson XIX

p126 2	恐れる	osoreru	fear
	逃げる	nigeru	flee, escape
3	くも	kumo	spider
	糸	ito	thread
	はらいのける	harainokeru	brush off
	とりのける	torinokeru	remove
4	へび	hebi	snake
	ねずみ	nezumi	mouse, rat
	有様	arisama	state, condition (what you see)
5	やがて	yagate	finally, after a while (yatto)
	最後	saigo	the last
	りっぱな	rippa na	magnificent
6	手をとりあう	te o toriau	take each other's hands
	喜ぶ	yorokobu	rejoice, be delighted

(日本美術の歴史で……と言われる)→夢殿の観音像

7	美術	bijutsu	art
	観音像	Kannonzō	statue of Kannon (the goddess of mercy)
9	作者	sakusha	creator, author
10	の上で	no ue de	in the field of
13	志賀直哉	Shiga Naoya	(novelist, 1883-)
	昭和	Shōwa	Shōwa Era (1926-)
	初年	shonen	~~early years~~ first year
p127 1	感じ	kanji	feeling
	起こす	okosu	give rise to, cause

jōken – restrictive conditions

p127

1　（今では 誰でも …… 有名 に なって いる）→ この 美しい 仏像

2　美しい　　　　　　　utsukushii　　　　　beautiful

5　フェノロサ　　　　　Fenorosa　　　　　　Ernest Fenollosa
　　　　　　　　　　　　　　　　　　　　　　(American educator and
　　　　　　　　　　　　　　　　　　　　　　art critic, 1853-1908)
6　岡倉覚三　　　　　　Okakura Kakuzō　　(philosopher, 1862-1913)

Supplement

p128

2　美術品　　　　　　　bijutsuhin　　　　　art object

4　五重塔　　　　　　　gojūnotō　　　　　　five-storied-pagoda

5　風呂屋　　　　　　　furoya　　　　　　　bathhouse

　　焚木　　　　　　　　takigi　　　　　　　firewood, wood (for fuel)
10　浮世絵　　　　　　　ukiyoe　　　　　　　ukiyoe
11　枚　　　　　　　　　-mai　　　　　　　　(counter for flat object)
p129
1　銭　　　　　　　　　sen　　　　　　　　　(Japanese monetary unit:
　　　　　　　　　　　　　　　　　　　　　　1/100 yen)
7　ビゲロー　　　　　　Bigerō　　　　　　　William Bigelow (1850-
　　　　　　　　　　　　　　　　　　　　　　1926)
9　コレクション　　　　korekushon　　　　collection

　　ボストン・ミュージアム　Bosuton　　　　　Boston Museum of Fine Arts
　　　　　　　　　　　　　myūjiamu

12　松方　　　　　　　　Matsukata　　　　　Matsukata Kōjirō
　　　　　　　　　　　　　　　　　　　　　　(businessman, art
p130　　　　　　　　　　　　　　　　　　　collector, 1865-1950)
1　逆に　　　　　　　　gyaku ni　　　　　conversely

2　許可する　　　　　　kyoka suru　　　　permit, allow

Based on Okakura Tenshin 岡倉天心, Nihon bijutsushi 日本美術史
(History of Japanese art), Tenshin zenshū 天心全集 (Complete works
of Tenshin), vol. 6, Sōgensha 創元社, 1944, p. 65, and Ernest F.
Fenollosa, Epochs of Chinese and Japanese Art, 2 vols., New York,
1921, vol. 1, p. 50.

Okakura Tenshin (1862-1913), the celebrated author of The Book of
Tea (1906), was a pioneer in the revaluation of traditional

Lesson XIX

Japanese art and its introduction abroad.

Ernest Fenollosa (1853-1908) was invited from the United States by the University of Tokyo in 1878 as a lecturer on philosophy, politics, and economics. Retiring from the University in 1886, he joined Okakura in his researches on Japanese art, and in 1890 returned to the United States to accept the position of curator of the Asiatic Department of the Museum of Fine Arts in Boston, a position which Okakura later held. The conservation and study of traditional art in Japan owes much to Fenollosa as well as to Okakura.

Lesson XX.   KUBUNDEN

1	口分田	kubunden	(rice fields distributed to the people after the Taika reform)
2	山の手	yama-no-te	bluffs, heights
	眺め	nagame	view, scene
3	あぜ道	azemichi	footpaths between rice fields
	真直に	massugu ni	straight
	通る	tōru	go through, pass
	囲む	kakomu	enclose, surround
4	田	ta	rice field
	枚	-mai	(counter for flat objects)
	一定の	ittei no	uniform, regular
	広さ	hirosa	area, extent
	丁度	chōdo	just
	碁盤の目	goban no me	square of a go board (resembles a checker board)
5	規則正しく	kisokutadashiku	systematically, regularly
	緑色	midoriiro	green color
6	所々	tokorodokoro	here and there
	溜池	tameike	irrigation pond
	碁石	goishi	go stone
7	正方形	seihōkei	square
8	長方形	chōhōkei	rectangle, oblong
9	自然に	shizen ni	naturally

86

1	特長	tokuchō	distinctive feature, strong point, forte, merit
	大体	daitai	generally, on the whole (outline, summary) in substance originally)

p131

9	古い	furui	(of) long (duration)
10	重要な	jūyō na	important
11	変革	henkaku	change, revolution
	起こる	okoru	occur
	大化の改新	Taika no kaishin	Taika reform (645-646)
12	古代	kodai	ancient times
	均田法	kindenhō	(Chinese) law of equal division of rice fields
	基づく	motozuku	be based on
	班田	handen	distribution of rice fields
	収授	shūju	appropriating and granting
	法	hō	law
13	採用する	saiyō suru	adopt
	公有	kōyū	publicly owned
	私有	shiyū	privately owned

p132

1	土地	tochi	land, estate
	人民	jinmin	people, subjects
	天皇家	tennōke	Imperial family
	改めて	aratamete	again, anew
2	男子	danshi	male
	段	-tan	(unit of area: 0.245 acres)
	女子	joshi	female
3	分け与える	wakeataeru	distribute
	定める	sadameru	prescribe, establish *decree*
	制度	seido	system
5	人毎に	hito goto ni	to each person

5 つまり　・　　*after all, eventually in short, that is*

Lesson XX

6	収める	osameru	*give* appropriate, collect
	授ける	sazukeru	grant
7	行なう	okonau	carry out

2	地方	chihō	provinces, district
3	間もなく	mamonaku	before long
5	正倉院	Shōsōin	Imperial Treasury at Nara
	為に	tame ni	in order to
	記録	kiroku	record, document
	間もなく	mamonaku	soon (after), presently, shortly, before long

Supplement

4	東大寺	Tōdaiji	(a temple in Nara)
5	能	nō	Nō play
8	神社	jinja	Shinto shrine
	芸術	geijutsu	art

4	井戸	ido	well
5	嫌い	kirai	dislike, hate
6	釘を打つ	kugi o utsu	drive a nail, nail
11	採り入れる	toriireru	adopt

Based on a Japanese schoolboy's composition, included in <u>Tsuzurikata fudoki</u> 綴方風土記 (School essays on Japanese geography), Heibonsha 平凡社 , 1953, vol. 5, pp. 266-67.

Lesson XXI. DEJIMA

1	出島	Dejima	(island in Nagasaki harbor)
2	長崎	Nagasaki	(seaport on west coast of Kyūshū)
	お蝶夫人	o-Chō fujin	Madam Butterfly

（お蝶夫人とか……有名な）→ 港

	' ピエル・ロティ	Pieru Roti	Pierre Loti (French novelist, 1850-1923)
	お菊さん	o-Kiku-san	(heroine of novel: <u>Madame Chrysanthème</u>, 1887)
	等	nado	and so forth, etc.
3	国際的に	kokusaiteki ni	internationally
	港	minato	port, harbor
	明治維新	Meiji ishin	Meiji Restoration
5	徳川幕府	Tokugawa bakufu	Tokugawa Shogunate
	鎖国	sakoku	national isolation
	政策	seisaku	(government) policy
	海外諸国	kaigai shokoku	overseas countries
7	ni shite mo = no baai demo		

8 （長崎の港……作られた）→ 小さな島

	人工的に	jinkōteki ni	artificially
9	居住する	kyojū suru	reside
	特別な	tokubetsu na	special
11	経済的	keizaiteki	economic
12	交際する	kōsai suru	associate with, mingle with
13	科学	kagaku	science
	主として	しゅとして	mainly, chiefly
	通して	とうして	thru, thru the medium for, of

当時 とうじ *in these (those) days, time*

Lesson XXI

p137
13 進んでいる　susunde iru　be advanced

p138
1 医学　igaku　study of medicine

3 知識人　chishikijin　intellectual (person)
　　　　　　　　　　　　(<u>chishiki</u> = knowledge)
　認識する　ninshiki suru　recognize, perceive

4 何とかして　nan toka shite　somehow or other

　進歩する　shinpo suru　progress, advance

　得る　eru, uru　obtain

5 (オランダ語を …… 集まった) → 人々

9 広がる　hirogaru　spread

10 国内に　kokunai ni　within the country

　混乱　konran　confusion

　一つには　hitotsu ni wa　for one thing

13 存在　sonzai　existence, place (in history, etc.)

p139
1 埋める　uzumeru　fill in (up)

mawari o uzumerarete = "land has been filled in all around it"
(the area around it has been filled in)

2 住む　sumu　live, reside

　扇　ōgi　(folding) fan

　港内に　kōnai ni　into the harbor, in the harbor

　つき出る　tsukideru　project

3 橋　hashi　bridge

4 出入口　deiriguchi　gateway

5 開国する　kaikoku suru　open a country (to foreign intercourse)

　に対して　ni taishite　toward

　開く　hiraku　open

90

p139
5	窓、	mado	window
6	光り	hikari	light
	さし込む	sashikomu	shine into

Supplement

p140
2	グラバー邸	Gurabā-tei	the mansion of (Thomas) Glover
6	輸出入	yushutsu-nyū	import and export
10	済む	sumu	be finished, be over
	カトリック	katorikku	Catholic
12	教会	kyōkai	church

p141
1	カトリック教	katorikkukyō	Catholicism
2	止める	tomeru	forbid
3	プチジャン	Puchijan	Bernard Thadée Petitjean (1829-84)
4	信者	shinja	believer, follower of a religion
7	申し込む	mōshikomu	request, ask for, apply for
9	サンタ・マリア	Santa Maria	Santa Maria

p142
1	現存する	genson suru	be in existence, remain intact

気がつく   notice, perceive, find

p143

1	封建制度	hōken seido	feudal system
3	一方においては	ippō ni oite wa	on the one hand (<u>ni oite</u> <u>wa</u> = <u>de wa</u>)
4	他方においては	tahō ni oite wa	on the other hand
	異なる	kotonaru	differ
5	発達	hattatsu	development, advancement
	速度	sokudo	(rate of) speed
7	根本的	konponteki	fundamental
8	初期	shoki	early stage
	封建制	hōkensei	feudal system (= <u>hōken</u> seido)
	高度に	kōdo ni	to a high degree, highly
	…に至るまで	ni itaru made	up to, until
10	とげる	togeru	achieve
	程度	teido	degree, level
11	to iu yō ni = "as may be seen from the fact that"		
12	足利時代	Ashikaga jidai	Ashikaga period (1338-1573)
13	末期	makki	final stage, end
	比較	hikaku	comparison

p144

2	すたれる	sutareru	die out, become obsolete

dochira ka to iu to = "if anything, rather (if one were to say which one)"

急速に	kyūsoku ni	rapidly
sunawachi	i.e., namely, that is to say	

p144
3	組織化する	soshikika suru	systematize
4	中央集権	chūōshūken	centralized power
7	急激に	kyūgeki ni	abruptly, precipitously
	たちまち	tachimachi	suddenly, at once
	終りをつげる	owari o tsugeru	come to an end, announce the end
8	段階	dankai	stage
9	歩み	ayumi	course, steps
11	容易に	yōi ni	easily
12	たがいに	tagai ni	mutually, with each other
	競争する	kyōsō suru	compete
13	地域	chiiki	region
	激しい	hageshii	keen, violent

p145
1	圧力	atsuryoku	pressure
2	孤立する	koritsu suru	be isolated
	外部	gaibu	outside
	蒙古襲来	Mōko shūrai	Mongol invasion (attack)
3	やって行く	yatte iku	go along
4	特に	toku ni	particularly
6	得る	-uru, -eru	be possible to (=koto ga dekiru) (literary)
	他の	ta no	other
	短期間に	tankikan ni	within a short period
7	過ぎ去る	sugisaru	pass, pass by

Supplement

p146

2	ベルツ	Berutsu	Erwin Bälz (physician, educator, 1849-1913)
4	気持	kimochi	feeling, idea, inclination
7	感じる	kanjiru	feel
11	学ぶ	manabu	learn
	理学	rigaku	natural science (obsolete)

p147

6	正月	shōgatsu	New Year's holidays
	馬琴	Bakin	Takizawa Bakin (novelist, 1767-1848)
7	売れる	ureru	sell
9	ブルジョワジー	burujowajī	bourgeoisie

p148

6	やってしまう	yatte shimau	accomplish, finish up

Based on the official U. S. Embassy translation of the speech delivered in English by Ambassador Edwin O. Reischauer at the University of Hiroshima, "Japanese history as viewed from abroad," October 16, 1961.

Edwin O. Reischauer (1910-   ), United States Ambassador to Japan, was formerly Professor of Japanese History, Harvard University. He is the author of Japan Past and Present, The United States and Japan, Ennin's Diary, etc.

Lesson XXIII.   DENPŌ NI TSUITE

1	電報	denpō	telegram
2	直ぐ	sugu	immediately
4	上京する	jōkyō suru	go to Tokyo, come to Tokyo (from another place in Japan)
	月末	getsumatsu	end of the month
5	足りる	tariru	be sufficient
	田舎	inaka	country, rural district
	父親	chichioya	father
	頼む	tanomu	ask, request
6	電報を打つ	denpō o utsu	send a telegram (utsu = strike)
	勿論	mochiron	of course
	頼信紙	raishinshi	telegram form
7	句読点を打つ	kutōten o utsu	put in punctuation
	一字分の料金を取られる	ichijibun no ryōkin o torareru	be charged for a syllable
9	届く	todoku	arrive, be delivered
	電文	denbun	text of a telegram
10	呉れる	kureru	give
11	飲む	nomu	drink
	そこで	sokode	so, thereupon
12	貯める	tameru	save (money)
	酒	sake	sake, liquor

95

Lesson XXIII

p149
13 貯金する   chokin suru   save money
p150
1   笑い話   waraibanashi   funny story, anecdote

種類   shurui   kind, sort

間違い   machigai   mistake

2   しばしば   shibashiba   frequently

片仮名だけで ‖ しかも句読点なしだ

3   切る   kiru   break, cut

4   反対の   hantai no   opposite

すら   sura   even (=<u>sae</u>) (literary)

6   普段   fudan   usually, commonly

一切   issai   wholly, entirely

表現   hyōgen   expression

7   文語   bungo   literary language

9   山田   Yamada   (surname)

10 山口   Yamaguchi   (surname)

相手   aite   the other party, partner
p151
1   口語   kōgo   colloquial language

に当る   ni ataru   correspond to

用法   yōhō   usage

2   したがって   shitagatte   accordingly, thus,
                                 consequently
4   六つ   muttsu   six

濁点   dakuten   (sign of voiced
                                 consonant)
5   半濁点   handakuten   (sign of "p" attached to
                                 <u>ha</u>, <u>hi</u>, <u>fu</u>, <u>he</u>, <u>ho</u>)
6   不   fu-   not

96

p151
8   jisū ga sukunakute sumu = "get along with a small number of syllables"

12	印象	inshō	impression
	与える	ataeru	give
	急ぐ	isogu	hurry
13	相当に	sōtō ni	fairly, rather

p152
2	その他	sonota	besides
5	組み合せる	kumiawaseru	combine
9	文	fumi	letter
	古語	kogo	archaic word

p153
1   nan no koto yara = "what on earth it is"

3	ローマ字に直す	rōmaji ni naosu	convert into roman letters, romanize
4	語	go	word

Supplement

p154
3	上野駅	Ueno-eki	Ueno Station
	吉田	Yoshida	(surname)
7	打電する	daden suru	send a telegram
8	テレフォンブック	terefonbukku	telephone directory
9	鉛筆	enpitsu	pencil
	野原	nohara	field, plain
	マッチ	matchi	match
	鶴亀	tsurukame	crane and tortoise
11	尾崎行雄	Ozaki Yukio	(statesman, 1859-1954)

97

p155

7	上松	Uenomatsu	(place name)
8	止す	yosu	give up, quit
9	大笑いする	ōwarai suru	have quite a laugh
10	洋酒	yōshu	Western liquors
	日本酒	Nihonshu	sake
11	飲料水	inryōsui	drinking water

Bungo 文語 (literary language) is the Japanese classical language based on the grammatical system of the Heian spoken language. Modern Japanese, though there are certain differences between hanashi-kotoba 話し言葉 (language used in conversation) and kaki-kotoba 書き言葉 (language used in writing), is inclusively called kōgo 口語, in contrast to bungo. However, certain bungo expressions are still found in kōgo and have become a part of it.

The following chart includes most of the "literary forms" which occur frequently in kōgo. The forms with solid underline are used both in hanashi-kotoba and kaki-kotoba, the forms with dotted underline are used only in kaki-kotoba, while the rest are not used in kōgo. The first column gives a rough indication of the English meaning of each of these literary suffixes (cf. the examples which follow), and columns 2 through 6 give its traditional conjugation, purely for reference. To summarize (note that a, c, and d are the regular adjectival conjugation in bungo, except that a2 -bekara- is contracted from -beku + ara[zu]); 2 = stem to which negative, tentative, or future endings are added; 3 = adverbial or clause-ending form; 4 = sentence-ending form; 5 = attributive (modifying) form; 6 = stem to which conditional or perfective endings are added.

	1	2	3	4	5	6
a	obligation	べから	べく	べし	べき	べけれ
b	negation	ず	ず	ず	ぬ (ん)	ね
c	desire	たく	たく	たし	たき	たけれ
d	similarity	ごとく	ごとく	ごとし	ごとき	ごとけれ
e	conjecture	——	——	む (ん)	む (ん)	め

98

Examples of hanashi-kotoba (these forms may also be used in kaki-kotoba):

a5	Anata wa ashita gakkō e ikubeki desu.	You ought to go to school tomorrow.
a5	Kore wa daigakusei no yomubeki hon desu.	This is a book a college student should read.
b3	Ame mo furazu (=furanaide) yuki mo furimasen deshita.	It neither rained nor snowed.
b3	Gakkō e ikazu ni (=ikanaide) eiga ni ikimashita.	I went to a movie instead of school.
b5	Shinakereba naran.	I must do it.
b6 b5	Ikaneba naranu (=ikanakereba naranai) toki ni ikimasen deshita.	I did not go when I should have.

Examples of kaki-kotoba:

a2 b4	Kono heya ni hairubekarazu.	Do not enter this room.
c3	Gozen kuji ni koraretaku onegai mōshiagemasu.	I should like to ask you to come at 9:00 a.m.
c4	Gozen kuji ni koraretashi.	You are requested to come at 9:00 a.m.
d5	Kare no gotoki gakusha demo kore wa wakaranai.	Even a scholar like him cannot understand this.
e5	Aran kagiri no koe o dashite yonda.	I called him in as loud a voice as possible.

p156

1	マケル	makeru	be beaten, be overcome
4	風	kaze	wind
5	夏	natsu	summer
	暑イ	atsui	hot

makenu = makenai (literary)

6	丈夫ナ	jōbu na	healthy, robust
7	欲	yoku	desire, greed
8	決シテ	kesshite	never (with negative)
	怒ル	ikaru	become angry (literary)
9	ワラウ	warau	laugh, smile
10	玄米	genmai	unpolished rice
	合	-gō	(unit of measure for grain and liquid: 0.18 litre)
11	味噌	miso	bean paste
	野菜	yasai	vegetable
	タベル	taberu	eat
12	アラユル	arayuru	every, all
13	カンジョウニ入レズニ	kanjō ni irezu ni	without taking into account

p157

1	mikiki shi = mikiki shite		*information*
3	野原	nohara	field, plain
	松	matsu	pine (tree)
	蔭	kage	shade
4	萱ブキノ小屋	kayabuki no koya	thatched hut
5	病気	byōki	sickness

100

p157

6	看病スル	kanbyō suru	care for, attend (the sick)
7	母	haha	mother
8	稲ノ束	ine no taba	sheaf of rice plants
	負ウ	ou	carry on one's back, bear
10	コワガル	kowagaru	be afraid
11	ケンカ	kenka	quarrel, fight
	ソショウ	soshō	lawsuit
12	ツマラナイ	tsumaranai	pointless, trivial
13	ヒデリ	hideri	drought
	ナミダヲナガス	namida o nagasu	shed tears

p158

1	サムサノナツ	samusa no natsu	a cold summer (damaging the rice in northern Japan)
	オロオロアルク	orooro aruku	walk about uneasily (in distress)
2	デクノボウ	deku no bō	simple-minded (man), blockhead (wooden figure)
3	ホメル	homeru	praise
4	クニスル	ku ni suru	consider (regard as) a nuisance

Supplement

p159

2	宮沢賢治	Miyazawa Kenji	(poet, 1896-1933)
	死後	shigo	after one's death
	発見スル	hakken suru	discover
3	東北地方	Tōhoku chihō	the north-eastern section of Japan
4	米	kome	rice
5	育ツ	sodatsu	grow up

p159
6 農学校　　　　　nō-gakkō　　　　agricultural school

　ツクス　　　　　tsukusu　　　　　serve, do much for
p160
2 満足スル　　　　manzoku suru　　be contented

Miyazawa Kenji 宮沢賢治, "Ame ni mo makezu" 雨ニモマケズ , Gendai
Nihon shijin zenshū 現代日本詩人全集(Anthology of modern Japanese
poets), 15 vols., Sōgensha, 1954-55, vol. 7, pp. 171-72.

　Miyazawa Kenji (1896-1933) was a poet and fairy-tale writer.

　As a farmer and teacher at an agricultural high school,
Miyazawa devoted his life to the education of farming people in
Northern Japan. Only two of his books appeared during his lifetime
(both at his own expense), but after his death his complete works
were published and received high critical praise. His poems are
deeply colored by Buddhist feeling.

　The poem "Ame ni mo makezu," dated November 3, 1931, was
found in one of his notebooks. It is the most famous of his poems.

102

p161

1	強制する	kyōsei suru	compel, force
2	バス	basu	bus
	に乗る	ni noru	ride on, board
	見廻す	mimawasu	look around at
3	週刊雑誌	shūkan zasshi	weekly magazine
	スポーツ	supōtsu	sports
	熱心に	nesshin ni	avidly, eagerly, enthusiastically
4	サラリーマン	sararīman	salary man, white collar worker
	をはじめ	o hajime	beginning with (from ... on)
6	なるほど	naruhodo	indeed
7	日刊	nikkan	daily (publication)
	に負ける	ni makeru	yield to, be less than
8	よく売れる	yoku ureru	sell well
9	不思議(な)	fushigi (na)	strange, odd
10	ラッシュ・アワー	rasshu awā	rush hour
	満員電車	man'in densha	full train
	大勢	ōzei	crowd, multitude (of people)
12	度に	tabi ni	every time (following a clause)
	何と	nan to	what a
	読書欲	dokushoyoku	passion for reading

103

p162

1	単行本	tankōbon	independent volume, book
	一生懸命に	isshōkenmei ni	intently, hard, with all one's energy
2	見かける	mikakeru	see, notice

to miruto = to omotte miru to

3	広告	kōkoku	advertisement
	ベスト・セラー	besuto serā	best-seller
	或るいは	aruiwa	or
4	映画	eiga	movie
	文学書	bungakusho	literary work (in book form)
5	家庭	katei	home
6	落ち着いた所	ochitsuita tokoro	quiet place
	専門的な	senmonteki na	professional, specialized
	書物	shomotsu	book, magazine
	社会	shakai	society
7	一員	ichiin	a member
	常識	jōshiki	good sense, common sense
	教養	kyōyō	(general) education, culture
	深める	fukameru	enrich, deepen
8	学問的な	gakumonteki na	scholarly
9	こんでいる	konde iru	crowded (with people)
10	一種の	isshu no	a sort of
11	暇つぶし	himatsubushi	pastime, (way of) killing time (hima = leisure, spare time)
	リクリエーション	rikuriēshon	recreation
	…の意味で	... no imi de	as, for the purpose of

104

p162

12	傾向	keikō	tendency
13	仕事	shigoto	work, labor

p163

1	遊ぶ	asobu	amuse oneself, play
	ゴルフ	gorufu	golf
	山のぼり	yamanobori	mountain climbing
2	映画館	eigakan	movie theater
	喫茶店	kissaten	coffee shop
	時間をつぶす	jikan o tsubusu	kill time (tsubusu = smash)
3	とにかく	tonikaku	anyhow, in any case
	本職	honshoku	one's regular occupation
4	とても...ない	totemo ... nai	certainly not
	落ち着く	ochitsuku	settle down, compose oneself
5	(何かを……ない)→"強制された"読書時間		
	外仕方のない	hoka shikata no nai	no other way, no alternative
6	楽しい	tanoshii	pleasant, enjoyable
7	頭	atama	head, brain
9	悲しむ	kanashimu	regret

Supplement

p164

2	月刊雑誌	gekkan zasshi	monthly magazine
3	専門	senmon	specialty, special field of study
8	ますます	masumasu	more and more
9	会社	kaisha	company, firm
13	いや	iya	rather

p165

2	出来事	dekigoto	happening, event
3	意見	iken	opinion
	結果	kekka	result
	テレビ	terebi	T.V.
6	属する	**zokusuru**	belong
	現象	genshō	phenomenon
8	個人	kojin	individual(s)
	独立した	dokuritsu shita	independent

Source: Suzuki Takeo 鈴木武雄, <u>Nihonjin to keizaikannen</u> 日本人と経済観念 (The Japanese people and their economic concepts), <u>Nihon bunka kenkyū</u> 日本文化研究 (Studies in Japanese culture), 9 vols., Shinchōsha 新潮社, 1958-61, vol. 6, pp. 5-6.

Suzuki Takeo (1901-   ), professor of economics at the University of Tokyo, is the author of <u>Gendai zaiseishi</u> 現代財政史 (History of modern finance) and <u>Shijō riron</u> 市場理論 (Market theory).

Suzuki, a leading specialist in finance, is also one of the advisers of the Japan Social Democratic Party. He is adept at explaining difficult economic theories by means of simple examples.

Lesson XXVI. ARU OSORE

1	おそれ	osore	fear, misgiving
2	真似する	mane suru	imitate
3	意見	iken	opinion, view
	いくらか	ikuraka	somewhat, to some extent
	心配	shinpai	anxiety, worry
	感じる	kanjiru	feel
4	過去	kako	past
	必ずしも…ない	kanarazushimo ...nai	not always, not necessarily
5	抒情性	jojōsei	lyricism
6	評価する	hyōka suru	value, evaluate
	杜甫	Toho	Tu Fu (Chinese poet, 712-770)
7	詩人	shijin	poet

dore dake = dore hodo, dore kurai

8	不正	fusei	injustice
	反抗	hankō	resistance
9	皆	mina	all
	平等 (な)	byōdō (na)	equal
10	つい	tsui	just, only (used with points in past time)
	認識する	ninshiki suru	recognize, perceive
12	少くとも	sukunakutomo	at least
	ニューアンス	nyūansu	nuance

107

p166
13 長男権 chōnanken rights of the eldest son, primogeniture

或るいは aruiwa in some cases

娘 musume daughter

p167
1 財産 zaisan property

言葉 kotoba speech

2 であり ‖ であった

男女 danjo male and female

身分 mibun social standing

3 夫妻 fusai husband and wife

4 お互 o-tagai each other

字 azana courtesy name, style (=tzu, usually derived from the given name)

ファースト・ネーム fāsuto nēmu first name

合う -au (do) each other

5 弟子 deshi pupil, disciple

友人 yūjin friend

見なす minasu consider, regard

四海 shikai the whole world (the four seas)

内 uchi inside

兄弟 kyōdai brothers

nari = de aru (literary)

6 紀元前 kigenzen before Christ, B.C. (before the era)

論語 Rongo the Analects of Confucius (Lun Yü)

地 chi earth

108

p167
6	生まれ落ちる	umareochiru	be born (into this world)
7	地上に	chijō ni	on the earth
8	肉身	nikushin	blood relative
	陶淵明	Tō Enmei	T'ao Yüan-ming (Chinese poet, 372-427)
9	伝統	dentō	tradition, convention
11	革命	kakumei	revolution
	床屋	tokoya	barbershop
	態度	taido	attitude
12	昨日	kinō	yesterday
	おい	oi	hey

p168
1	同調する	dōchō suru	share (feeling), sympathize
	ないとはかぎりない	nai to wa kagiranai	it is not impossible, it may be
2	大急ぎで	ōisogi de	in a great hurry
	とり入れる	toriireru	take in, incorporate

Source: Yoshikawa Kōjirō 吉川幸次郎, "Aru osore" あるおそれ, Asahi Shinbun 朝日新聞, January 1, 1955, reprinted in Raihōtō 雷峯塔 (Thunder Peak pagoda), Chikuma Shobō 筑摩書房, 1956, pp. 82-83.

Yoshikawa Kōjirō (1904-   ) is professor of Chinese literature at the University of Kyoto.

Yoshikawa is a leading scholar of classical Chinese literature. As an essayist, he is notable for his limpid prose style, a style enriched but not overburdened by the proper and refined use of Chinese compounds.

Lesson XXVII.   GENJITSU TO IMĒJI

p169

1	現実	genjitsu	reality
	イメージ	imēji	image
2	日常の話	nichijō no hanashi	everyday talk
	ソ連	Soren	the Soviet Union (=Sobietto Renpō ソビェット連邦)
3	気安く言う	kiyasuku iu	speak casually (about)
	一定の	ittei no	fixed
	像	-zō	image, picture of
	前提	zentei	premise
5	一致する	itchi suru	correspond (to), coincide (with)
6	確かめる	tashikameru	ascertain
	機会	kikai	opportunity, chance
7	手段	shudan	means
9	アイク	Aiku	Ike (Eisenhower)
10	フルシチョフ	Furushichofu	Khrushchev
	ネール	Nēru	Nehru
p170 2	平和	heiwa	peace
	運動	undō	movement
	保守の	hoshu no	conservative
3	ジャーナリスト	jānarisuto	journalist
5	悪い	warui	bad
6	現実の	genjitsu no	actual

p170

7	厚い層	atsui sō	thick layer
8	に従って	ni shitagatte	as, while
	もとの	moto no	original, former
9	と離れて	to hanarete	apart from
	独自の	dokuji no	individual, peculiar
10	原物	genbutsu	the original
	別の	betsu no	different, other
	無数の	musū no	numberless
	区別する	kubetsu suru	distinguish, differentiate
	化け物	bakemono	monster, apparition
11	ひとり歩きする	hitoriaruki suru	be independent, stand on one's own feet
12	生きる	ikiru	live, be alive
	言い過ぎる	iisugiru	overstate, exaggerate
13	対象	taishō	object

p171

1	共通する	kyōtsū suru	have (something) in common
3	リアリティー	riaritī	actuality, reality (=genjitsusei 現実性)
	本物自身	honmono jishin	the real thing itself
5	判断する	handan suru	judge
	行動する	kōdō suru	act, behave
6	イリュージョン	iryūjon	illusion
7	iyō to = ite mo		
8	作り出す	tsukuridasu	produce, create
9	リアル	riaru	real
	状態	jōtai	situation, state (of things, affairs)

111

Source: Maruyama Masao丸山眞男 , "Shisō no arikata ni tsuite"
思想のあり方について (On modes of thought), lecture delivered in
June, 1958, reprinted in <u>Nihon</u> <u>no</u> <u>shisō</u> 日本の思想 , Iwanami Shinsho
岩波新書 Series 434, 1961, pp. 126-28.

    Maruyama Masao (1914-   ) is professor of political science
at the University of Tokyo. His <u>Nihon</u> <u>shisōshi</u> <u>kenkyū</u> 日本思想史研究
(Studies in the history of Japanese thought), which deals with the
history of Japanese thought from the Edo period to the present, is
the leading work in this field.

    This text is written in a characteristic lecture style:
chiefly the polite conversational style, but with occasional use
of the plain style.

p172			
1	僕	boku	I (used by boys and men)
2	今に	ima ni	in time, sooner or later
6	おおよそ	ōyoso	approximately, roughly
9	それ故に	sore yue ni	for that reason
11	濁音	dakuon	voiced consonant
12	殊に	koto ni	especially, particularly
	音を濁る	on o nigoru	voice a sound
13	バ行	bagyō	line of <u>ba</u>, <u>bi</u>, <u>bu</u>, <u>be</u>, <u>bo</u>
	好まれている	konomarete iru	be liked, be popular

p173			
1	始まる	hajimaru	begin
	気を付ける	ki o tsukeru	pay attention, be careful
	御覧なさい	gorannasai	look (=<u>minasai</u>) (polite)
	半分	hanbun	half
	有難くない	arigatakunai	unwelcome (<u>arigatai</u> = worthy of gratitude)
3	どうして又	dōshite mata	how on earth
4	我が国	waga kuni	our country
5	漢文	kanbun	literary-style Chinese writing
	向う	mukō	the other (here, Chinese)
6	真似る	maneru	take after, imitate
7	文章	bunshō	writing, sentence
	使用人	shiyōnin	servant, employee

113

p173

8	尊敬する	sonkei suru	honor, respect
	召使い	meshitsukai	servant

9 meue demo nan demo nai = "not in any way (at all) a superior"

10	唯の同輩	tada no dōhai	a mere equal
	乱用	ran'yō	improper use, abuse
11	敬語	keigo	term of respect, honorific expression
12	殆ど…ない	hotondo ...nai	hardly (hotondo = almost)
13	下男	genan	manservant

p174

1	別に	betsu ni	separately
	書生	shosei	student, student-dependent
	即ち	sunawachi	namely
8	遊び半分	asobihanbun	half in fun
	何時か	itsuka	at a certain time, some time
9	姉妹	shimai (kyōdai)	sisters
	変 (な)	hen (na)	strange
10	弟	otōto	younger brother
	先ず	mazu	before any others, first
11	聞き馴れる	kikinareru	be (become) used to hearing
12	耳	mimi	ear
13	大多数	daitasū	great majority

p175

1 shūkan ni natte ori = shūkan ni natte ite

	代りの	kawari no	substitute

3 kono mama ni to = kono mama ni shite okō to omotte

	改める	aratameru	correct
4	嫌 (な)	iya (na)	disagreeable

114

p175

4	なりかける	narikakeru	about to become
5	今にも	ima ni mo	at any moment
	決っている	kimatte iru	I am sure, it is certain
7	ショウ（妾）	shō	I (used by women, obsolete)
9	見える	mieru	seem
	広まる	hiromaru	spread
	廃れる	sutareru	go out of fashion
11	足りない	tarinai	(be) lacking

Source: Yanagida Kunio 柳田国男 , "Jishō no daimeishi" 自稱の代名詞 (First person pronouns), Akatonbo 赤とんぼ , August, 1946, reprinted in Kotoba no iroiro 言葉のいろいろ (All kinds of language), Tadeshina Shobō 蓼科書房 , 1949, pp. 65-69.

Yanagida Kunio (1875-1962) was active as a leading ethnologist from the end of the Meiji era until his death. He also published many books on language, of which Kotoba no iroiro is one.

This selection is characteristic in its old-fashioned essay style, which relies rather on traditional methods of persuasion than on scientific or logical rigor.

p176

1	能力	nōryoku	ability
2	学ぶ	manabu	learn
	しかも	shikamo	and yet
3	発想する	hassō suru	begin thinking, conceive ideas
4	協力する	kyōryoku suru	cooperate
5	調査報告	chōsa hōkoku	research report
	一見する	ikken suru	take a look at
6	最新の	saishin no	newest
7	結果	kekka	findings, result
8	疑う	utagau	doubt
	マッチ	matchi	match

katakana kara = katakana kara hajimatte

9	履歴書	rirekisho	curriculum vitae
10	正確に	seikaku ni	correctly, accurately
11	全国民	zenkokumin	the whole population
	国民	kokumin	a national, people (of a nation)
12	兵隊	heitai	soldier, military enlisted man
13	徴兵検査	chōhei kensa	draft examination
	文盲	bunmō (monmō)	illiterate (person), illiteracy

p177

1	満点、	manten	a perfect score, one hundred points
2	義務教育	gimu kyōiku	compulsory education

116

p177

2	普及する	fukyū suru	become widespread
3	いわゆる	iwayuru	so-called
	率	ritsu	rate
	極めて	kiwamete	extremely
4	驚く	odoroku	be surprised
5	高知	Kōchi	(city in Kōchi-ken, Shikoku)
	日教組	Nikkyōso	Japan Teachers' Union (=Nihon kyōshokuin kumiai 日本教職員組合)
	集まり	atsumari	assembly
	卒業生	sotsugyōsei	graduate
6	習得する	shūtoku suru	learn, master
	以下	ika	less than
	発表する	happyō suru	announce
	戦前	senzen	before the war, before (and during) World War II
7	誠之小学校	Seishi Shōgakkō	(a primary school in Tokyo)
9	いとなむ	itonamu	carry on, conduct
	コミュニケイション	komyunikeishon	communication
10	技術	gijutsu	technique
11	頭が悪い	atama ga warui	slow-witted, dull
13	勤勉	kinben	diligence

p178

1	表記法	hyōkihō	method of written expression
2	厳しい	kibishii	harsh
	生き延びる	ikinobiru	survive
	発展する	hatten suru	develop, flourish

117

p178

3	上層部	jōsōbu	upper classes
	インテリ	interi	educated people, intellectuals (=<u>interigenchia</u>)
	優秀 (な)	yūshū (na)	excellent
4	ダメ (な)	dame (na)	no good
	知的水準	chiteki suijun	intellectual level
5	(表記法が‥‥‥ない)→イタリア		
6	イタリア	Itaria	Italy
	入学する	nyūgaku suru	enter school
7	ドイツ	Doitsu	Germany
	イギリス	Igirisu	United Kingdom
8	入学後	nyūgakugo	after entering school
	ないし	naishi	from ... to (with numerical measures)
9	デモクラシー	demokurashī	democracy
	何とか	nantoka	somehow or other

nantoka aratamenakutewa = "Unless you make some change (the future looks bleak)."

| 10 | 当然 | tōzen | natural, a matter of course |

Source: Kuwabara Takeo 桑原武夫, "Minna no Nihongo" みんなの日本語, <u>Bungei Shunjū</u> 文藝春秋, April, 1953, reprinted in <u>Shinsen Nihon gendai bungaku zenshū</u> 新選日本現代文学全集 (New anthology of modern Japanese literature), 38 vols., Chikuma Shobō, 1958-60, vol. 34, pp. 257-58.

Kuwabara Takeo (1904-   ) is a literary critic and professor of French literature at the University of Kyoto.

Kuwabara's works range from translations of Stendhal to

118

popular studies of Japanese culture. His "Daini geijutsu ron" 第二芸術論 (Second-class literature) (1946), pointing out the limitations of <u>haiku</u> poetry, brought about a great debate on Japanese traditional culture.

This selection is part of an essay by Kuwabara supporting the official policy of limiting the number of Chinese characters in ordinary use. Controversy over the radical reforms of the Japanese writing system which were carried out after World War II has continued to the present. Further views on this problem will be found in Lessons 45 to 47.

Lesson XXX.   HEIWARON NI TSUITE

1	平和論	heiwaron	discussion on peace, the question of peace
2	先年	sennen	some years ago
	訪問する	hōmon suru	visit (formally)
	首相	shushō	prime minister
	モスクワ	Mosukuwa	Moscow
3	語る	kataru	talk, talk about
	とは限らない	to wa kagiranai	not necessarily, not always
4	伝える	tsutaeru	report
5	誠実 (な)	seijitsu (na)	sincere, faithful
8	度々	tabitabi	frequently
	名よりも実	na yori mo jitsu	the reality rather than the name
10	均衡	kinkō	balance
	保つ	tamotsu	maintain
11	理想的の	risōteki no	ideal, perfect
	人類愛	jinruiai	love for mankind, sense of human brotherhood
12	理解	rikai	understanding

hajimete = "only"

1	事実	jijitsu	fact, actual situation
	に満足する	ni manzoku suru	be satisfied (content) with
2	無視する	mushi suru	ignore, disregard

p180

4	軍備	gunbi	(national) armaments
	撤廃する	teppai suru	abolish
	兵器	heiki	arms, weapons
	捨てる	suteru	throw away, discard

5   sekai wa heiwa to naru ka no yō ni shuchō suru = "who hold that the world may achieve peace"

6	果して	hatashite	really, in reality
	本気で言う	honki de iu	say seriously
	問う	tou	ask, question, doubt
8	願う	negau	wish, hope (for)

9   naranai = ikenai

	議論	giron	discussion, argument
10	ざるを得ない	zaru o enai	cannot help ...ing (literary)
13	ただし	tadashi	however
	成否	seihi	success or failure, result

p181

6	軍縮	gunshuku	reduction of armaments
	実行	jikkō	practice, realization
7	成績	seiseki	record, result
8	現実の	genjitsu no	actual
	守る	mamoru	protect, defend
	現実的	genjitsuteki	practical, realistic
9	核	kaku	nuclear
	解決する	kaiketsu suru	solve, settle

Source: Koizumi Shinzō 小泉信三, "Shinnen shokan" 新年所感
(Thoughts on New Year's Day), <u>Mainichi</u> <u>Shinbun</u> 毎日新聞, January 3,
1958, reprinted in <u>Jinseiron</u> <u>tokuhon</u> 人生論読本(Readings on problems
of human life), 12 vols., Kadokawa Shoten 角川書店, 1960-61, vol.
11, pp. 196-98.

Koizumi Shinzō (1888-1966), economist, formerly president of
Keiō University, is an adviser of the Board of the Crown Prince's
Affairs.

Koizumi is an "old liberal" of the sort known as "Meiji no
hito." He advocates revision of the Japanese constitution to permit
national rearmament.

Notice that this essay includes such <u>bungo</u> expressions as
<u>hatashite</u> ... <u>ka dōka</u> <u>o</u> ... <u>towareneba</u> <u>naranu</u> (180.6-7), ... <u>mono</u>
<u>de aru ga</u> (180.8), and <u>motazaru</u> <u>o enai</u> (180.10-11).

p182

1	憲法	kenpō	constitution (of a country)
2	戦後	sengo	after the war, after World War II
3	押しつける	oshitsukeru	impose, force (on)
	ちょいちょい	choichoi	now and then, from time to time
	前文	zenbun	preamble
	冒頭	bōtō	beginning (of a composition, speech)
5	行為	kōi	action, conduct
	再び	futatabi	again, a second time
	惨禍	sanka	calamity, horror
6	決意する	ketsui suru	resolve, determine
	一体	ittai	really, after all, (how, what) on earth
	受け取る	uketoru	take, understand
7	(戦争という)→あの恐ろしいこと		
	恐ろしい	osoroshii	terrible
9	で ‖ ではない		
10	そのもの	sonomono	itself
12	底	soko	bottom, depths
	共鳴する	kyōmei suru	echo, respond sympathetically
	現在のところ	genzai no tokoro	for the present
13	否定する	hitei suru	deny

p183
1   itte iru ijō = "as long as it says"

p183

2　(政府が……得る)→こと

行為に出る　　　kōi ni deru　　　act, take steps

保証　　　　　　hoshō　　　　　　guarantee

3　一番大きな　　　ichiban ōkina　　largest, main

4　関心　　　　　　kanshin　　　　　concern

主権　　　　　　shuken　　　　　　sovereignty

to iu no ga = to itte iru koto ga

5　最大　　　　　　saidai　　　　　　largest, maximum

いわば　　　　　iwaba　　　　　　in short, that is to say

7　唯一無二の　　　yuiitsu muni no　the one and only, the unique

貴重な　　　　　kichō na　　　　　precious

目標　　　　　　mokuhyō　　　　　goal, aim

8　kara itte = kara kangaete

9　推論　　　　　　suiron　　　　　　(line of) reasoning, deduction

12　指導者　　　　　shidōsha　　　　　leader

欺す　　　　　　damasu　　　　　　deceive

13　(平和で安定した)→生活

安定する　　　　antei suru　　　　be stabilized

政権　　　　　　seiken　　　　　　political authority

p184

1　動かす　　　　　ugokasu　　　　　control, move

Source: Ukai Nobushige 鵜飼信成, <u>Kenpō o tsukuru chikara to kowasu chikara</u> 憲法をつくる力とこわす力 (The power to create the constitution and the power to destroy it), Kawade Shinsho 河出新書 Series (Kyōyō) 124, 1955, pp. 184-85.

Ukai Nobushige (1906-　　), the president of the International Christian University, was formerly professor of law at the University of Tokyo.

Some persons who advocate rearmament call the post-war Japanese constitution the "MacArthur constitution," implying that it should be revised because it was dictated by the Americans. Ukai represents liberal scholarly opinion favoring retention of the permanent disarmament cause.

p185

1	森鷗外	Mori Ōgai	(physician, novelist, 1862-1922)
	殉死	junshi	suicide upon the death of one's lord
2	明治天皇	Meiji Tennō	Emperor Meiji (Mutsuhito, 121st emperor of Japan, 1852-1912)
	亡くなる	nakunaru	die (honorific)
	大正	Taishō	Taishō era (1912-1926)
	改まる	aratamaru	change (to something new)
3	年	toshi	year
	葬式	sōshiki	funeral
	乃木大将	Nogi Taishō	General Nogi (Nogi Maresuke, hero of Russo-Japanese War, 1849-1912)
	大将	taishō	lieutenant general
	大名	daimyō	feudal lord
5	普段から	fudan kara	always (fudan = usually)
	家臣	kashin	retainer
	死後	shigo	after death
6	仕える	tsukaeru	serve (a master)
	自殺する	jisatsu suru	commit suicide
7	隷属する	reizoku suru	be subject (to)
8	野蛮な	yaban na	uncivilized, savage
9	主人	shujin	master
	個人	kojin	individual

p185

9	純粋な	junsui na	pure
10	友情	yūjō	friendship
	信頼	shinrai	reliance, trust
11	表われ	araware	expression, manifestation
	かえって	kaette	on the contrary (contrary to expectations)
13	気持	kimochi	feeling

p186

2	感動する	kandō suru	be moved, be impressed
3	留学	ryūgaku	study abroad
	親しみ	shitashimi	friendly feeling, intimacy
4	知らせ	shirase	news, tidings
5	興津弥五右衛門の遺書	Okitsu Yagoemon no Isho	Last Testament of Okitsu Yagoemon (1921) (isho = posthumous writing, note left behind at death)
6	細川	Hosokawa	(surname)
7	武士	bushi	samurai, warrior
	題材	daizai	material (for a literary work, etc.)
8	次々と	tsugitsugi to	one after another
	事件	jiken	incident
9	(封建時代の……出来ない)→人々		
10	義理	giri	duty, obligation
	意地	iji	self-will, refusal to yield
	名誉心	meiyoshin	love of fame, ambition
	等	-tō, -nado	and so forth, etc.
11	姿	sugata	appearance, figure
	冷静な	reisei na	cool, composed
	立場	tachiba	attitude, standpoint

p186

11	描く	egaku	describe, depict
12	取り扱う	toriatsukau	deal with
13	風ではない	fū de wa nai	does not seem
	無意味に	muimi ni	meaninglessly

p187

1	争う	arasou	fight
2	阿部一族	Abe Ichizoku	The Abe Clan (1913)
	何でもない	nan demo nai	trifling
3	悲惨な	hisan na	tragic, miserable
	大塩平八郎	Ōshio Heihachirō	Ōshio Heihachirō (1914)
	仲間	nakama	comrades, colleagues
4	果す	hatasu	accomplish
	わかれわかれになる	wakarewakare ni naru	become separated (from one another)
5	奉天	Hōten	Mukden
	強いて言えば	shiite ieba	if anything, if I must describe it (shiite = muri ni)
	極み	kiwami	extremity, height
10	同感	dōkan	agreement, the same feelings

Source: Sugimori Hisahide 杉森久英, Mori Ōgai 森鴎外, Fukumura Shoten 福村書店, 1961, pp. 113-16.

Sugimori Hisahide (1912-   ) is a literary critic and biographer.

Mori Ōgai is commonly regarded, with Natsume Sōseki, as one of the two greatest writers in modern Japanese literature. After taking a degree in medicine at the University of Tokyo, Ōgai studied in Germany for four years as a medical officer, later became surgeon-general, and, after his retirement from the army, occupied such high positions as curator of the Imperial Museum (now the

128

National Museum) and head librarian of the Imperial Library. His
fame as a man of letters had meanwhile increased with his many
translations of Western literature, that of Goethe's Faust among
others, with his own rather sentimental fiction, his literary
criticism, and in later years a notable series of historical novels.

Sugimori has recently become well known as a writer of
fictional biography. In this text he deals with Ōgai's attitude
toward the old custom of junshi, a problem Ōgai had to confront
upon the death of General Nogi. Sugimori takes the view that Ōgai
was basically opposed to junshi. Mori Ōgai was written for high-
school students.

Lesson XXXIII. ISHO (SONO ICHI)

2	心理	shinri	mental state, psychology
	ありのままに	ari-no-mama ni	frankly, exactly as is
3	自尊心	jisonshin	pride, self-respect
	自尊心 ‖ 不足		
4	不足	fusoku	lack, insufficiency
6	動機	dōki	motive, incentive
	レニエ	Renie	Henri de Régnier (French poet, novelist, 1864-1936)
7	主人公	shujinkō	hero (of a novel, drama)
9	三面記事	sanmenkiji	police news, human interest stories (formerly appearing on the "third page" of a Japanese newspaper)
	生活難	seikatsunan	difficulty in (earning a) living
	病苦	byōku	suffering of illness
	精神的苦痛	seishinteki kutsū	anguish, mental suffering
10	発見する	hakken suru	find, discover
11	大抵	taitei	in most cases, in general
12	至る	itaru	arrive at, get to
	過程	katei	process

1	複雑な	fukuzatsu na	complex, complicated
2	ぼんやりとした	bon'yari to shita	vague, indistinct
	不安	fuan	uneasiness, unquietness

p189

4 或るいは   aruiwa   perhaps, I suppose

5 boku ni chikai hitobito de ... inai kagiri = "unless people are close to me and in similar circumstances to me"

境遇	kyōgū	situation, circumstances
ない限り	-nai kagiri	unless, in so far as (they are) not

6
歌	uta	song
消える	kieru	vanish, disappear

7 咎める   togameru   blame

8
しみじみした	shimijimi shita	keen, deep (feeling)
マインレンデル	Mainrenderu	Philipp Mainländer (real name: Philipp Batz; philosopher, 1841-1876)

9 抽象的な   chūshōteki na   abstract

10
死に向う	shi ni mukau	go towards death, approach death
うまい	umai	skillful

11
具体的に	gutaiteki ni	concretely
家族達	kazokutachi	family members
同情	dōjō	sympathy, pity

12 欲望   yokubō   desire

p190

1
非人間的	hiningenteki	inhuman
一面には	ichimen ni wa	in one aspect, one side

Source: Akutagawa Ryūnosuke 芥川龍之介, "Aru kyūyū e okuru shuki" 或舊友へ送る手記 (A note to a certain friend), Akutagawa Ryūnosuke zenshū, 19 vols., Iwanami Shoten, 1954-55, vol. 6, pp. 170-73.

Akutagawa Ryūnosuke (1892-1927) was perhaps the greatest short-story writer of modern Japan.

Akutagawa's early stories are often ironic versions of

traditional Japanese tales, but in his last years he wrote in a more nihilistic and autobiographical vein. This letter (intended for publication) was written just before his suicide.

p191

2	苦しむ	kurushimu	suffer
	云う	iu	say (=言う)
3	縊死	ishi	death by hanging (mostly suicide)
	合う	au	suit, be suitable
4	美的嫌悪	biteki ken'o	aesthetic aversion
5	愛する	aisuru	love
	彼女	kanojo	she
	急に	kyū ni	suddenly
	愛	ai	love
6	失う	ushinau	lose
	溺死	dekishi	death by drowning
	水泳	suiei	swimming (as a sport)
	到底	tōtei	by any possibility
	達する	tassuru	fulfill, attain
	筈はない	hazu wa nai	it is not likely that
	のみならず	nominarazu	moreover, not only that (=sore nomi narazu)
	万一	man'ichi	by some remote chance, one chance in ten thousand
	成功する	seikō suru	succeed
8	轢死	rekishi	death by being run over (by train or car)
	何よりも先に	nani yori mo saki ni	first of all, before anything else

133

p191

9   ataezu ni wa inakatta = "couldn't help giving (me a feeling of)"

ピストル	pisutoru	pistol
ナイフ	naifu	knife
10 震える	furueru	tremble
失敗する	shippai suru	fail
ビルディング	birudingu	(office) building (large Western style)
11 飛び下りる	tobioriru	jump down
見苦しい	migurushii	unsightly, ugly
に違いない	ni chigai nai	must be
これ等の事情	korera no jijō	these reasons, these circumstances
等	-ra	(plural ending)
12 薬品	yakuhin	drugs
13 苦しい	kurushii	painful, torturing

p192

1 求める	motomeru	acquire, seek out
2 内心	naishin	in the heart
定める	kimeru	determine
3 手に入れる	te ni ireru	obtain
5 遺産	isan	estate, property (of a dead person)
坪	tsubo	(unit of measure for land, floor space: 6 shaku square --- a shaku is .994 English feet)
6 著作権	chosakuken	copyright
7 苦にする	ku ni suru	worry
8 おかしさ	okashisa	absurdity, ludicrousness
10 事実上	jijitsujō	actually

p192			
10	不便	fuben	inconvenience
	避ける	sakeru	avoid
11	出来るだけ	dekiru dake	as much as possible
	死体	shitai	dead body, corpse
12	工夫する	kufū suru	devise, plan
13	気付く	kizuku	notice (=<u>ki</u> <u>ga</u> <u>tsuku</u>)
	数ヶ月	sūkagetsu	(for) several months
p193			
1	準備する	junbi suru	prepare
	兎に角	tonikaku	anyhow, in any case
	自信	jishin	assurance, self-confidence
	冷ややかに	hiyayaka ni	coolly
2	この先の心もち	kono saki no kokoromochi	feeling from this point on

p194

2	資本主義	shihonshugi	capitalism
3	遅れる	okureru	be backward
	前	zen-	pre-
	広範に	kōhan ni	to a large extent, extensively
	残す	nokosu	retain
5	に於ては	ni oite wa	in, at (=de wa, ni wa) (literary)
	資本家的	shihonkateki	capitalistic
	経営	keiei	management, operation; enterprise
	無い	nai	be nonexistent, be lacking
7	農民	nōmin	farmers, farm people
8	就業人口	shūgyō jinkō	working population
	程度	teido	around, approximately (=gurai) (literary)
10	漁業	gyogyō	fishing (industry)
	林業	ringyō	forestry
	生産	seisan	production
11	企業	kigyō	enterprise
12	鉱工業	kōkōgyō	mining and manufacturing
	商業	shōgyō	commerce
	多数の	tasū no	many
	中小企業	chūshō kigyō	small and medium enterprises

p195

1	町工場	machi kōba	small scale factory (town factory)

p195

1	小売の店	kouri no mise	retail store
2	直接に	chokusetsu ni	directly
	働く	hataraku	work, labor
	むしろ	mushiro	rather
3	含む	fukumu	include
4	生産額	seisangaku	amount of production
5	農林業	nōringyō	agriculture and forestry
	兆	chō	trillion
	億	oku	hundred million
	鉱山業	kōzangyō	mining
6	工業	kōgyō	(manufacturing) industry
	家内工業	kanai kōgyō	household industry
	生産物	seisanbutsu	products
8	圧倒的に	attōteki ni	overwhelmingly
	明らか (な)	akiraka (na)	clear, apparent
9	支配する	shihai suru	dominate, control
11	基本的な	kihonteki na	basic, fundamental

tokushoku to itte ii = tokushoku de aru to ieru

p196

1	完全に	kanzen ni	entirely, perfectly
2	典型的に	tenkeiteki ni	typically
4	ますます	masumasu	even more
5	欧米	Ōbei	Europe and America
	きわだっている	kiwadatte iru	be conspicuous, be prominent

137

Source: Ōuchi Tsutomu 大内力 , <u>Nihon</u> <u>no</u> <u>shakai</u> 日本の社会 , Mainichi Shinbunsha, 1957, pp. 56-59.

Ōuchi Tsutomu (1918-   ) is professor of economics at the University of Tokyo.

Lessons 35, 36, and 37 deal with some of the chief economic problems of modern Japan. Here Ōuchi discusses the double structure of the Japanese economy, against the contrasting background of conditions in Western countries, where the farming populations have been smaller and large capital enterprises have gone further toward absorbing small and medium ones. However, economic conditions in Japan have changed rapidly even in the few years since this study was written.

Lesson XXXVI.   PĀMANENTO ENPUROIMENTO

1	パーマネント・エムプロイ メント	pāmanento enpuroimento	permanent employment
4	従業員	jūgyōin	staff member, employee
	会社	kaisha	company (business)
	定年	teinen	age limit, retirement age
	給与	kyūyo	pay, compensation
5	上る	agaru	go up, increase
	不利 (な)	furi (na)	disadvantageous
6	採用する	saiyō suru	employ, engage
	たとえ…(ても)	tatoe ... (temo)	even if
7	適当な	tekitō na	suitable, appropriate
	やとう	yatou	hire, employ
	刑法	keihō	criminal law, penal code
	刑法上の	keihōjō no	criminal
8	罪	tsumi	offense, crime, sin
	犯す	okasu	commit (an offense)
	やめる	yameru	quit, resign
9	恩情主義	onjōshugi	paternalism, employer's sympathy toward his employees (onjō = warm feeling, kindliness)
	精神	seishin	spirit
	秩序	chitsujo	(social) order

139

p197

10	に限らず	ni kagirazu	not only
	官庁	kanchō	government office
	機関	kikan	institution, organ
11	組織	soshiki	organization
	ほぼ	hobo	almost, nearly (=daitai)
	共通して	kyōtsūshite	commonly
12	破る	yaburu	violate, break
	損をする	son o suru	lose, suffer
13	合理的な	gōriteki na	rational
	営利	eiri	(making) profit, gain
	民間企業	minkan kigyō	private enterprise

p198

2	多年	tanen	(for) many years
3	昇給	shōkyū	increase in salary
	恩恵感	onkeikan	feeling of benefit, of having received a favor
4	本採用の	honsaiyō no	regular, permanent (permanently employed)
	に応じて	ni ōjite	in response to
	臨時(の)	rinji (no)	temporary
5	コントロールする	kontorōru suru	control
	下請工場	shitauke kōba (kōjō)	subcontract plant
6	景気	keiki	business conditions
	安全弁	anzenben	safety valve
7	労働者	rōdōsha	laborer
8	日本独特の	Nihon dokutoku no	peculiar to Japan
	組合	kumiai	union

140

p198

9	産業別大組合	sangyōbetsu daikumiai	large industrial union
	流動性	ryūdōsei	mobility, fluidity
10	成立する	seiritsu suru	be formed, organized
	ジェネラル・モーターズ	Jeneraru Mōtāzu	General Motors
11	フォード	Fōdo	Ford
12	ルーサー	Rūsā	Walter Reuther
13	団体交渉	dantai kōshō	collective bargaining

Source: Tsuru Shigeto 都留重人, "Nihon shakai no hikage" 日本社会の日蔭 (The dark side of Japanese society), Ekonomisuto エコノミスト, May 26, 1959, reprinted in Keizai o ugokasu mono 経済を動かすもの (Motivating forces in the economy), Iwanami Shinsho Series 359, 1961, pp. 85-86.

Tsuru Shigeto (1912-   ) is professor of economics at Hitotsubashi University.

Japanese people often say that changing jobs is a stain on a man's record, a view which no doubt reflects the traditional one that a faithful subject never serves two masters.

Lesson XXXVII.   DEKASEGIGATA RŌDŌ

1 出稼　　　　　dekasegi　　　　working away from home
　　　　　　　　　　　　　　　　(temporary employment
　　　　　　　　　　　　　　　　away from permanent
　　　　　　　　　　　　　　　　residence)
　型　　　　　　-gata, -kata　　type, pattern

2 賃労働　　　　chinrōdō　　　　wage labor

3 出稼人　　　　dekaseginin　　laborer away from home

4 従う　　　　　shitagau　　　　be engaged in

(農家経済と結びついた)→出稼労働者

　農家　　　　　nōka　　　　　　farm family, farmhouse
　結びつく　　　musubitsuku　　be connected
　性格　　　　　seikaku　　　　characteristic, character

6 賃銀　　　　　chingin　　　　wages
　占める　　　　shimeru　　　　make up, occupy

7 例外　　　　　reigai　　　　　exception

　農村 ‖ それも条件の悪い農村

　農村　　　　　nōson　　　　　farm village, rural
　　　　　　　　　　　　　　　community
　貧農　　　　　hinnō　　　　　poor farmer

8 貧しい　　　　mazushii　　　poor, needy
　助ける　　　　tasukeru　　　help

9 嫁入り　　　　yomeiri　　　　marriage (of a woman)
　一定期間　　　itteikikan　　for a prescribed period
　離れた　　　　hanareta　　　remote, distant

142

p200
9 工場へ ‖ それも主として紡績工場 などへ

10	紡績	bōseki	spinning
11	職業	shokugyō	(paid) occupation, profession
12	契約	keiyaku	contract
13	主婦	shufu	housewife

p201
2	同じく	onajiku	likewise, in the same way
3	本質	honshitsu	essence
4	鉱山	kōzan	mine
5	過剰	kajō	surplus
	流出する	ryūshutsu suru	flow out
6	次・三男	jisannan	second and third sons, younger sons
7	好景気	kōkeiki	prosperity, good times
8	職	shoku	job, employment
	不景気	fukeiki	bad times, depression
9	職場	shokuba	working place, job
	帰農	kinō	return to farming (from another occupation), return to the country farming
10	農	nō	farming
12	一時	ichiji	for a while
	頼る	tayoru	depend on, rely on
	回復する	kaifuku suru	recover

13 農民として……のではなく ‖ 失業者として……のである

	失業者	shitsugyōsha	unemployed (person)

p202
2	につれて	ni tsurete	with, in accordance with

p202

2 流入する　　　　　ryūnyū suru　　　　flow in

4 （無限の深さを持った）→ 貯水池

　　無限の　　　　　　mugen no　　　　　limitless

　　貯水池　　　　　　chosuichi　　　　　reservoir

5 役割　　　　　　　　yakuwari　　　　　role

9 チャンス　　　　　　chansu　　　　　　(good) chance

　　幸運な　　　　　　kōun na　　　　　　fortunate, lucky

11 恐慌　　　　　　　　kyōkō　　　　　　panic, crisis

　　長期の　　　　　　chōki no　　　　　long, prolonged

Source: Ōkōchi Kazuo 大河内一男 , <u>Reimeiki no Nihon rōdō undō</u>
黎明期の日本労働運動 (The Japanese labor movement in its dawning
period), Iwanami Shinsho Series 115, 1952, pp. 4-5.

Ōkōchi Kazuo (1905-　　　　) is professor of economics at the
University of Tokyo.

Ōkōchi, a specialist in labor problems, uses the metaphor of
a reservoir to explain surplus population in the farming villages
as a source of cheap labor. If permanent employment has been
characteristic of most white-collar work in Japan, the historical
pattern described here has been typical of an important sector of
Japanese labor.

144

Lesson XXXVIII.   TSUBOUCHI SHŌYŌ

1	坪内逍遙 (雄蔵)	Tsubouchi Shōyō (Yūzō)	(novelist, 1859-1935)
2	予定	yotei	schedule, plan
	数え年	kazoedoshi	(old Japanese way of counting age)
3	卒業する	sotsugyō suru	be graduated
	文学士	bungakushi	Bachelor of Arts (in humanities)
	在学中に	zaigakuchū ni	while at school, during his school days
4	教師	kyōshi	teacher
	試験	shiken	examination
5	ガートルード	Gātorūdo	Gertrude
	王妃	ōhi	queen (wife of a king)
	批評する	hihyō suru	comment on, criticize
6	儒教的な	Jukyōteki na	Confucian
	道徳意識	dōtoku ishiki	sense of morality
	善悪	zen'aku	good and evil
7	批判する	hihan suru	criticize
	答案	tōan	examination paper
8	点	ten	mark, grade
9	考えなおす	kangaenaosu	reconsider
	(滝沢馬琴に …… とは違った)→立場		
	滝沢馬琴	Takizawa Bakin	(novelist, 1767-1848)
10	代表する	daihyō suru	represent

p203

11	リアリズム	riarizumu	realism
	解釈する	kaishaku suru	interpret, elucidate
	幾つかの	ikutsu ka no	several
13	シェークスピア	Shēkusupia	Shakespeare

p204

1	注釈書	chūshakusho	commentary (in book form)
	フォートナイト・レビュー	Fōtonaito Rebyū	The Fortnightly Review (founded in 1865)
2	フォラム	Foramu	The Forum
3	のる	noru	appear (in a publication)
4	評論	hyōron	criticism, comment, review
	読みあさる	yomiasaru	read in wide-ranging fashion (asaru = fish, search for)
5	ノートする	nōto suru	take notes on
	次第に	shidai ni	gradually
6	理論	riron	theory
7	前年	zennen	the previous year
	創立する	sōritsu suru	found, establish
	東京専門学校	Tōkyō Senmon Gakkō	Tokyo Technical School
	後の	nochi no	later
	早稲田大学	Waseda Daigaku	Waseda University
8	講師	kōshi	lecturer
9	翻訳	hon'yaku	translation
10	完成する	kansei suru	complete, accomplish
11	自由太刀余波鋭鋒	Jiyū no tachi nagori no kireaji	(a kabuki-style title, literally: the lingering sharpness of the sword of liberty)

146

11	題	dai	title
	出版する	shuppan suru	publish
13	原作	gensaku	the original (work)

1	忠実な	chūjitsu na	faithful
	歌舞伎	kabuki	<u>kabuki</u> drama
	せりふ	serifu	speech, one's lines
2	巧みに	takumi ni	skillfully, adroitly
	移し変える	utsushikaeru	transform, transfer
5	翌年	yokunen	the year after, the following year
6	当世書生気質	Tōsei shosei katagi	<u>The Character of Present-Day Students</u> (1885)
	描き出す	egakidasu	describe, portray
	寄宿舎	kishukusha	dormitory
	ぬけ出す	nukedasu	slip out
	遊郭	yūkaku	gay quarter, prostitution quarter
10	泊る	tomaru	stay at, put up (at)
	知り合い	shiriai	acquaintance
11	借りる	kariru	borrow
	参考書	sankōsho	reference book
	質に入れる	shichi ni ireru	pawn
12	(坪内自身や……体験した)→学生生活		
	体験する	taiken suru	experience personally or directly
13	場面	bamen	scene

2	数少い	kazu sukunai	the few, small number of
	のみ	nomi	only (=<u>dake</u>)

p206

3	センセーション	sensēshon	sensation
5	恋愛	ren'ai	(amatory) love
	扱う	atsukau	deal with
	出身	shusshin	(class, institution, or other) origin, background
	下等	katō na	low class, vulgar
	文士	bunshi	man of letters
	堕落する	daraku suru	degenerate
6	通念	tsūnen	common notion
8	不愉快な	fuyukai na	unpleasant, disagreeable
	ショック	shokku	shock
9	新思想家	shin-shisōka	modern thinker

to arō mono = "one who enjoys the reputation of being"

10	何事だ	nanigoto da	What kind of behavior is it...?
	非難する	hinan suru	criticize, censure
11	語り伝えられる	kataritsutae-rareru	be handed down orally

Source: Itō Sei 伊藤整, <u>Kindai Nihon no bungakushi</u> 近代日本の文学史, Kōbunsha 光文社, 1958, pp. 58-61.

Itō Sei (1905-   ) is a novelist and literary critic.

Japanese literature of the Meiji era remained close to the tradition of Edo literature until about 1885, when Tsubouchi published his influential critical study <u>Shōsetsu shinzui</u> 小説神髄 (The essence of the novel). In this work Tsubouchi pointed out a new path for the novel by advocating its independence as an artistic genre, freed from the <u>kanzen-chōaku</u> 勧善懲悪 (reward the good and punish the wicked) moralizing of popular Edo fiction. He is also famous as the first translator of the complete works of Shakespeare.

148

p207

2	私生活	shiseikatsu	private life
	告白	kokuhaku	confession
	場	ba	place
	生命	seimei	life, (animate) existence
3	仮構	kakō	fictitiousness
	芸術	geijutsu	arts

(芸術化された)→自叙伝あるいは日記

	自叙伝	jijoden	autobiography
4	花袋	Katai	(Tayama Katai, novelist, 1872-1930)

(花袋の……主流になる)→こと

5	蒲団	Futon	The Quilt (1907)
	私小説	shishōsetsu	"I-novel" (novel depicting the author's own life experience)
	藤村	Tōson	(Shimazaki Tōson, poet and novelist, 1872-1943)
	春	Haru	Spring (1908)
6	泡鳴	Hōmei	(Iwano Hōmei, novelist, 1873-1920)
	耽溺	Tandeki	Indulgence (1909)
	放浪	Hōrō	Wandering (1910)
7	秋声	Shūsei	(Tokuda Shūsei, novelist, 1872-1943)
	黴	Kabi	Mold (1911)
	生	Sei	Life (1908)
8	主流	shuryū	main stream

149

p207

9	妨げる	samatageru	prevent, hinder
10	読者	dokusha	reader
11	むろん	muron	= <u>mochiron</u>
	引く	hiku	attract, draw
12	凡人	bonjin	ordinary person, plebeian
	かつ	katsu	and, moreover
13	(これらの……である)→こと		
	求道者	kyūdōsha	seeker after truth

p208

1	(このように……とされる)→という我国に独自な現象		
2	排する	haisuru	reject, push aside
	単に	tan ni	simply
3	本道	hondō	main road, orthodoxy
4	現象	genshō	phenomenon
	背景	haikei	background, setting
	おそらく	osoraku	probably (in my opinion)
5	(明治時代……持っていた)→大きな過信		
	過信	kashin	overestimation, credulity
	風潮	fūchō	current, trend
7	(自然主義の……生まれた)→こと		
	思潮	shichō	current of ideas
8	(科学的思考……生んだ)→民族		
	思考	shikō	(way of) thinking
9	内部	naibu	interior
	生む	umu	bear, give birth to

150

p208

9 黒船　　　　　kurofune　　　　black ship (Edo term for Western ships)

（黒船……経験した）→ 民族

鉄道　　　　　tetsudō　　　　　railroad

電信　　　　　denshin　　　　　telegraph

10 外形　　　　 gaikei　　　　　external form

模倣　　　　　mohō　　　　　　imitation

11 現われる　　 arawareru　　　be revealed, appear

12 詳しく　　　 kuwashiku　　　in detail

要するに　　　yōsuru ni　　　in short

13 故郷　　　　 kokyō　　　　　native place, homeland

p209

1 魔術　　　　　majutsu　　　　magic, sorcery

表面　　　　　hyōmen　　　　　surface

作用する　　　sayō suru　　　act, have effect on

3 （自然科学と…… 感じさせた）→ こと

権威　　　　　ken'i　　　　　authority, prestige

4 動揺させる　 dōyō saseru　　shake, disturb

鋭敏な　　　　eibin na　　　　sensitive, keen, sharp

良心　　　　　ryōshin　　　　conscience

懐疑　　　　　kaigi　　　　　doubt, skepticism

幻滅　　　　　genmetsu　　　　disillusionment

5 両者　　　　　ryōsha　　　　both

（それに代る……とする）→ 努力

6 代る　　　　　kawaru　　　　replace

体系　　　　　taikei　　　　system (of ideas, beliefs)

p209

6	努力	doryoku	effort
7	欠ける	kakeru	lack
8	(科学を……組織だてる)→ コントやテーヌの努力		
	基礎	kiso	basis
	組織だてる	soshikidateru	systematize
	コント	Konto	Auguste Comte (French philosopher, sociologist, 1798-1857)
	テーヌ	Tēnu	Hippolyte Taine (French philosopher, 1828-1893)
10	人心	jinshin	people's minds, public feeling
	及ぼす	oyobosu	exert, extend
	破壊力	hakairyoku	destructive power

sore dake ni = "in so far as (it was an intellectual phenomenon)"

	全般	zenpan	the whole, entire
11	一部の	ichibu no	a part of, some
	階級	kaikyū	class, rank
12	目覚める	mezameru	awaken, be awakened

13 taru = to aru ("as") (literary)

	逆説的な	gyakusetsuteki na	paradoxical
	自負	jifu	pride, self-esteem

p210

1	実証精神	jisshō seishin	positivist spirit (jisshō = actual proof)
	酔う	you	be intoxicated
	ロマン派	romanha	romantic school
	派	-ha	group, school
2	形式	keishiki	form

152

p210
2 (何よりも ‥‥‥ とした) ⟶ 詩人たち

3 動かす   ugokasu   move

4 除く   nozoku   remove, eliminate

Source: Nakamura Mitsuo 中村光夫 , <u>Nihon no kindai shōsetsu</u>
日本の近代小説 , Iwanami Shinsho Series 177, 1961, pp. 135-37.

Nakamura Mitsuo (1911-   ) is a literary critic and
professor of French literature at Meiji University.

Nakamura has attempted to define the character of Japanese
Naturalism by contrasting it with French Naturalism of the
nineteenth century, pointing out that novelists in Japan turned
from realistic observation of society to introspective and
confessional fiction.

Nakamura's essays are customarily written in the polite
conversational style.

2 貴方がた   anatagata   you (plural)

jiyū ni aran = jiyū de aru (literary)

切望する   setsubō suru   desire earnestly

3 義務   gimu   duty, obligation

納得する   nattoku suru   understand, consent to (納＝納)

願って已まない   negatte yamanai   desire sincerely (ceaselessly)

5 公言する   kōgen suru   declare, pronounce

はばかる   habakaru   hesitate to, shrink from (doing)

6 此の   kono   this

誤解   gokai   misunderstanding, misconception (誤＝誤)

7 に對して   ni taishite   toward, to

吹き込む   fukikomu   instill, infuse

8 私が濟みません   watakushi ga sumimasen   it would be inexcusable of me, I could not forgive myself

其の邊は   sono hen wa   in that regard (邊＝辺)

注意   chūi   attention

9 個性   kosei   individuality

發展   hatten   development

10 幸福   kōfuku   happiness

關係   kankei   influence, relation

11 他に   ta ni   to others, on others

p211
11　（他に影響の……ない位の）→自由

を向く	o muku	turn toward, look toward

12　差支ない　sashitsukae nai　be all right, be free to (there is no hindrance, no objection)

把持する　haji suru　grasp, hold

他人　hito　other person

附與する　fuyo suru　grant, give

13　とりもなほさず　tori mo naosazu　precisely, nothing other than

p212
1　金力　kinryoku　power of money

權力　kenryoku　(political) power, influence

2　俺　ore　I (vulgar, used by men)

好かない　sukanai　find disagreeable, dislike

奴　yatsu　guy, fellow (vulgar, used by men)

疊んでしまふ　tatande shimau　beat (him) up, silence (vulgar) (tatamu = fold)

氣に食はない　ki ni kuwanai　be unable to stomach

3　やっつけてしまふ　yattsukete shimau　beat up, crush

惡い　warui　bad

warui koto mo nai no ni = "although he is blameless"

4　亂用する　ran'yō suru　abuse

破壞する　hakai suru　destroy, demolish

5　不幸　fukō　unhappiness, misfortune

其所　soko　there, that point

6　不都合を働く　futsugō o hataraku　do wrong, misconduct oneself

單に　tan ni　merely, simply

氣に入る　ki ni iru　please, suit

155

p212

7	警視總監	keishi sōkan	chief of the Metropolitan Police (監=監)
	巡査	junsa	policeman
	取り巻く	torimaku	surround, besiege (巻=卷)
9	德義	tokugi	morality, honor
10	三井	Mitsui	(famous <u>zaibatsu</u> family)
	岩崎	Iwasaki	(famous <u>zaibatsu</u> family)
	豪商	gōshō	merchant prince
	嫌ふ	kirau	dislike
11	買收する	baishū suru	bribe, buy
	事ごとに	kotogoto ni	in everything
12	背後に	haigo ni	behind, at the back of
	人格	jinkaku	character, personality
13	無法	muhō	injustice, illegality

p213

2	弊害	heigai	evil (practice), abuse (害=害)
	道義	dōgi	morality, moral principles
3	一般	ippan	the public
	おし廣める	oshihiromeru	aggrandize, extend (by force)
4	我儘	wagamama	selfishness

ni hoka naran = ni hoka naranai ("is nothing other than") (literary)

5	俗人	zokujin	vulgar (ordinary) people
6	國家	kokka	nation
	危險	kiken	danger (險=険)
7	解釋	kaishaku	understanding, interpretation
8	立派な	rippa na	fine, splendid

p213

9	黨派心	tōhashin	factionalism (tōha = party clique)
	理非	rihi	(judgment of) right and wrong, reason
10	裏面	rimen	other side, the back
	淋しい	sabishii	lonely
	潛む	hisomu	lurk, lie behind
11	我	ware	I (literary)
	勝手に	katte ni	as one pleases, wilfully
13	ばらばらになる	barabara ni naru	become scattered

Source: Natsume Sōseki 夏目漱石, "Watakushi no kojinshugi" 私の個人主義, lecture delivered at Gakushūin (the Peers' School), Tokyo, November 27, 1914, included in Sōseki zenshū, 34 vols., Iwanami Shoten, 1961-62, vol. 21, pp. 151-56.

Natsume Sōseki (1867-1916) was probably the greatest novelist of modern Japan.

Sōseki studied English literature at the University of Tokyo, then in England (1900-03), and was a professor at the University of Tokyo from 1903 to 1907. From 1907 until his death, Sōseki wrote a series of brilliant psychological novels under contract with the Asahi Shinbunsha. Well read both in Western and Oriental literature, he exerted a powerful influence on the culture of the Meiji and Taishō eras. Unlike Mori Ōgai, his chief rival as a man of letters, Sōseki had numerous followers (deshi 弟子) who were active in such fields as literature, philosophy, and education.

In "Watakushi no kojinshugi" Sōseki relates his efforts to establish a philosophy of life which would resolve the conflicting values of Japan and the West, of traditional thought and the morality of modern society, and of the nation and the individual. It is notable that he firmly asserted the dignity of the individual in spite of the rising nationalism of the years after the Russo-Japanese war.

Lessons 40 to 44 and 45 to 59 are written in the orthography standard before the language reforms, with kyūkanji 旧漢字 (old kanji)

157

and kyūkanazukai 旧 仮名づかい (old kana usage).

Characters not included in the official list of 1,850 tōyō kanji (characters for practical use) are called kyūkanji. These may be divided into two categories: (1) characters of which the new (abbreviated) forms are prescribed as tōyō kanji, and (2) characters which are supposed to be replaced by kana or, in some cases, by tōyō kanji. The following table shows a few examples of how words formerly written in kyūkanji are written in the new orthography:

	OLD	NEW
hatten	發展 →	発展
kankei	關係 →	関係
hisomu	潛む →	ひそむ
henshū	編輯 →	編集

More or less wide variations in kana usage have always been characteristic of Japanese writing, partly because of phonetic changes such as the loss of the distinction between the vowels お o and を (w)o, い i and ゐ (w)i, and え e and ゑ (w)e. Notable attempts to regulate kana usage according to historical principles were made by Fujiwara Teika 藤原定家 (1162-1241) and Keichū 契沖 (1640-1701), among others, and a system of "historical spelling" of the kana was adopted by the government at the beginning of the Meiji era. That system remained standard until the new rules for kana usage (shinkanazukai) were established after World War II. The major differences between the old and new systems are summarized in the following table. (However, it will be noticed that inconsistencies in the use of both kanji and kana are occasionally found even in the most determinedly up-to-date practice.)

In the traditional kana orthography:		OLD	NEW
1. O is written を instead of お in many words (as well as for the particle を), similarly i (ゐ for い) and e (ゑ for え).	okashii	をかしい	おかしい
	osamaru	をさまる	おさまる
	iru	ゐる	いる
	gurai	ぐらゐ	ぐらい
	inui	いぬゐ	いぬい
	ehagaki	ゑはがき	えはがき
2. The long vowel ō is also written o + ho, a + u (or fu), e + u (or fu), etc.	ōi	おほい	おおい
	ōkii	おほきい	おおきい
	ikō	行かう	行こう
	sōda	さうだ	そうだ
	darō	だらう	だろう

	deshō	で せう	で しょう
	ikimashō	行きませう	行きましょう

3. Ha は , hi ひ , fu ふ, he ヘ , ho ほ are often used, especially in verbal inflections, where wa わ , i い , u う , e え , and o お would now be standard.

omowareru	思はれる	思われる
iimasu	言ひます	言います
iu	言ふ	言う
omou	思ふ	思う
kangaeru	考へる	考える

4. Ji and zu are written ぢ and づ (instead of じ and ず) in many words.

jā	ぢゃあ	じゃあ
mazu	まづ	まず

5. Ka is often ku + wa (ga = gu + wa).

Kannon	くわんのん	かんのん
gaijin	ぐわいじん	がいじん

6. Double consonants are not only indicated by the symbol つ (usually written the same size as other kana) but by き , く , or ち , chiefly in compounds of which the first member ends with one of these symbols in its basic reading.

gekkō	げつくわう	げっこう
nikkō	につくわう	にっこう
sakka	さくか	さっか
gakkō	がくかう	がっこう
nitchū	にちちゆう	にっちゅう

2	かつて	katsute	once, at one time
	朝日新聞	Asahi Shinbun	the <u>Asahi</u> (newspaper)
	文藝欄	bungeiran	literary column, section
	擔任する	tannin suru	take charge of, be in charge of
	誰であったか	dare de atta ka	someone (I don't remember who)
3	三宅雪嶺	Miyake Setsurei	(writer, 1860-1945)
	悪口	warukuchi	criticism, abuse
	人身攻撃	jinshin kōgeki	personal attack (撃 = 擊)
5	たった	tatta	only (=<u>tada</u>)
	すると	suru to	then, thereupon
	日本及び日本人	Nihon oyobi Nihonjin	<u>Japan</u> <u>and</u> <u>the</u> <u>Japanese</u> (magazine edited by Miyake Setsurei)
6	連中	renjū, renchū	party, company, set
	怒る	okoru	become angry
7	下働き	shitabataraki	assistant
	取消	torikeshi	retraction
	申し込む	mōshikomu	demand, propose
8	本人	honnin	the person himself
	子分	kobun	follower, henchman
	何だか	nandaka	somehow or other
9	博奕打	bakuchiuchi	gambler, gangster
	まあ	mā	well

160

p215 9	同人	dōjin	associate, member of the staff (of the magazine)
10	事實	jijitsu	fact, actual situation; in fact
	もっとも(な)	mottomo (na)	reasonable
12	此方の	kochira no	our, my
	途	michi	way
p216 1	一部	ichibu	some (people), a part
	毎號	maigō	every issue (號 = 号)
	なほのこと	nao no koto	still more
2	といふのは	to iu no wa	for, because
3	に反して	ni hanshite	as opposed to
5	載せる	noseru	print (in a magazine, newspaper)
6	評語	hyōgo	critical remarks
7	失禮ながら	shitsurei nagara	although it is rude (禮 = 礼)
8	時代後れ	jidaiokure	out-of-date
	團隊	dantai	body, group
9	遂に	tsui ni	after all
10	脱却する	dakkyaku suru	get out of, escape
	譯に行かない	wake ni ikanai	be impossible, cannot manage (to)
11	防ぐ	fusegu	prevent, avert
	一言する	ichigon suru	say a word
12	反對	hantai	opposite
13	取る	toru	take, consider, regard
	理窟の立たない	rikutsu no tatanai	unreasonable, illogical

161

p216			
13	漫然とした	manzen to shita	incoherent, rambling
p217			
2	立ち行く	tachiyuku	can maintain itself, support itself
	云ひふらす	iifurasu	spread (a report or an idea)
3	naru mono = to iu mono (literary)		
	蹂躙する	jūrin suru	trample underfoot
	亡びる	horobiru	perish
4	唱道する	shōdō suru	advocate
	馬鹿げた	bakageta	silly, foolish
5	ariyō = aru to iu yō na koto		
	私共	watakushi-domo	we
7	sore hodo ... nai = "be not too (sore hodo = sonna ni, "so much")"		
	安泰(な)	antai (na)	stable, secure
	貧乏(な)	binbō (na)	poor
8	従って	shitagatte	accordingly
10	今が今	ima ga ima	any moment
	潰れる	tsubureru	collapse
	滅亡	metsubō	destruction, fall
	憂目	ukime	bitter experience, misery
11	國柄	kunigara	national character, national heritage
	さわぎ廻る	sawagimawaru	run around making a lot of noise
13	御注意までに	go-chūi made ni	to your attention
p218			
1	段	dan	level
2	元來	ganrai	originally, essentially
	辭令	jirei	(diplomatic) language

p218

2	やかましい	yakamashii	strict, punctilious
3	德義心	tokugishin	moral sense, sense of honor

ariya shimasen = ari wa shimasen

	詐欺	sagi	fraud
	誤魔化し	gomakashi	deception, trickery
4	ペテンにかける	peten ni kakeru	swindle, cheat (peten = fraud, swindle, trick)
	滅茶苦茶な	mechakucha na	chaotic, confused
5	標準	hyōjun	standard
	一團	ichidan	body, group
	よほど	yohodo	very, greatly
	低級な	teikyū na	low, inferior
6	甘んじる	amanjiru	be content with, put up with
	平氣な	heiki na	composed, unperturbed
8	平穩な	heion na	peaceful, tranquil
9	重きを置く	omoki o oku	stress, place emphasis on

Lesson XLII. "SOREKARA" YORI (I)

3 默る   damaru   be silent (默 = 默)

6 -tte = to iu to

  sorya = sore wa

世の中   yo no naka   the times, world

7 大袈裟に   ōgesa ni   on a large scale, exaggeratedly

對   tai   between, versus

駄目   dame   no good

8 借金   shakkin   debt

こしらへる   koshiraeru   raise (money), make

貧乏震ひ   binbōburui   nervous trembling of a poor man (metaphor for poverty)

10 外債   gaisai   foreign debt

12 sorede ite = "in spite of that"

一等國   ittōkoku   a first-class power

13 を以て任じる   o motte ninjiru   profess to be

仲間入りをする   nakamairi o suru   join the ranks

1 方面   hōmen   area, direction

  mukatte = oite

奧行   okuyuki   depth, length

削る   kezuru   cut down, reduce

2 間口   maguchi   width, frontage

p220

2	張る	haru	stretch, display, put up (a good front)
	なまじひ	namajii	superficially, in a half-baked way
3	牛	ushi	cow, ox
	蛙	kaeru	frog
	腹	hara	abdomen, belly
	裂ける	sakeru	split
4	反射する	hansha suru	mirror, reflect
5	給へ	tamae	(imperative suffix used by men on a friendly level)
	壓迫	appaku	pressure, oppression
	餘裕	yoyū	room, margin
6	ろくな	roku na	satisfactory (always used with negative)
	ことごとく	kotogotoku	entirely, one and all
	切りつめる	kiritsumeru	cram, economize
7	目が廻る	me ga mawaru	be dizzy
	こき使ふ	kokitsukau	drive (a person) hard, keep (a person) overbusy
	そろって	sorotte	all (without exception)
	神經衰弱	shinkei suijaku	nervous prostration, neurasthenia (suijaku = weakening, debility)

natchimau = natte shimau

8	馬鹿	baka	fool
9	只今の	tadaima no	present, immediate
10	疲勞する	hirō suru	become exhausted, be tired
	困憊	konpai	exhaustion, fatigue
	身體	shintai, karada	body

165

p220

11	不幸にして	fukō ni shite	unfortunately
	伴ふ	tomonau	go together, accompany (each other)
	敗退	haitai	collapse, rout
	一所に	issho ni	= 一緒に
12	見渡す	miwatasu	look out over, glance over

miwatashitatte = miwatashite mo

	輝く	kagayaku	shine, glitter
	斷面	danmen	section, phase
13	一寸四方	issun shihō	one <u>sun</u> (about one inch) square
p221 1	しやうがない	shō ga nai	useless, no good (=<u>shikata ga nai</u>) (colloquial)
	怠けもの	namakemono	lazy fellow
	いや	iya	or rather
2	往來する	ōrai suru	associate, communicate (with)
	時分	jibun	time, those days
3	景氣をつける	keiki o tsukeru	make a show of high spirits (<u>keiki</u> = liveliness)
4	有爲多望の 社會	yūi tabō no shakai	capable and promising society (會 = 会)
5	大體の上に於て	daitai no ue ni oite	on the whole
	健全 (な)	kenzen (na)	healthy (of society, etc.)
	依然として	izen to shite	still, as before
6	遣る	yaru	do (=<u>suru</u>)(informal)
7	怠惰性	taidasei	idleness, laziness
	打ち勝つ	uchikatsu	overcome
	丈	dake	extent
	刺激	shigeki	stimulus

166

p221

| 8 | 然し | shikashi | but, however |
| | 是 | kore | this |

mushiro jibun dake ni natte iru = "I'd rather keep to myself"

10	適する	tekisuru	suit, be suitable
11	接觸する	sesshoku suru	contact, touch (觸＝触)
	満足する	manzoku suru	be satisfied, content
	進んで	susunde	deliberate, by choice
12	なんて	nante	＝ <u>nado</u>
13	代助	Daisuke	(man's first name)
	一寸	chotto	a little, a bit
	息	iki	breath
	息を繼ぐ	iki o tsugu	catch breath, pause
	窮屈さうに	kyūkutsusō ni	awkwardly, constrained
	控へる	hikaeru	wait on

p222

1	三千代	Michiyo	(woman's first name)
	御世辭を遣ふ	o-seji o tsukau	flatter, pay a compliment
2	隨分	zuibun	very
	吞氣	nonki	carefree, free and easy, happy-go-lucky
	宜い	ii	good
3	賛成する	sansei suru	agree (with), approve (賛＝賛)
4	厭世の	ensei no	pessimistic
	樣	yō	it appears
	妙な	myō na	strange, curious
5	胡魔化す	gomakasu	camouflage, cover up

167

p222

6	へえ、	hē	is that so, you think so
	何處	doko	where (處 = 処)
7	平岡	Hiraoka	(surname)
8	盃	sakazuki	<u>sake</u> cup
9	酌をする	shaku o suru	fill (a person's) cup (with <u>sake</u>)

Source: Natsume Sōseki, <u>Sorekara</u> それから , <u>Asahi</u> <u>Shinbun</u>, June-October, 1909, included in <u>Sōseki</u> <u>zenshū</u>, vol. 8, pp. 75-79.

Daisuke, the hero of <u>Sorekara</u>, is an uneasy intellectual of the last years of the Meiji era. Although he has grown up in a wealthy family and has received an excellent education, he is in despair over the insecurity of Japanese society and has no interest in working or marrying. One day he meets his old friend Hiraoka and Hiraoka's wife Michiyo, who have recently come back to Tokyo after three years' absence. For the sake of their friendship, Daisuke once helped Hiraoka to win Michiyo's love, in spite of his own love for her. When he finds that Michiyo is now unhappy because of illness and Hiraoka's debauchery, his old love revives. This time he resolves to shake off his apathy and marry her. As a result, he is rejected by his family and cut off from financial assistance. He begins to look for a job.

This extract is from the scene in which Daisuke meets Hiraoka and Michiyo shortly after their return to Tokyo.

3	そいつ	soitsu	it (=sore)
	大いに	ōi ni	very, greatly
	僕みたいに	boku mitai ni	like me
	局部	kyokubu	limited part (of the society)
	當る	ataru	face, deal with
4	悪闘する	akutō suru	fight desperately, struggle
	餘地がない	yochi ga nai	no room (to, for)
5	貧弱(な)	hinjaku (na)	poor, meager
	弱蟲	yowamushi	weakling, coward
	氣が附く	ki ga tsuku	notice, become aware of
7	暇人	himajin	man of leisure
8	氣になる	ki ni naru	weigh on one's mind, feel uneasy about (something); be inclined to
	用のない	yō no nai	have no business, free
	傍觀者	bōkansha	spectator
9	顔	kao	face
	鏡	kagami	mirror
10	なんか	nanka	such ... as (=nado)
12	薄笑ひ	usuwarai	wan (thin) smile
13	附け加へる	tsukekuwaeru	add
p224			
1	不自由する	fujiyū suru	be in need (of), be lacking (in)

p224
1	不可ない	ikenai	hopeless
2	坊ちゃん	botchan	(sheltered young man who knows little of the world)
	品の好い	hin no yoi	high-brow, refined
4	突然	totsuzen	suddenly
	中途で	chūto de	halfway, in the middle
	さへぎる	saegiru	interrupt
5	名譽	meiyo	honor, credit
6	神聖な	shinsei na	sacred, holy
	勞力	rōryoku	labor, effort
	パン	pan	bread
10	論理学	ronrigaku	logic
	命題	meidai	proposition

mita yō na = mitai na

12	食ふ	kuu	eat (familiar)
13	まるで	marude	entirely, completely
	猛烈に	mōretsu ni	strongly, violently

p225
6	それ見給へ	sore mitamae	see, I told you so
	方便	hōben	expedient
7	合せる	awaseru	match, fit
8	構ふ	kamau	matter
9	歸着する	kichaku suru	arrive (at a conclusion)
	方向	hōkō	direction, course
10	乃至	naishi	or
	制肘する	seichū suru	control, restrain

170

Lesson XLIII

12	どうも	dō mo	somehow
	一向	ikkō	at all (with negative)
	差支ない	sashitsukae nai	there is nothing wrong
13	ごく	goku	very, extremely
	上品な	jōhin na	high-brow, elegant
	古臭い	furukusai	old, stale
	覺え	oboe	memory
	織田信長	Oda Nobunaga	(warrior-politician: 1534-1582)
	料理人	ryōrinin	cook (ryōri = cuisine)

p226

2	抱へる	kakaeru	engage, employ
3	すこぶる	sukoburu	very, extremely
	まづい	mazui	tasteless
	小言を云ふ	kogoto o iu	scold, rebuke
4	最上の	saijō no	of the highest class
	叱る	shikaru	scold
5	二流	niryū	second-class
	もしくは	moshiku wa	or (else)
	三流	sanryū	third-class
	あてがふ	ategau	provide, furnish
	始終	shijū	always
6	ぬけ目のない	nukeme no nai	shrewd, smart
9	だって	datte	but, still
	解雇する	kaiko suru	dismiss, discharge
10	衣食	ishoku	food and clothing

171

p226

10	物ずきにやる	monozuki ni yaru	do because it strikes his fancy
11	眞面目な	majime na	serious, earnest
13	なあ	nā	don't you think so?

p227

1	もどる	modoru	return, come back
5	かく	kaku	scratch
	たうとう	tōtō	finally
	お仕舞になる	o-shimai ni naru	come to an end

Lesson XLIV.　　HANABI

1	花火	hanabi	fireworks
2	午飯	hirumeshi	noon meal
	箸	hashi	chopsticks
	ポン	pon	bang! pop!
	音	oto	sound
3	梅雨	tsuyu	the rainy season (梅=梅)
	漸く	yōyaku	finally, at long last
	明けぢかい	akejikai	nearly over, almost ended
	曇る	kumoru	be cloudy
	涼しい	suzushii	cool (凉=涼)
	絶えず	taezu	ceaselessly
4	簾	sudare	bamboo blind

mireba = (ki ga tsuite) miru to

	路地裏の家々	rojiura no ieie	houses facing the alley (roji = alley, lane)
	軒並に	nokinami ni	at every house
	國旗	kokki	national flag
5	わが家	wagaya	my (our) house
	格子戸	kōshido	lattice gate
6	市	-shi	city
	欧洲	Ōshū	Europe
	講和	kōwa	peace negotiations

173

p228

6	記念祭	kinensai	celebration, commemoration (祭 = 祭)
	當日	tōjitsu	the day, appointed day
8	静か(だ)	shizuka (da)	quiet
	表通り	omotedōri	street

nani ka koto areba = nani ka kawatta koto ga areba

9	あっちこっち	atchikotchi	here and there
	明く	aku	open
	駆け出す	kakedasu	run out
	下駄	geta	Japanese wooden clogs
10	今日に限って	kyō ni kagitte	on this particular day
	騒ぐ	sawagu	make a noise, clamor, be excited (騷 = 騒)
	女房	nyōbō	wife, housewife (房 = 房)
11	話聲	hanashigoe	voice (in conversation)
	日比谷	Hibiya	(district of Tokyo)
	上野	Ueno	(district of Tokyo)
	出掛ける	dekakeru	go out, set out
12	耳をすます	mimi o sumasu	prick one's ears
	かすかに	kasuka ni	faintly
	叫ぶ	sakebu	shout
13	ふと	futo	suddenly, unexpectedly
	身の上	mi no ue	one's lot, circumstances
	いかに	ika ni	how (much)
	世間	seken	world, society, community
	掛離れる	kakehanareru	be far removed (from)

p229

1	われながら	ware nagara	although I say so myself
2	鞏固な	kyōko na	strong, firm
	意志	ishi	will
3	殊更	kotosara	intentionally, purposely
	いっとなく	itsu to naku	unnoticed, before one is aware
4	知らず知らず	shirazushirazu	without knowing (it)
	孤獨	kodoku	solitude, loneliness
	孤獨の身	kodoku no mi	solitary existence
5	連絡	renraku	communication, liaison
6	慶應義塾	Keiō Gijuku	Keio University
	通勤する	tsūkin suru	commute to work
	道すがら	michisugara	on the way
7	折々	oriori	occasionally, sometimes
	市ヶ谷	Ichigaya	(district of Tokyo)
	囚人	shūjin	prisoner
	馬車	basha	coach, carriage, cart
	臺	-dai	(counter for vehicles and machines)
	引續いて	hikitsuzuite	in succession
	裁判所	saibansho	courthouse, court
8	見聞する	kenbun suru	see and hear, experience
	世上の	sejō no	worldly, earthly
9	折	ori	occasion
	云ふに云はれない	iu ni iwarenai	unutterable, inexpressible

175

9	厭な	iya na	disgusting, unpleasant
	黙する	mokusuru	be silent (=<u>damaru</u>)
11	naranai = ikenai		
	ゾラ	Zora	Emile Zola (French novelist, 1840-1902)
	ドレフュー	Dorefyū	Alfred Dreyfus (French army officer, 1859-1935)
	正義	seigi	justice
12	國外	kokugai	outside the country, abroad
	亡命する	bōmei suru	exile oneself, seek refuge
	世の文學者	yo no bungakusha	contemporary man of letters
13	何となく	nan to naku	somehow, for some reason or other

1	たへる	taeru	bear, endure
	氣がする	ki ga suru	feel
2	甚しい	hanahadashii	intense, terrible
	羞恥	shūchi	shame
	品位	hin'i	grade of quality, dignity
3	戯作	gesaku	light literature (戯=戯)
	引下げる	hikisageru	lower, reduce
	に如くはない	ni shiku wa nai	there is nothing like, nothing as good as
	思案する	shian suru	reflect, ponder
4	煙草入	tabakoire	tobacco pouch
	さげる	sageru	wear, carry (hanging from the sash)
	浮世繪	ukiyoe	<u>ukiyoe</u>, genre picture
	集める	atsumeru	collect
	三味線	shamisen	three-string musical instrument

176

p230

4　ひく　　　　　　hiku　　　　　　play (a stringed instrument)

5　（江戸末代の……来ようが‖櫻田……されようが‖そんな事は……

をかいてゐた）→其の瞬間の胸中

末代　　　　　　matsudai　　　the last years (of an era, etc.)

淨世繪師　　　　ukiyoeshi　　　ukiyoe artist

浦賀　　　　　　Uraga　　　　　(seaport town 16 miles south-west of Yokohama)

6　櫻田御門　　　Sakurada Gomon　Sakurada Gate (of the Imperial Palace, Tokyo)

大老　　　　　　tairō　　　　　chief minister (in the Tokugawa government, here Ii Naosuke, 1815-1860)

暗殺する　　　　ansatsu suru　assassinate

下民　　　　　　gemin　　　　　common people, vulgar classes

與リ知る　　　　azukarishiru　concern, be the business of

7　否　　　　　　ina　　　　　　no, nay

とやかく　　　　toyakaku　　　this and that, complaints, criticism

おそれ多い　　　osoreōi　　　　impious, lacking in respect

8　すまして　　　sumashite　　indifferently

春本　　　　　　shunpon　　　pornographic book

春畫　　　　　　shunga　　　　pornographic picture

瞬間　　　　　　shunkan　　　instant, moment

胸中　　　　　　kyōchū　　　　feeling; bosom, heart

9　oba = o (emphatic)

呆れる　　　　　akireru　　　be shocked by, be disgusted with

思立つ　　　　　omoitatsu　　set one's mind on, resolve

Source: Nagai Kafū 永井荷風, "Hanabi"花火, Kaizō 改造, December, 1919, included in Azabu zakki 麻布襍記 (Azabu miscellany), Kafū zenshū, 27 vols., Iwanami Shoten, 1963- , vol. 15, pp. 7-12.

Nagai Kafū (1879-1959) was a novelist and essayist of the first rank.

Kafū's writings are influenced both by later nineteenth-century French literature and by the decadent aesthetic tendencies of Edo culture. On returning to Japan after studying in the United States and France from 1903 to 1907, Kafū became a professor at Keiō University and then editor-in-chief of the periodical Mita bungaku 三田文学. Early in the Taishō era, however, he began to devote himself entirely to literature, often writing on such subjects as geisha, prostitutes, and dancing girls. Though forbidden to publish his works during World War II, he continued writing and enjoyed renewed success after the war.

"Hanabi" is an essay in which Kafū reflects on his life until middle age against the background of social and political events. The "Kōtoku incident" occurred in 1910 when Kōtoku Shūsui 幸徳秋水 and twenty-three other anarchists were arrested on the charge of plotting the assassination of the Emperor; twelve of them were executed the following year after a secret trial.

p231

2	ざっと	zatto	approximately, roughly
	審議	shingi	deliberation
	審議会	shingikai	deliberation association, council
	委員	iin	member (of a committee)
	命じる	meijiru	appoint, order
3	既に	sude ni	already
	発足する	hossoku suru	start functioning
4	国字	kokuji	(characters not of Chinese origin used in Japanese writing)
	表音化する	hyōonka suru	phoneticize
	方針	hōshin	policy, principle
5	決定する	kettei suru	decide (upon)
	仮名遣	kanazukai	the use of <u>kana</u>
	決まる＝決る		
6	線	sen	line
	その線に沿って	sono sen ni sotte	along those lines, in accord with those principles (<u>sou</u> = follow along)
	進める	susumeru	carry on, go forward

（一八五〇字の……書けないとする）→ 私

7	異端	itan	heresy
	異端視を受ける	itanshi o ukeru	be regarded as a heretic

179

p231			
9	無くす	nakusu	eliminate, remove
10	一掃する	issō suru	sweep away
12	構成する	kōsei suru	compose, constitute
13	成行き	nariyuki	the course (of events)
	成行きまかせの	nariyuki makase no	letting (something) take its course
p232	追随する	tsuizui suru	follow along
1	実施する	jisshi suru	put into effect, enforce
3	訓む	yomu	read (pronounce) Chinese characters in Japanese
4	お姉さん	o-nēsan	elder sister (honorific)
	お兄ちゃん	o-nīchan	elder brother (chan= san, familiar)
	然り	shikari	the same, likewise
5	便宜	bengi	convenience, advantage
	機能	kinō	function
7	過激な	kageki na	extreme, radical
9	戦術	senjutsu	tactics
10	忠孝	chūkō	loyalty and filial piety
11	観念	kannen	concept, idea
	思いおこす	omoiokosu	call to mind
12	庶民	shomin	the common people, masses
	幸福	kōfuku	happiness
	押しまげる	oshimageru	bend, distort
	専制の	sensei no	despotic, tyrannical
	君主	kunshu	lord, master
13	利益	rieki	profit, advantage

p232 13	貪る	musaboru	covet, be greedy for
p233 1	柱	hashira	pillar
	拘束する	kōsoku suru	restrict, bind
2	逸脱する	itsudatsu suru	escape, deviate
	カラクリ	karakuri	tricky system
	恐るべき	osorubeki	frightful, terrible
3	直截に	chokusetsu ni	directly, straightforwardly
	なくなす	nakunasu	remove, do away with
5	カナガキ	kanagaki	_kana_ writing
	エフェクト	efekuto	effect
7	まして	mashite	furthermore, moreover
8	罪悪、	zaiaku	evil, crime
9	死滅する	shimetsu suru	die out, become extinct
10	作り直す	tsukurinaosu	rebuild, remake
11	不自然な	fushizen na	unnatural
	押売り	oshiuri	pressured sale
12	廃止	haishi	abolition
	無謀な	mubō na	thoughtless, reckless
	焦土	shōdo	burnt land
	焦土戦術	shōdo senjutsu	scorched earth tactics
13	白痴	hakuchi	idiocy, idiot
p234 1	玉石混淆	gyokuseki konkō	a jumble of gems and stones, mixture of wheat and chaff
2	断絶	danzetsu	break, rupture
3	けしからん	keshikaran	blameworthy, outrageous

181

p234

4	帝国主義	teikokushugi	imperialism
	求刑	kyūkei	prosecution
5	価値	kachi	value
	顛倒	tentō	inversion
	謀る	hakaru	plan, plot
6	伝承	denshō	tradition, transmission
	絶つ	tatsu	sever, cut off
	空白	kūhaku	vacuum, blank
	麻酔	masui	anesthesia
7	痙攣	keiren	convulsions
	役立てる	yakudateru	make use of, turn to account
8	推測	suisoku	conjecture, supposition
9	簡素 (な)	kanso (na)	simple, plain
10	幼稚 (な)	yōchi (na)	crude, childish
11	目下の	mokka no	of this moment
	普遍的	fuhenteki	universal, general
12	あり方	arikata	attitude, state
13	暴走する	bōsō suru	run recklessly (blindly)
	陳弁する	chinben suru	plead their case, argue (in defense)
p235			
2	送りがな	okurigana	(kana added to kanji to complete a word)
3	行きすぎ	ikisugi	extreme, going too far
	標本	hyōhon	specimen, example
	執着する	shūjaku suru	be tenaciously attached to
	墓穴	boketsu	grave

182

p235

3　掘る　　　　　　horu　　　　　　　　dig

Source: Funahashi Seiichi 船橋聖一, "Kokugo mondai to minzoku no shōrai" 国語問題と民族の将来, Chūōkōron 中央公論, May, 1961, pp. 48-56.

Funahashi Seiichi (1904-　　) is a popular novelist.

Funahashi attracted the attention of literary circles when he founded, with Abe Tomoji 阿部知二 and other anti-Fascist writers, the monthly review Kōdō 行動 (Action) shortly before the outbreak of World War II. After a silence during the war, Funahashi has continued his career as a novelist.

Attempts to reform the Japanese writing system date from the beginning of the Meiji period. Some first-rate scholars, Nishi Amane 西周　for instance, advocated even the use of rōmaji, not to mention those who merely proposed to limit the number of Chinese characters. In 1902 the government established the Japanese Language Investigation Committee, which was abolished in 1913 before taking any action to reform the writing system. A new committee was established in 1921, with various tentative plans for reform, and has continued to function ever since. Still, because of powerful conservatism both within and without the committee, actual reforms had to wait until 1946, when the Ministry of Education, as a link in the chain of democratic policy, issued regulations simplifying and limiting the number of Chinese characters and fixing kana usage. These regulations, however, were drawn up so hastily that they have certain defects and disadvantages, which have been pointed out by many scholars, writers, and critics.

Lesson XLVI.   GENGO SEISAKU NI TSUITE (I)

2	結論	ketsuron	conclusion
5	あたりまえのこと	atarimae no koto	natural thing, a matter of course
6	構造	kōzō	structure
	本来	honrai	essentially, primarily, originally
7	大切な	taisetsu na	important, precious
	道具	dōgu	tool
8	差	sa	difference
9	所有物	shoyūbutsu	possession, property
10	属する	zokusuru	belong (to)
12	独創的	dokusōteki	creative, original
	文法	bunpō	grammar
13	せいぜい	seizei	at most, at best
	若干	jakkan	some, a number (of)

1	味	aji	flavor, taste
	生み出す	umidasu	produce, create
	度がすぎる	do ga sugiru	go to excess
2	詩	shi	poem, poetry
3	好ききらい	sukikirai	likes and dislikes, taste
4	語い	goi	vocabulary
	同様	dōyō	the same
5	特定の	tokutei no	certain, specific

184

p237

5	よしあし	yoshiashi	good or bad
6	基準	kijun	standard, basis
7	さて	sate	well, then, now
	固有の	koyū no	characteristic, peculiar, native
8	支える	sasaeru	support
9	認定	nintei	recognition
10	いまさら	imasara	by now, at this time
12	民衆的	minshūteki	popular
	芝居	shibai	play (here: Kabuki)
	狂言	kyōgen	comedy ("mad words" = comic interludes performed between Nō plays)
13	西鶴	Saikaku	Ihara Saikaku (novelist, 1642-1693)
	諸作	shosaku	(various) works

p238

2	唯一の	yuiitsu no	the only, unique
	選択	sentaku	choice
	自体	jitai	itself
3	意識的に	ishikiteki ni	consciously, intentionally
	変化	henka	change
	統御する	tōgyo suru	control
4	それとも	soretomo	or (alternatively)
7	致命的に	chimeiteki ni	vitally, mortally
	重大な	jūdai na	important, weighty
	最善	saizen	the best

(最善と思われる)→ 方法

p238
8 | 処理する | shori suru | manage, settle

一般に | ippan ni | in general

特徴 | tokuchō | characteristic

11 | 実質的に | jisshitsuteki ni | substantially

12 | 急 (な) | kyū (na) | urgent

13 | 無責任な | musekinin na | irresponsible

p239
1 | 野放し | nobanashi | leaving (something) to take care of itself; pasturing

不都合 | futsugō | inconvenience

いよいよ | iyoiyo | more and more, all the more

3 | 改革 | kaikaku | reform

6 | 当座 | tōza | for the present, temporarily

8 | 亀井勝一郎 | Kamei Katsuichirō | (critic, 1907-   )

魅力 | miryoku | charm

10 | 意中の女 | ichū no onna | sweetheart, woman in one's heart

13 | 女一般 | onna ippan | women in general

ひき出す | hikidasu | draw (out), pull (out)

p240
1 | 冒す | okasu | make, commit

toshite dake aru no de wa nai = "are not only (do not merely exist as)"

5 | 学問 | gakumon | learning, scholarship

金もうけ | kanemōke | moneymaking

夫婦 | fūfu | husband and wife, couple

6 | 考慮 | kōryo | consideration

186

Source: Katō Shūichi 加藤周一, "Gengo seisaku ni tsuite"
言語政策 について Tōkyō Shinbun 東京新聞, July 24, 1958, reprinted
in Kokugo kaikaku ronsō 国語改革論争, (The language reform
controversy), Kuroshio Shuppan くろしお出版, 1960, pp. 110-116.

    Katō Shūichi (1919-   ) is a poet and literary critic.

    Katō made his debut as a member of the "matinée poétique"
group which, taking Mallarmé and Valéry as its masters, played an
active part in the chaotic post-war literary world. After earning
a doctorate in medicine, Katō wrote literary criticism while
working at the Tokyo University Hospital. He holds a secure
position among contemporary critics for his knowledge of Western
literature and thought.

Lesson XLVII.   GENGO SEISAKU NI TSUITE (II)

p241
2　話を文学に限リ‖問題の……ということにかぎって

に かぎる	ni kagiru	limit to
問題 の	mondai no	in question, controversial
著しい	ichijirushii	marked, conspicuous
制限	seigen	limitation, restriction

3　(の) おかげで　(no) o-kage de　due to, owing to

4　豊富 (な)　hōfu (na)　rich, abundant

さかんに　sakan ni　vigorously, extensively

5　(漢字による……生みだしている)→の

6

感情	kanjō	emotion, feeling
文体	buntai	literary style

7　石川淳　Ishikawa Jun　(writer, 1899-　　　)

(江戸時代の……ラテン語程度の)→[もの]‖それ

和製	wasei	made in Japan
ラテン	Raten	Latin

8　らくに　raku ni　easily, freely

9　大言壮語する　taigensōgo suru　rant, rave

10　勇気　yūki　courage

11　今の日本文学‖または……小説戯文の類

俗に	zoku ni	commonly, popularly
賞	shō	prize

188

p241

12	戯文	gibun	burlesque, parody
	類	tagui, rui	kind, sort
	…どころか	... dokoro ka	far from ... but, not at all ... but
13	およそ	oyoso	altogether, on the whole
	無知	muchi	ignorance
	鈍感	donkan	insensitivity
	展覧会	tenrankai	exhibition

p242

4	事ここに至る	koto koko ni itaru	things come to such a pass
5	周囲	shūi	surroundings, environment
	壊れる	kowareru	be ruined, be broken (down)
6	(漢字に頼ることの多かった)→ 伝統的文章		
7	規範	kihan	standard, norm
8	見出す	miidasu	find
	あきらめる	akirameru	give up, abandon
10	でたらめさ	detaramesa	haphazardness
11	残存	zanson	survival
	不在	fuzai	absence
12	矛盾	mujun	contradiction
	生じる	shōjiru	produce, bring about
13	害	gai	harmful effect, injury
	及ぶ	oyobu	extend

p243

1	漢詩	kanshi	Chinese poem, Chinese poetry
4	なくなる	nakunaru	disappear, vanish
5	漢語	kango	"Chinese word" (written in Chinese characters,

p243
5   read in <u>on</u>)

7	観点	kanten	point of view
	算える	kazoeru	enumerate, count
8	暇	hima	time
9	事務	jimu	business, office work
	能率	nōritsu	efficiency
	ひどい	hidoi	terrible
	害する	gaisuru	impair, harm
	印刷	insatsu	printing
	分類	bunrui	classification
11	あいまい (な)	aimai (na)	ambiguous, vague
	…がち (な)	… gachi (na)	apt to
12	ハッコウイチウ (八紘一宇)	hakkō ichiu	the eight corners of the world under one roof (metaphor for governing by tennō)
	ドウコク(慟哭)	dōkoku	lamentation
13	ふんい気	fun'iki	atmosphere

p244

2	三つ	mittsu	three (items)
3	限り	kagiri	limit
5	授業時間	jugyō jikan	school hours
	犠牲	gisei	sacrifice
6	語学的に	gogakuteki ni	as an object of language study
	奪う	ubau	rob, deprive of
8	だまされ易い	damasareyasui	easy to be deceived
9	民主主義	minshushugi	democracy

190

p244

9	希望	kibō	hope, expectation, prospect
10	電話帳	denwachō	telephone directory
	探す	sagasu	look for
11	約束する	yakusoku suru	make an engagement, promise
	あいびき	aibiki	date, rendezvous

p245

3	論じ去る	ronjisaru	discuss (and dispose of)
4	式	-shiki	type, kind
5	現に	gen ni	actually
6	有難い	arigatai	desirable, welcome
	涙もろい	namida moroi	easily moved to tears
7	気分	kibun	feeling, mood
	根拠	konkyo	foundation, ground
8	活動写真	katsudōshashin	motion picture
	略して	ryakushite	for short
9	ばかばかしさ	bakabakashisa	absurdity
11	浪費	rōhi	waste
	用語	yōgo	term, word
	定義	teigi	definition
	要求する	yōkyū suru	ask, demand
	ひとたまりもなく	hitotamari mo naku	without the least resistance

2	土台	dodai	foundation, basis
3	定まる	sadamaru	be fixed, determined
	さらに	sara ni	moreover, in addition
4	向い合う	mukaiau	face (each other), be opposite
	つながり	tsunagari	link, bond
6	決める	kimeru	determine
9	考察する	kōsatsu suru	consider, examine
10	(資本主義 …… ひきずってきている)→ところ		
	立前	tatemae	principle, policy
	なかば	nakaba	half
11	名残り	nagori	remains, traces
	ひきずる	hikizuru	drag, trail
13	いり混る	irimajiru	be intermixed, mingled

1	デリケートな	derikēto na	delicate
	つり合い	tsuriai	balance
2	目立つ	medatsu	be conspicuous
3	(日本の人間関係で近代化されていない)→要素		
	要素	yōso	element, factor
4	大ざっぱに	ōzappa ni	roughly
	結局	kekkyoku	after all
	約束	yakusoku	convention

192

7	権利	kenri	legal rights, privilege
	裏づけ	urazuke	backing, support
8	微妙に	bimyō ni	delicately, subtly
	からみあう	karamiau	be intertwined, become intertwined
11	(社会生活の‥‥‥ 行動すべきであるかについての)→ 約束		
	各人	kakujin	each person
12	居る	oru	(=<u>iru</u>)

2	自己	jiko	self, oneself
4	世間体	sekentei	(public) appearance, face
6	親類	shinrui	relative
7	何れにしても	izure ni shite mo	in any case
8	(昔からきめられた‥‥‥行動する)→ こと		
	リクツ抜きに	rikutsu nuki ni	without argument, without discussion

arubekiyō ni = "as it should be (as one ought to be)"

10	恩愛	on'ai	kindness and affection (for a child)
	孝心	kōshin	filial feeling
	孝行	kōkō	filial piety
11	愛情	aijō	affection
12	人情	ninjō	human feeling, human nature
13	家長	kachō	head of a household

1	服従	fukujū	obedience, submission
2	加わる	kuwawaru	be added, join
3	義父母	gifubo	father- and mother-in-law
	嫁	yome	daughter-in-law

p249

3	しゅうとめ	shūtome	mother-in-law
4	勝つ	katsu	prevail
	量	ryō	amount, quantity
5	に比例して	ni hirei shite	in proportion to
	冷厳さ	reigensa	coldness, sternness
	増加する	zōka suru	increase
6	相応する	sōō suru	be suitable, proper
	奉公	hōkō	service, devotion
8	(「人情」からくる・・・・・・思うの)→孝行		
	血のつながった	chi no tsunagatta	related by blood
10	漁村	gyoson	fishing village
12	はるかに	haruka ni	far more, by far
	位置	ichi	position, status

p250

1	久しく	hisashiku	for a long time
	男尊女卑	danson johi	predominance of man over woman
3	男を上げる	otoko o ageru	honor oneself, build one's reputation
	未だに	imada ni	still, even now
	国会	kokkai	the Diet
	一つ一つの	hitotsu hitotsu no	individual, each and every
	閉じこめる	tojikomeru	confine
7	・・・にわたって	-ni watatte	extending to, ranging over
	ヒナ型	hinagata	pattern, model
8	拡がる	hirogaru	extend, spread
	主	shu	primary

194

p250

9　集合体　　　　　shūgōtai　　　　group, collective body,
　　　　　　　　　　　　　　　　　　　collectivity

10　孝道　　　　　　kōdō　　　　　　filial way

　　重んずる　　　　omonzuru　　　　stress, attach
　　　　　　　　　　　　　　　　　　　importance to

12　（家族の集団を……それになぞらえる）→やり方

　　集団　　　　　　shūdan　　　　　group, body

13　なぞらえる　　　nazoraeru　　　pattern after, model
　　　　　　　　　　　　　　　　　　　after

Source: Minami Hiroshi 南博 , <u>Nihonjin no shinri</u> 日本人の心理,
Iwanami Shoten, 1960, pp. 186-97.

　　　Minami Hiroshi (1914-　　) is professor of social psychology
at Hitotsubashi University.

Lesson XLIX.   NIHONJIN NO NINGEN KANKEI (II)

2	親分	oyabun	boss, chief
	おとな	otona	a grown-up, adult
5	ニセの	nise no	false, counterfeit
7	せせこましい	sesekomashii	narrow-minded, fussy
	なれ合い	nareai	collusion, acting in league
	植えつける	uetsukeru	plant, implant
8	親心	oyagokoro	parental affection
	温情	onjō	warm feelings
11	商人	shōnin	merchant, tradesman
	客	kyaku	customer; guest
13	某	bō	a certain
	デパート	depāto	department store

1	尊称	sonshō	honorific title
3	店員	ten'in	clerk
	さとす	satosu	admonish, advise
4	ほんの	honno	mere, only
5	年配の	nenpai no	elderly
	世論	seron	public opinion
6	所	-jo	institute, center
	統計	tōkei	statistics
9	情けない	nasakenai	lamentable, grievous

196

p253

10	年令	nenrei	age, years of age
	回答者	kaitōsha	respondent
	割	-wari	tenth, ten per cent
11	設問	setsumon	question
	多分に	tabun ni	in large measure
12	誘導的	yūdōteki	leading
13	数字	sūji	figure, numeral
	割引きする	waribiki suru	discount, reduce

p254

1	増減	zōgen	increase and decrease, variation
2	名物	meibutsu	special product, specialty
3	根強い	nezuyoi	tenacious, deeply rooted
7	対人的な	taijinteki na	interpersonal
8	環境	kankyō	environment
	拡がり	hirogari	extent, area
9	とりどり(の)	toridori (no)	varied
10	市民	shimin	townsman, citizen
	向う三軒両隣	mukō sangen ryōdonari	one's nearest neighbors, the three houses opposite and the two houses flanking
13	範囲	han'i	limits, extent

（「近所の手前 …… ようにする）→ 近所づきあいの「あるべきよう」

p255

1	の手前	no temae	out of consideration for, in deference to
	工合	guai	decency; state, condition
	工合がわるい	guai ga warui	feel awkward, be improper
	近所づきあい	kinjozukiai	neighborhood association

197

p255

3	かかわる	kakawaru	reflect on
	申しわけない	mōshiwake nai	no apology, inexcusable
6	お蔭	okage	indebtedness
	こもる	komoru	be implied
7	何らかの形で	nanra ka no katachi de	in some form (or other)
8	守る	mamoru	keep
	奉仕する	hōshi suru	serve
9	先祖	senzo	ancestor
10	バクゼンとした	bakuzen to shita	vague, obscure
12	挙げる	ageru	mention, cite

p256

1	問い	toi	question
2	利己主義	rikoshugi	selfishness, egoism
3	恩返し	ongaeshi	repayment of a favor

(恩返しと……行動である)→と考える人

Lesson L. NIHON NO SHINJŌ

p257

1	心情	shinjō	feeling, sentiment
2	儒者	jusha	a Confucian
	何もの	nanimono	something, someone
3	信ずる	shinzuru	believe (in)
	神	kami	god
4	あける	akeru	open
	聖書	seisho	the Bible
6	清浄な	seijō na	pure
	光景	kōkei	scene, sight

(それはやはり…… 偉大さを示すもの)→と考えている

7	且つ	katsu	also, moreover
	すばらしい	subarashii	splendid, wonderful
8	偉大(な)	idai (na)	great, grand
9	実在の	jitsuzai no	real, actual

10 (それは一つの便宜にすぎない)→と考えている

11	気	ki	ch'i, ether (material principle of Neo-Confucian metaphysics)
	物質	busshitsu	matter, material
12	体内の	tainai no	internal
13	肉体	nikutai	the flesh, body
	消散	shōsan	dissipation, disappearance

199

Lesson L

p258

1	とめる	tomeru	stop, put a stop to
2	仏教	Bukkyō	Buddhism
3	説く	toku	expound, explain
4	無宗教者	mushūkyōsha	person without religion, non-believer
5	善意	zen'i	good will
	動物	dōbutsu	creature, animal
7	充分に	jūbun ni	fully, amply
8	論証	ronshō	proof
13	証拠	shōko	evidence
	もちだす	mochidasu	bring out, produce (evidence)

(完全に……実在したという)→ 一つの設定

p259

1	聖人	seijin	sage, saint
	の名の下で	no na no moto de	in the name of, under the color of
2	設定	settei	hypothesis, proposition
8	キリスト教	Kirisutokyō	Christianity
	信者	shinja	believer
9	やや	yaya	a little, slightly
	新興	shinkō	newly rising, new
	宗教	shūkyō	religion

10 (普通の意味でいう)→ いかなる宗教

11	いかなる	ikanaru	any kind of, any
	無縁な	muen na	without relations
12	相互の	sōgo no	mutual

p260

1	ほかならない	hokanaranai	be nothing but

p260

2	こうした	kōshita	such, of this sort (kono yō na)
3	何程かの	nanihodo ka no	any (degree of)
4	こまかに	komaka ni	in detail, minutely
	分析する	bunseki suru	analyze
5	現存の	genson no	actual, present
7	おおむね	ōmune	in general
8	出発する	shuppatsu suru	depart, start
	東方	Tōhō	the East, Orient
	類似する	ruiji suru	resemble, be similar to
9	探究	tankyū	research, inquiry

Source: Yoshikawa Kōjirō, "Nihon no shinjō" 日本の心情, <u>Jinmin</u>人民, no. 12 (1958), reprinted in <u>Nihon no shinjō</u>, Shinchōsha, 1960, pp. 171-76.

p261
2　（われわれ日本人が……くり返している）→ 生活

なにげなく	nanige naku	casually, without paying attention
3　とりあげる	toriageru	take up
5　貸家	kashiya	rental house
引越す	hikkosu	move into, move to
6　神棚	kamidana	(household) altar (Shinto)
つくりつけになる	tsukuritsuke ni naru	be fixed, built-in
台所	daidokoro	kitchen
のぞく	nozoku	peep in, look in
7　残す	nokosu	leave
お札	o-fuda	charm, talisman
ひきつぐ	hikitsugu	take over
8　仏壇	butsudan	Buddhist altar
家財道具	kazai dōgu	household belongings, effects
毎朝	maiasa	every morning
あげる	ageru	offer
9　ご飯	gohan	cooked rice
お初をそなえる	o-hatsu o sonaeru	offer on an altar the first portion (of food)
カネ	kane	bell
ならす	narasu	ring (bell)
合掌する	gasshō suru	join the palms of the

202

p261
9   hands, fold hands in prayer

季節	kisetsu	season
初物	hatsumono	the first product (of the season)
到来物	tōraimono	a present (received), gift
おそなえをする	o-sonae o suru	make an offering
いただく	itadaku	eat, accept, receive
息子	musuko	son

(息子が……報告する)→母親の姿

月給袋	gekkyūbukuro	pay envelope
せがれ	segare	son (familiar)
涙をうかべて	namida o ukabete	with tears (in one's eyes), tearfully
格	kaku	standing, rank

p262

盆	bon	the Festival of the Dead
彼岸	higan	the equinoctial week
経	kyō	sutra
お経をあげる	o-kyō o ageru	chant a sutra
墓まいり	hakamairi	visit to a grave
親しむ	shitashimu	be close to, intimate with
童話	dōwa	children's story
絵本	ehon	picture book
漫画	manga	cartoon, caricature
教科書	kyōkasho	textbook, schoolbook
仏	hotoke	Buddha
お化け	obake	specter, (inhuman) apparition

p262

7	ラジオ	rajio	radio
	演劇	engeki	play, drama
	講談	kōdan	storytelling (historical)
	落語	rakugo	comic storytelling
	浪花節	naniwabushi	narrative chanting accompanied by shamisen
8	神仏	shinbutsu	gods and buddhas
	奇蹟談	kisekidan	miracle story
	歴史もの	rekishimono	historical story category
	神社	jinja	Shinto shrine
	祭る	matsuru	enshrine, honor
9	英雄	eiyū	hero, great man
	忠臣	chūshin	loyal retainer
	平素から	heiso kara	in everyday living
	身近な	mijika na	close to oneself, familiar
10	両親	ryōshin	(both) parents
	氏神	ujigami	tutelary deity
	宮	miya	Shinto shrine (=jinja, less formal)
	宮まいり	miyamairi	(newborn baby's first visit to its tutelary shrine, about a month after the birth)
11	七・五・三	shichi go san	(gala day for children of seven, five, and three years of age: November 15)
	お祝	o-iwai	celebration

te o awaseru = gasshō suru

| 12 | 拝む | ogamu | bow, worship |

p262 13	しつける	shitsukeru	train, discipline
	氏子	ujiko	parishioner
p263 1	祭り	matsuri	festival
	花	hana	flower
	提灯	chōchin	collapsible paper lantern
	軒	noki	eaves (of a house)
	そろいの	soroi no	uniform, of the same pattern
	浴衣	yukata	unlined cotton kimono
2	太鼓	taiko	drum
	ひっぱる	hipparu	pull
	御輿	mikoshi	portable shrine
3	かつぐ	katsugu	bear, carry on the shoulder
	楽しむ	tanoshimu	enjoy oneself, enjoy
	幼稚園	yōchien	kindergarten
	通う	kayou	attend, go to
4	教会	kyōkai	church
6	禁止する	kinshi suru	forbid, prohibit
	遠足	ensoku	hike, day outing
	修学旅行	shūgaku ryokō	school excursion (overnight trip)
7	生徒	seito	pupil
	名所	meisho	noted place
	古蹟	koseki	historical spot
	神宮	jingū	Shinto shrine (high ranking)
	寺院	jiin	temple

p263

8	たちよる	tachiyoru	stop by, drop in
	絵はがき	ehagaki	picture postcard
	記念スタンプ	kinen sutanpu	souvenir seal (of temple or shrine, etc.)
9	押す	osu	stamp, impress
	もの心がつく 以前から	monogokoro ga tsuku izen kara	before one can remember (i.e. while still a little child)
10	自覚する	jikaku suru	be aware of, realize
	いつしか	itsushika	before one is aware
11	浸みこむ	shimikomu	soak into, permeate
	御利益	goriyaku	divine favor
	授かる	sazukaru	be bestowed, granted
12	積極的な	sekkyokuteki na	positive, active
	参拝	sanpai	worship (at shrines and temples)
13	客商売	kyakushōbai	entertainment business

p264

1	招き猫	manekineko	("beckoning cat": statue of cat with right paw raised)
	福の神	fuku no kami	god of wealth
	エビス	Ebisu	(god of commerce)
	大黒	Daikoku	(Mahākāta, god of wealth)
2	隅	sumi	corner
	お稲荷さん	o-inari-san	fox deity
3	初詣で	hatsumōde	the first shrine visit of the New Year
	節分	setsubun	the day before the beginning of spring
	参詣者	sankeisha	visitor (to shrines and temples)
	群	mure	crowd

206

p264

4	おしよせる	oshiyoseru	push into
	各地	kakuchi	every locality, each place
	遊覧	yūran	sightseeing
5	ウグイス嬢	uguisujō	Miss Nightingale (nickname for female guide)
	美声	bisei	beautiful voice
	はりあげる	hariageru	raise (the voice)
	解説	kaisetsu	explanation, commentary
	有難さ	arigatasa	value, dignity
6	カメラ	kamera	camera
	とりだす	toridasu	take out, put out
	撮影	satsuei	taking a picture, photographing
7	破魔矢	hamaya	arrow charm against bad luck
	お守り	o-mamori	talisman
	持ち帰る	mochikaeru	take home
	結婚式	kekkonshiki	marriage ceremony, wedding
8	神式	shinshiki	Shinto style
	仏式	busshiki	Buddhist style
9	(最近では……お参りをしているという)→人たち		
	洋装	yōsō	Western dress
	式を挙げる	shiki o ageru	hold a ceremony
11	新婚旅行	shinkon ryokō	honeymoon (trip)
	さきざき	sakizaki	places one goes to
12	お参り	o-mairi	visit (to temples and shrines)

Source: Takagi Hiroo 高木宏夫, <u>Nihon</u> <u>no</u> <u>shinkō</u> <u>shūkyō</u> 日本の新興宗教 (New religions in Japan), Iwanami Shinsho Series 365, 1961, pp. 3-5.

    Takagi Hiroo (1922-   ) is professor of sociology at Tōyō University.

p265

1	郵便局	yūbinkyoku	post office
	窓口	madoguchi	window, counter
5	鴉	karasu	crow, raven
	零落する	reiraku suru	fall low
6	運命	unmei	destiny, fate
	すり切れる	surikireru	wear out

chatta = te shimatta

7	煤煙	baien	sooty smoke
	空	sora	sky
10	父上	chichiue	father (honorific, literary)
11	人生	jinsei	life, human existence
12	虚無感	kyomukan	feeling of nothingness, emptiness
13	財布	saifu	wallet, purse

p266

1	銅貨	dōka	copper (coin)
	かえる	kaeru	change, alter
2	道路	dōro	street, road
	敷石	shikiishi	pavement, paving stone
	叩きつける	tatakitsukeru	throw at, hurl at
4	老いたまえる	oitamaeru	old (honorific, literary)
7	空気	kūki	air
	蹌踉として	sōrō to shite	falteringly, vaguely

209

p266

8	波止場	hatoba	wharf, pier
	憂鬱な	yūutsu na	melancholy
10	出帆する	shuppan suru	set sail
	汽船	kisen	steamship
11	笛	fue	whistle
	吠えさけぶ	hoesakebu	wail, howl
	響	hibiki	sound, reverberation

Hagiwara Sakutarō 萩原朔太郎, "Yūbinkyoku no madoguchi de"
郵便局の窓口で, <u>Gendai</u> <u>Nihon</u> <u>shijin</u> <u>zenshū</u>, vol. 4, p. 242.

Hagiwara Sakutarō (1886-1942) was one of the finest poets of modern Japan.

Modern Japanese poetry began in the 1880's along with the translation of Western poetry, and was called <u>shintaishi</u> 新体詩 (new-style poetry) in contrast to the traditional <u>kanshi</u> 漢詩, <u>waka</u> 和歌, and <u>haiku</u> 俳句 genres. However, shintaishi remained wedded to bungo and the five-seven syllable meter, and a new poetry of artistic value, fervently Romantic, began to flourish only around the turn of the century. A decade later Japanese poets came under the strong influence of French symbolism, deliberately indulging in difficult words and ambiguous expressions. A reaction toward <u>kōgo-shi</u> 口語詩 (colloquial poetry) followed soon after, and has determined the line of modern Japanese poetry ever since.

Hagiwara, a symbolist with hypersensitive nerves, is regarded as the poet who perfected the kōgo-shi.

p267

1	文化財	bunkazai	cultural treasures
	保護	hogo	protection
2	法華堂	Hokkedō	(a temple in Tōdaiji, area of Nara)
3	永久に	eikyū ni	permanently
	保存する	hozon suru	preserve
	憂鬱な	yūutsu na	melancholy
4	塑像	sozō	clay figure, clay image
	弁財天	Benzaiten	(Sarasvatī, Buddhist goddess of speech and learning)
	吉祥天	Kisshōten, Kichijōten	(Laksmī, Buddhist goddess of fortune)
	一層	issō	more, even more
8	今後の	kongo no	future, coming
	貢献する	kōken suru	contribute, render service
	功成り名とげた人	kō nari na togeta hito	person who rendered service and won fame
	(功成り名……こき使う)→感じ		
9	無慙な	muzan na	pitiful, merciless
10	ぼろぼろになる	boroboro ni naru	crumble, fall to pieces
	いい加減に	ii kagen ni	before overdoing it, in moderation
	勘弁する	kanben suru	excuse, release
11	土	tsuchi	earth, soil
13	負担	futan	burden, obligation

211

p268

1	役目	yakume	role, duty
	役目に廻る	yakume ni mawaru	be placed in a position
	つくづく	tsukuzuku	deeply, keenly
2	断片	danpen	fragment, piece
	整理する	seiri suru	arrange, put in order
3	国庫	kokko	national treasury
	貰う	morau	have (done), receive
4	重税	jūzei	heavy tax
	一家心中	ikka shinjū	family suicide
5	(これまで …… 残った) → 物		
8	ボロ布れ	borogire	rag, ragged cloth
9	救う	sukuu	save, relieve
	全力	zenryoku	all one's power
	集中する	shūchū suru	concentrate
10	青臭い	aokusai	raw, immature
	書生論	shoseiron	sophomoric argument
11	軽重	keijū	relative importance
12	愉快 (な)	yukai (na)	pleasant, comfortable
	終戦	shūsen	end of war (especially of World War II)
	直後	chokugo	immediately after
	敗戦	haisen	defeat, lost battle
	償金	shōkin	indemnity
13	法隆寺	Hōryūji	(temple in Nara)
	そっくり	sokkuri	just as it is, the whole thing

p268

13	如何	dō	how
	説	setsu	view, opinion
	梅原龍三郎	Umehara Ryūzaburō	(painter, 1888-)

p269

1	軽減する	keigen suru	reduce
3	余裕	yoyū	margin (for comfort, luxury)
5	ギリシア彫刻	Girisha chōkoku	Greek sculpture
	始末がいい	shimatsu ga ii	easy to deal with, easy to manage
7	fushigi to ieba	fushigi na toki da = "may well be called a strange time"	
8	徹底的な	tetteiteki na	thorough, complete
9	原子爆弾	genshi bakudan	atomic bomb
	水素	suiso	hydrogen
	まさか	masaka	surely (not)

Source: Shiga Naoya 志賀直哉, "Watakushi no shinjō" 私の信条, <u>Sekai</u>, October, 1950, reprinted in <u>Watakushi</u> <u>no</u> <u>shinjō</u>, Iwanami Shinsho Series 75, 1951, pp. 47-48.

Shiga Naoya (1883-   ) is a major novelist and essayist.

Shiga was one of the founding members of the Shirakaba 白樺 ("White Birch") literary group, which was organized by graduates of the Peers' School in 1910 as an idealistic humanitarian reaction to the then current Naturalism. He is much admired for his sharp, unsentimental observation, his accurate descriptive style, and his firm character.

Lesson LIV.   KOBAYASHI TAKIJI E NO TEGAMI

1	小林多喜二	Kobayashi Takiji	(novelist, 1903-33)
3	オルグ	Orugu	The Organizer (1931) (orugu = Communist organizer)
	蟹工船	Kanikōsen	The Cannery Boat (1929) (kani = crab)
	小品	shōhin	short piece
	三・一五	San ichi go	March 15, 1928 (1928) (full title =一九二八年三月十五日)
4	拝見する	haiken suru	see, read (humble)
6	念入りに	nen'iri ni	carefully, elaborately
	描写	byōsha	description
	生々と	ikiiki to	vividly
9	プロレタリア	puroretaria	proletarian, proletariat
10	主人持ち	shujinmochi	subservient, having a master
	好む	konomu	like
11	たずさわる	tazusawaru	take part in, be concerned with
	止むを得ぬ	yamu o enu	inevitable
12	不純 (な)	fujun (na)	impure

ni naru ga tame ni = ni naru tame ni (emphatic)

	効果	kōka	effect, efficacy
	弱い	yowai	weak
13	大衆	taishū	the masses

| 1 | 弱身 | yowami | weak point |

p271

2 小児病   shōnibyō   infantilism

   里見   Satomi   (Satomi Ton, novelist, 1888-   )

   今年竹   Kotoshidake   <u>A</u> <u>New</u> <u>Bamboo</u> (1919)

3 (ある男が……感激する)→事

   感激する   kangeki suru   be deeply moved

4 不服   fufuku   dissatisfaction, complaint

5 別に   betsu ni   particularly

6 しきりに   shikiri ni   repeatedly, strongly

7 力を入れる   chikara o ireru   put effort into

11 芸術品   geijutsuhin   work of art

13 イデオロギー   ideorogī   ideology

p272

1 如何なる   ikanaru   any, whatever (=<u>donna</u>)

2 作家   sakka   writer

   肉   niku   flesh, meat

3 はとも角   wa tomokaku   setting aside, aside from

   (何かある……主張する)→事

5 独立する   dokuritsu suru   become independent

7 トルストイ   Torusutoi   (Leo Tolstoy, 1828-1910)

   to shite = "granting that"

8 (完全に……仕事されている)→点、

   おさえる   osaeru   suppress, control

9 偉い   erai   great, remarkable

   若し   moshi   if

   のさばる   nosabaru   be overbearing, be

215

p272

10				high-handed
11	薄っぺら (な)	usuppera (na)		shallow, thin
12	稀薄(な)	kihaku (na)		weak, diluted

p273

4	正視する	seishi suru	look straight at, look in the face
	ザンギャクな	zangyaku na	cruel
5	産物	sanbutsu	product
6	na mono no = de aru keredomo		
	かたづく	katazuku	be settled, be disposed of
8	本位で	hon'i de	on the basis of
9	望む	nozomu	wish, hope
	老婆心	rōbashin	old womanly solicitude

Source: A letter of Shiga Naoya to Kobayashi Takiji, August 7, 1931, reprinted in <u>Shiga Naoya zenshū</u>, 17 vols., Iwanami Shoten, 1955-56, vol. 16, pp. 219-22.

This letter is drawn from Shiga's private correspondence, and was a blow to proletarian literature when it was first published in 1931. The phrase <u>shujinmochi no bungaku</u> came into fashion among novelists and critics.

Kobayashi Takiji, the most influential of the proletarian writers, respected Shiga and, though they met only once, remained on friendly terms with him through correspondence. Kobayashi was arrested on February 10, 1933, while on a secret errand for the communist underground movement, and died of torture the same day.

216

Lesson LV.　KAMIGATAGO

1	上方	kamigata	the Kyōto-Ōsaka area
2	言葉	kotoba	language
3	緻密 (な)	chimitsu (na)	precise, minute
	物事	monogoto	a matter, things
4	純	jun-	pure, genuine
	日本風	nihonfū	Japanese style
	奥床しい	okuyukashii	refined, graceful
5	甚だ	hanahada	exceedingly
	不向 (な)	fumuki (na)	unsuitable, unfit
6	おしゃべり	oshaberi	chattering, talkativeness
	過ぎる	sugiru	be excessive, exceed
9	大阪	Ōsaka	Osaka
	てにをは	te-ni-o-ha	(general term for particles 助詞 in Japanese grammar)
	使ひ分け	tsukaiwake	differentiation of usage
10	神経質 (な)	shinkeishitsu (na)	nervous, fussy
11	あたし	atashi	=watakushi (familiar, mainly used by women)
12	然るに	shikaru ni	however (literary)
13	恐らく	osoraku	probably
	うち	uchi	I (Kamigata dialect)

uchi wakarehen = watashi wa wakarimasen

217

p275

1	訂正する	teisei suru	correct
2	卍	Manji	<u>Whirlpool</u> (1928)
4	粗い	arai	coarse, loose
6	ついでながら	tsuide nagara	by the way, incidentally
	略す	ryakusu	omit, abbreviate
10	わっし	wasshi	=<u>watakushi</u> (vulgar, used by men)

wasshā = watashi wa

bokā = boku wa

	却って	kaette	on the contrary
11	伸ばす	nobasu	lengthen
	仮に	kari ni	granting that, (even) if
12	クォーテーション	kuōtēshon	quotation
13	省く	habuku	omit
	何々と仰しゃいました	naninani to osshaimashita	(he) said so and so (honorific)

p276

1 iyaharimashiten = iwaremashita

	谷崎	Tanizaki	(surname)
3	区別をつける	kubetsu o tsukeru	make a distinction

4 sore yattara = sore dattara

5	丁寧な	teinei na	polite
	云ひ廻し	iimawashi	(manner of) expression
6	意外 (な)	igai (na)	surprising, unexpected
7	遊ばせ言葉	asobase kotoba	polite language (used by women)
8	変化	henka	variety, diversity
	実に	jitsu ni	very, really

218

p276
12 shiyagaru = suru (vulgar)
p277

1	単語	tango	word
3	女学生	jogakusei	high school girl
	友達	tomodachi	friend
	めったに…ない	metta ni ... nai	seldom
4	お召し物	o-meshimono	clothes (honorific)
	おみ足	o-mi-ashi	leg, foot (honorific)
	歳	toshi	age, years of age
7	推量	suiryō	guess
	酌み取る	kumitoru	grasp (another's idea); dip out
8	隙間	sukima	gap, empty space
9	優れる	sugureru	be superior
11	下品な	gehin na	vulgar, coarse
12	無言	mugon	silence, reticence
13	美徳	bitoku	virtue, fine trait
	東洋	Tōyō	the Orient

p278

2	備はる	sonawaru	be endowed with, possess
	美点	biten	virtue, merit
3	通用する	tsūyō suru	be acceptable, admissible
	さすがに	sasuga ni	as might be expected
	婦人	fujin	lady
4	昔ながらの	mukashi nagara no	as it was before, as formerly
5	口へ出す	kuchi e dasu	mention (=kuchi ni suru)
	残り	nokori	remainder

219

p278
5　沈黙　　　　　chinmoku　　　　silence

　　ほのかに　　　honoka ni　　　faintly

　　ただよふ　　　tadayou　　　　drift

6　伝はる　　　　tsutawaru　　　be handed down,
　　　　　　　　　　　　　　　　　transmitted

Source: Tanizaki Jun'ichirō 谷崎潤一郎, "Watakushi no mita Ōsaka oyobi Ōsaka-jin" 私の見た大阪及大阪人 , Chūōkōron, February-April, 1932, reprinted in Tanizaki Jun'ichirō zenshū, 30 vols., Chūōkōronsha, 1957-59, vol. 17, pp. 257-59.

　　　Tanizaki Jun'ichirō (1886-1965) is not only one of the most distinguished novelists of modern Japan but an eloquent advocate of traditional Japanese culture, particularly that of the Kyoto-Osaka region.

p279

1 夢の浮橋	Yume no Ukihashi	The Bridge of Dreams (1919)(also title of last book of Genji Monogatari)
2 五十四帖	gojū-yon jō	fifty-four chapters (=Genji Monogatari)
讀み終り侍りて	yomiowari haberite	having finished reading (humble)
3 ほとゝぎす	hototogisu	cuckoo
(ほとゝぎす‥‥‥来啼く)→今日		
五位	goi	a kind of heron
庵	iori	cottage, retreat
啼く	naku	sing (bird)
4 渡りをへ(たる)	watarioe(taru)	(to have) finish(ed) crossing
5 詞書	kotobagaki	foreward to waka or haiku
伴ふ、	tomonau	be accompanied by
首	-shu	(counter for waka)
詠	ei	poem, song
但し	tadashi	but, however
生みの母	umi-no-haha	one's real mother
6 まゝ母	mamahaha	stepmother
7 仔細	shisai	details, circumstances
8 追ひ追ひ	oioi	gradually, by and by
詳かにする	tsumabiraka ni suru	make clear in detail
擧げる	ageru	mention, cite

221

p279
9　生母　　　seibo　　　one's real mother
　　　　　　　　　　　　(=<u>umi</u>-<u>no</u>-<u>haha</u>) (literary)
　継母　　　keibo　　　stepmother (=<u>mamahaha</u>)
　　　　　　　　　　　　(literary)
　茅渟　　　Chinu　　　(woman's first name)

　幼童　　　yōdō　　　young child

　一家　　　ikka　　　family

11　濱寺　　　Hamadera　　(town in the suburbs of
　　　　　　　　　　　　Osaka) (濱=浜)
　別荘　　　bessō　　　villa, country house
　　　　　　　　　　　　(荘=莊)
　茅渟の海　Chinu no umi　(ancient name for Osaka
　　　　　　　　　　　　Bay)
　に因んで名づける　ni chinande　name after
　　　　　　　　nazukeru
12　戸籍　　　koseki　　　family register

　記載　　　kisai　　　statement, record

13　正しく　　masashiku　certainly

　嫁ぐ　　　totsugu　　become a bride
p280
1　經子　　　Tsuneko　　(woman's first name)

　實名　　　jitsumei　　real name

2　宛てる　　ateru　　　address (to)

　消息　　　shōsoku　　letter (literary)

3　どの　　　dono　　　(formal honorific title
　　　　　　　　　　　　used mostly by men)
5　區別がつく　kubetsu ga　be distinguishable
　　　　　　　tsuku
　さう云ふ譯で　sō iu wake de　for that reason

　歌　　　　uta　　　　poem (=<u>waka</u>)

6　記す　　　shirusu　　record, write down

　色紙　　　shikishi　　(square paper used for
　　　　　　　　　　　　writing and painting)

Lesson LVI

p280

6	女	-jo	(suffix to woman's name, in literary usage)
8	詠歌	eika	song, composition
9	傳はる	tsutawaru	be handed down
10	うやうやしく	uyauyashiku	respectfully, reverently
	裱具する	hyōgu suru	mount
	遺る	nokoru	remain
11	六十餘歳	rokujūyosai	age of more than sixty years
	存生する	zonjō suru	live, be still living
	乳母	uba	wet nurse
12	越前	Echizen	(present Fukui-ken)

(越前の……依った)→本式の墨流しの紙

	武生	Takeo	(place name)
	取り寄せる	toriyoseru	order, send for (and obtain)
	手法	shuhō	technique
	に依る	ni yoru	according to
	本式の	honshiki no	orthodox, regular
13	墨流し	suminagashi	("ink-running" technique of transferring wave pattern in dilute ink to paper or silk) (墨 = 墨)

p281

1	苦勞をする	kurō o suru	have difficulty
2	なかなか	nakanaka	easily (with negative)
	讀み下す	yomikudasu	read through
3	近衞三藐院	Konoe Sanmyakuin	(Konoe Nobutada, calligrapher, 1565-1614)
	流れ	nagare	a school, style

223

p281

3	の流れを汲む	no nagare o kumu	follow in the style of
	字體	jitai	style of calligraphy, form of a character
	萬葉假名	Man'yōgana	Chinese characters used phonetically in Man'yōshū to write Japanese
4	澤山	takusan	many
	交る	majiru	be mingled, intermingled
	大人	otona	adult
5	ima no yo = gendai		
7	巧拙	kōsetsu	degree of skill
	兎角のこと	tokaku no koto	this and that
	資格	shikaku	qualification
8	近衞流	Konoe ryū	Konoe school, style

(近衞流の……お書きこなしやす)→お方

Konoe ryū no jī o konai jōzu ni okakikonashiyasu okata wa
oiya itashimahen sō ni gozarimasse = Konoe ryū no ji o konna
ni jōzu ni okakikonashi ni naru okata wa oide ni naranai sō
de gozaimasu yo.

	書きこなす	kakikonasu	write skillfully
9	おゐや致しまへん	oiyaitashima-hen	= oide ni narimasen
10	しろうと考	shirōto kangae	layman's view
	能筆	nōhitsu	skillful brushwork
11	行成流	Kōzei ryū	school of Fujiwara Kōzei (972-1027)
	細い	hosoi	slender, delicate
	しなやかな	shinayaka na	graceful, flowing
	選ぶ	erabu	choose
12	肉の厚い	niku no atsui	thick, fleshy

224

p281
12　(肉の厚い……漢字の多い)→書體

	たっぷりと	tappuri to	abundantly, fully
	肥える	koeru	become fat
13	漢字	kanji	Chinese character
	書體	shotai	calligraphic style
	奇異 (な)	kii (na)	strange

p282

1	特殊 な	tokushu na	particular
2	和歌	waka	Japanese (31-syllable) poem
	猶更	naosara	even more (猶=猶)
	不案内	fuannai	ignorant, unfamiliar (with)
3	秀歌	shūka	excellent <u>waka</u>
4	源氏	Genji	<u>The</u> <u>Tale</u> <u>of</u> <u>Genji</u> by Murasaki Shikibu (10th century) (=<u>Genji</u> <u>Monogatari</u>)
	最終巻	saishūkan	the last book
	讀み終へる	yomioeru	finish reading
6	至って	itatte	very, extremely
9	五位鷺	goisagi	a kind of heron (=<u>goi</u>)
	飛ぶ	tobu	fly
10	祖父	sofu	grandfather
	邸	yashiki	residence
	庵	-an	cottage, retreat
	呼び習はす	yobinarawasu	be used to call, accustomed to call
11	鷺	sagi	heron
12	があ	gā	(sound of the heron)

225

Source: Tanizaki Jun'ichirō, <u>Yume</u> <u>no</u> <u>ukihashi</u> 夢の浮橋,
Chūōkōronsha, 1960, pp. 3-13.

p283

2	池	ike	pond
	土管	dokan	earthen pipe
3	溢れる	afureru	overflow
	落す	otosu	let fall, drop
4	杉	sugi	Japanese cedar
	丸太	maruta	log
	正門	seimon	outside gate, front gate
	這入る	hairu	enter
	石甃	ishidatami	stone pavement
	奥	oku	end (of the lane)
	中門	chūmon	middle gate (between outside gate and front door)
5	兩側	ryōgawa	both sides
	さゝやかな	sasayaka na	small, dwarf
	竹	take	bamboo
	植わってゐる	uwatte iru	be planted
	朝鮮	Chōsen	Korea
6	運ぶ	hakobu	transport, carry
	李朝	Richō	Yi Dynasty (1392-1910)
	官人	kanjin	government official
	石像	sekizō	stone statue

227

p283

6	相對する	ai-taisuru	face each other
7	杉皮	sugikawa	cedar bark
	檜肌葺	hiwadabuki	cypress-bark roof
	葺く	fuku	thatch (a roof)
8	とざす	tozasu	close
	聯	ren	(a pair of oblong boards of calligraphy on walls or pillars)
	懸る	kakaru	hang
9	禽鳥	kinchō	birds
10	塵	jin	dust
	竹松	chikushō	bamboo and pine
	清シ	kiyoshi	pure, clean
11	書	sho	writing, calligraphy
13	横	yoko	side
	ベル	beru	doorbell
	押す	osu	push
	開ける	akeru	open

p284

1	橡の木	tochi no ki	horse chestnut tree
	くぐる	kuguru	pass through, pass under
	玄關	genkan	entrance way, vestibule
	三疊の間	sanjō no ma	three-mat room (疊 = 畳)
2	疊	-jō	(counter for <u>tatami</u>)
	壁間に	hekikan ni	on the wall
	鳶	tobi	kite (kind of bird)

228

p284

2	魚	uo	fish
	躍ル	odoru	jump, leap
	頼山陽	Rai San'yō	(historian, 1780-1832)
	額	gaku	framed picture or calligraphy
	眼	me	eye
3	値打	neuchi	value
	林泉	rinsen	landscape garden
	平屋造り	hirayazukuri	one-story house
4	母屋	omoya	main house
	間数	makazu	number of rooms
	女中部屋	jochūbeya	maidservants' room
	内玄関	naigenkan	side entrance
5	板の間	itanoma	wooden floor
6	料理屋	ryōriya	Japanese restaurant
	コック場	kokkuba	kitchen (of a restaurant)
	なみに	nami ni	on the scale of
	走り元	hashirimoto	kitchen sink
	に接して	ni sesshite	touching
	掘り抜き井戸	horinukiido	artesian well
7	佛光寺室町	Bukkōji-Muromachi	(district of Kyoto)
8	別業	betsugyō	villa, country house (=bessō) (literary)
	後年	kōnen	later, in later years
	譲る	yuzuru	hand over, let go (讓=譲)
9	本邸	hontei	one's principal residence

p284

9	隣りの	tonari no	adjoining, next
	乾	inui	northwest
	角地面	kadojimen	corner of a lot
	三階建ての	sangaidate no	three-story
	土蔵	dozō	Japanese storehouse, warehouse (蔵 = 藏)
	建て増す	tatemasu	build on, build (an extension)
10	まことに	makoto ni	truly, really
	是非とも	zehitomo	= _zehi_
12	乳母	uba	wet nurse
	上 (女中)	kami (jochū)	lady's maid
	中 (女中)	naka (jochū)	housemaid
	下 (女中)	shimo (jochū)	kitchen maid
13	ゆったり	yuttari	ample, comfortable

p285

1	銀行	ginkō	bank
	顔を出す	kao o dasu	show one's face, put in an appearance
	つきあひ	tsukiai	association, connection
2	客	kyaku	guest, visitor
	招く	maneku	invite
3	茶事	chaji	tea ceremony
	道樂	dōraku	hobby, pastime
4	由緒(の)ある	yuisho (no) aru	of distinguished history, of good lineage
	茶席	chaseki	teahouse, place for performing tea ceremony
	引く	hiku	transfer, move
5	のほとりに	no hotori ni	by, near

230

p285

5	建てる	tateru	erect, set up
	巽	tatsumi	southeast
	合歡亭	Gōkantei	(Silk-Tree Pavilion)
	離れ家	hanareya	detached house
6	代	dai	generation, time
	折角の	sekkaku no	precious, prized
7	(たからの) 持ちくされ	(takara no) mochikusare	useless possession, (rotting in one's possession)
	の形で	no katachi de	in the state of
	晝寢	hirune	nap, siesta (寢 = 寝)
	手習ひ	tenarai	writing practice
8	稽古場	keikoba	training place
9	ひとへに	hitoe ni	wholly, solely
	注ぐ	s:sogu	concentrate (on); pour
	琴	koto	(zither-like instrument with thirteen strings)
	奏でる	kanaderu	play (stringed or wind instrument)
	聽き入る	kikiiru	listen attentively (聽 = 聴)
12	娛樂	goraku	recreation, pastime (娛 = 娯)
13	植惣	Ue-Sō	Gardener Sō
	造園	zōen	landscape gardening

p286

1	庭師	niwashi	gardener
	丹精	tansei	exertion, effort
	凝らす	korasu	devote, concentrate
2	奥深い	okufukai	deep

p286

2	幽邃な	yūsui na	secluded, retired and quiet
	表玄關	omote genkan	main entrance, front entrance
	襖	fusuma	(opaque) sliding door
3	奥に	oku ni	beyond, in back
	座敷	zashiki	drawing room parlor (Japanese style)
4	廣間	hiroma	large room, hall
	御殿	goten	palace
5	緣	en	(=engawa) veranda
	廻らす	megurasu	surround, enclose
	欄干	rankan	railing
	勾欄	kōran	balustrade (of type used in temples and shrines)
6	わざと	waza to	purposely, intentionally
	棚	tana	lattice, shelf
	さしかける	sashikakeru	extend over, hang over
7	野木瓜	mube	gourd-vine, akebia
	葉	ha	leaf
	一ぱいに	ippai ni	in profusion
	繁る	shigeru	grow thick
8	際	kiwa	edge
	寄せる	yoseru	be close
	欄	ran	railing
	もたれる	motareru	lean against
	眺める	nagameru	view, gaze at
9	木深い	kobukai	(thickly) wooded

232

9	瀧	taki	waterfall
	落ちる	ochiru	fall
	春	haru	spring
	八重山吹	yaeyamabuki	double yellow rose
	秋	aki	autumn, fall
	秋海棠	shūkaidō	begonia
10	暫く	shibaraku	(for) a little while
	せせらぎ	seseragi	shallow, and murmuring brook
12	糺	Tadasu	(man's first name)

Tadasu-san, sonna toko e ite oike e hamattara ikimahen e = Tadasu-san, sonna tokoro e itte oike ni hamattara taihen desu yo.

	はまる	hamaru	fall into
13	頻りに	shikiri ni	repeatedly, strongly
	制する	seisuru	restrain, control
	飛び出す	tobidasu	rush out

1	築山	tsukiyama	artificial hill (in a garden)
	熊笹	kumazasa	low and striped bamboo
	ふち	fuchi	edge
	寄る	yoru	approach
2	これこれ	kore-kore	Here, here! Look here!
	危い	abunai	dangerous

hitori de ikuno ya arashimahen = hitori de iku mono de wa arimasen.

4	びっくりする	bikkuri suru	be alarmed, be startled
	追ひかける	oikakeru	run after

p287
5 兵兒帯 hekoobi (informal <u>obi</u> for children and men made with silk or cotton)

押へる osaeru hold back, hold down

伸す nobasu stretch

6 覗き込む nozokikomu peer into

7 片時も katatoki mo even for a moment

眼を離す me o hanasu take eyes off

注意を怠る chūi o okotaru relax attention, be inattentive

9 お兼どん o-Kane don (maid's name plus <u>don</u>, a form similar to <u>san</u> and used for servants)

Kore o-Kane don, bon'yarishitetara akahen ya nai ka = Kore o-Kane don, bon'yari shitetara ikenai ja nai ka.

ぼんやりする bon'yari suru be inattentive

10 中程 nakahodo (around the) middle

土橋 dobashi earthen bridge

11 向う岸 mukōgishi other shore, opposite bank

12 浅い asai shallow (浅=浅)

13 一箇所 ikkasho one spot, one place

背 se height; back

掘り下げる horisageru dig down

p288
1 涸れる kareru dry up (a body of water)

鯉 koi carp

鮒 funa crucian, Prussian carp

2 穴 ana hole

3 Ako e hamattara erai koto e, otona katte dete korarehen e =
Asoko ni hamattara taihen na koto desu yo, otona datte dete

234

p288
3   koraremasen yo.

2	正直に	shōjiki ni	frankly, honestly
6	佛典	butten	Buddhist scripture
7	深く到る	fukaku itaru	go deep, be deep-rooted
8	(日本の……なかに入ってゐる)→ 哀調的な要素		
	風俗	fūzoku	manners, morals
	哀調的な	aichōteki na	plaintive, melancholy
9	濃い	koi	strong, heavy
	センチメンタリズム	senchimentari-zumu	sentimentalism
10	流行歌	ryūkōka	popular song
	軍歌	gunka	war song
	いつか	itsuka	one time, once
11	赤十字	sekijūji	Red Cross
12	反戦	hansen	anti-war
	非戦	hisen	renunciation of war
13	しょっちゅう	shotchū	always (=<u>shijū</u>)

2	筋	suji	plot, story
3	千羽鶴	Senbazuru	<u>Thousand</u> <u>Cranes</u> (1951)
4	引伸ばす	hikinobasu	stretch out, draw out
	雪國	Yukiguni	<u>Snow</u> <u>Country</u> (1947)
5	連載	rensai	serial (publication)
6	(新聞でひどく受けた)→ 小説		

236

p290

6	受ける	ukeru	be well received, be popular
	冊	-satsu	(counter for books)
7	可笑しい	okashii	odd, funny
8	啞然とする	azen to suru	be dumbfounded
9	(初期の……をとった)→もの		
	身邊	shinpen	one's surroundings
	材	zai	material
	モデル	moderu	model
10	人物	jinbutsu	person, character
	ヒント	hinto	hint, idea
11	(「千羽鶴」が……ヒントをえた)→といふ話		
12	円覺寺	Enkakuji	(temple in Kamakura)
	茶会	chakai	tea ceremony gathering
	お孃さん	ojōsan	young lady
13	物語	monogatari	tale, story

p291

1	空想	kūsō	fabrication, imagination
	伊豆	Izu	(place name)
	踊子	odoriko	dancer (female)
3	駒子	Komako	(woman's first name)
	にしたところで	ni shita tokoro de	(even) in the case of
	實在する	jitsuzai suru	(actually) exist
5	脚色	kyakushoku	dramatization
	上演する	jōen suru	perform
	花柳章太郎	Hanayagi Shōtarō	(actor, 1894-)

237

p291
6 がっかりする   gakkari suru   be disappointed

   止す   yosu   give up, discontinue

7 温泉   onsen   hot spring (resort)

   聞き出す   kikidasu   find out about

9 娘   musume   young girl

   鼻   hana   nose

10 兄   ani   elder brother

   梅毒   baidoku   syphilis

   風呂   furo   Japanese bath

11 いやでたまらない   iya de tamaranai   cannot bear, cannot stand

12 浅草紅団   Asakusa Kurenaidan   Asakusa <u>Scarlet</u> <u>Gang</u> (1930) (name of Kawabata's novel)

13   hitori to shite inai = hitori mo inai

   不良少年団   furyōshōnendan   gang of juvenile delinquents

p292
1 文献   bunken   literature, documents

Source: Kawabata Yasunari 川端康成, "Watakushi no sakuhin" 私の作品, reprinted in <u>Gendai</u> <u>no</u> <u>sakka</u>, Iwanami Shinsho Series 212, 1961, pp. 234-36.

     Kawabata Yasunari (1899-   ) is one of the major novelists of modern Japanese literature. His works are notable for their poignant lyricism, their subtle, elliptical style, and their psychological insight.

Lesson LIX. YAMA NO OTO

2	信吾	Shingo	(man's first name)
	枕もと	makuramoto	(at the) head of the bed
	拾ふ	hirou	pick up
	むし暑い	mushiatsui	sultry, muggy
	起き出す	okidasu	get up out of bed
3	雨戸	amado	sliding shutter
	しゃがむ	shagamu	squat, crouch
	月夜	tsukiyo	moonlit night
4	ぎゃあっ	gyā	(screech of bird, etc.)
	鳴聲	nakigoe	song, cry (of bird, insect)
5	櫻	sakura	cherry (tree) (櫻 = 桜)
	幹	miki	trunk (of a tree)
	蟬	semi	cicada
	不氣味な	bukimi na	uncanny, eerie
6	惡夢	akumu	nightmare
	怯える	obieru	be frightened (by)
7	飛びこむ	tobikomu	jump into
	蚊帳	kaya	mosquito net
	裾	suso	bottom, skirt
	とまる	tomaru	perch, light
8	つかむ	tsukamu	seize, grasp

239

p293

8	おし	oshi	mute (hence a female cicada)
	つぶやく	tsubuyaku	mutter
10	力いっぱい	chikara ippai	with all one's strength
11	高み	takami	top, height
	向けて	mukete	towards
	投げる	nageru	throw
	手答へ	tegotae	(feeling of) response
13	つかまる	tsukamaru	hold on (to)

p294

2	横向けに	yokomuke ni	horizontally
	遠く	tōku	distance, distant place
3	木の葉	konoha	leaf (of a tree)
	夜露	yotsuyu	night dew
6	満月	mangetsu	full moon
	しめっぽい	shimeppoi	humid, damp
	夜氣	yaki	night air
	小山	koyama	hill
7	輪郭	rinkaku	outline
	ぼやけてゐる	boyakete iru	blurred, dim
9	廊下	rōka	corridor
	しだ	shida	fern
10	谷	yato	valley
	波	nami	wave
12	地鳴り	jinari	rumbling of the ground
	底力	sokojikara	latent energy

240

p294			
13	耳鳴り	miminari	ringing in the ears
p295			
1	振る	furu	shake
2	やむ	yamu	stop
	恐怖	kyōfu	fear, panic
	おそはれる	osowareru	be seized (with), be attacked (by)
3	死期	shiki, shigo	time of death
	告知する	kokuchi suru	announce
	寒け	samuke	chill
7	魔	ma	demon, evil spirit
	通りかゝる	tōrikakaru	pass by
	鳴らす	narasu	cause to rumble
8	急な	kyū na	steep
	勾配	kōbai	slope
	水氣	suiki	moisture
	夜色	yashoku	(shades of) night
	前面	zenmen	front, face
9	暗い	kurai	dark
	壁	kabe	wall
	をさまる	osamaru	able to be accommodated, put in
10	卵形	tamagogata	egg shape
	立てる	tateru	stand, set up
12	裏山	urayama	hill in back
p296			
1	頂上	chōjō	hilltop, summit
	星	hoshi	star

p296

1 透けて見える   sukete mieru   be visible through

Source: Kawabata Yasunari, <u>Yama no oto</u> 山の音 , Iwanami Bunko 岩波文庫
Series 5738-40, 1962, pp. 11-13.

Ogata Shingo, the hero of the novel from which this extract
has been taken, is sixty-two years old, the director of a company,
and lives in Kamakura, a seaside residential and resort city near
Tokyo.

242

Lesson LX.　ZADANKAI

1	座談会	zadankai	round-table talk
2	竹山道雄	Takeyama Michio	(literary critic, 1903-　　)
	日露戦争	Nichiro sensō	Russo-Japanese War (1904-1905)
	ごく	goku	very, extremely
	少数	shōsū	a small number, a few
3	散発的に	sanpatsuteki ni	sporadically
4	境	sakai	border line, boundary
	情熱	jōnetsu	enthusiasm, passion
6	安倍能成	Abe Yoshishige	(educator, 1883-　　)
	北村透谷	Kitamura Tōkoku	(poet and critic, 1869-1894)
	先駆者	senkusha	forerunner
8	勝本清一郎	Katsumoto Seiichirō	(literary critic, 1899-　　)
	内部生命論	naibu seimeiron	theory (in favor) of the inner life
9	肯定	kōtei	affirmation
11	外	-gai	outside

(それを世界内へ……破滅するから)→という抑制的な考え方

	内	-nai	inside, in
12	衝突し合う	shōtotsu shiau	clash with one another
13	収拾する	shūshū suru	put in order
	闘争	tōsō	conflict
	持ち来らせる	mochikitaraseru	produce, bring forth

243

p298

1	破滅する	hametsu suru	be ruined
	抑制的な	yokuseiteki na	restraining
2	十年代	jūnendai	second decade (period from 10th year through 19th)
3	(人間の……闘争させた)→方		
4	解放する	kaihō suru	release, liberate
	成長する	seichō suru	grow
	考え難い	kangaegatai	difficult to think
7	漱石	Sōseki	(Natsume Sōseki, novelist, 1867-1916)
	エゴイズム	egoizumu	egoism
8	目の敵にする	me no kataki ni suru	regard as a mortal enemy (to be attacked on sight) (kataki = enemy, rival)
9	(個人主義的……許され難い)→社会		
12	ラフカディオ・ハーン	Rafukadio Hān	Lafcadio Hearn (writer, 1850-1904)
	の最中に	no saichū ni	in the midst of, middle of

p299

2	ガタつく	gatatsuku	be rickety, unstable
3	憂慮	yūryo	fears, anxiety
4	叩き直す	tatakinaosu	correct, restore to proper shape by beating
5	生まれ変わる	umarekawaru	be reborn, regenerated
	精華	seika	essence, flower
	発揮する	hakki suru	manifest, display
7	目につく	me ni tsuku	catch the eye
	盛ん(な)	sakan (na)	popular, flourishing
8	与謝野晶子	Yosano Akiko	(waka poetess, 1878-1941)

ya nan ka no = ya sono ta no hitobito no

p299

9	ロマンチシズム	romanchishi-zumu	Romanticism
12	ガン	gan	malignancy; cancer

p300

1	伝記	denki	biography
3	ネガチブ	negachibu	negative
6	固定する	kotei suru	stabilize, fix
7	総領	sōryō	eldest son, heir
8	受け継ぐ	uketsugu	inherit
	世話する	sewa suru	take care of, look after
9	不文律	fubunritsu	unwritten law
12	かなり	kanari	considerably

p301

4	唐木順三	Karaki Junzō	(literary critic, 1904-　　)
	行住坐臥	gyōjūzaga	daily life (walking, stopping, sitting, and lying)
5	食べる	taberu	eat
	訓練	kunren	training
6	…は別として	... wa betsu to shite	putting aside

（二十四時間の……　いかん）→　というデシプリン

7	格	kaku	rule, norm
8	デシプリン	deshipurin	discipline

（個人あるいは人間を訓練する）→デシプリン
9

11	勝手放題	kattehōdai	as one pleases
12	崩壊する	hōkai suru	collapse, crumble

（そういう……　訓練した）→もの
13

	単位	tan'i	unit
	メンバー	menbā	member

245

p302

3	民法	minpō	civil law, civil code
4	醇風美俗	junpū bizoku	good morals and manners, good customs
	養う	yashinau	cultivate, foster
8	しつけ	shitsuke	upbringing, discipline
9	虐待する	gyakutai suru	maltreat
10	中期	chūki	middle period
	重圧	jūatsu	oppression, pressure
	逃れる	nogareru	escape
11	全体主義	zentaishugi	totalitarianism
12	育つ	sodatsu	grow
	時勢	jisei	times, conditions of life
13	白樺	Shirakaba	<u>White Birch</u> (literary magazine, 1910-1923)
	菊池	Kikuchi	(Kikuchi Hiroshi, novelist, 1888-1948)
	芥川	Akutagawa	(Akutagawa Ryūnosuke, short-story writer, 1892-1927)

p303

1	一頃	hitokoro	at one time
2	何かを約束するような‖オプティミズムを楽に持たせるような		
3	オプティミズム	oputimizumu	optimism
5	不満	fuman	discontent, dissatisfaction
7	ほれこむ	horekomu	be strongly attracted, fall deeply in love
	下れる	kudareru	downhill
9	機縁(にする)	kien (ni suru)	(take as an) opportunity
10	エネルギー	enerugī	energy
11	たるみ	tarumi	slackening, letdown
12	凡庸(な)	bon'yō (na)	mediocre

246

p303
13 天子様　　　　　tenshi-sama　　　　emperor (old term for tennō)

（明治時代 …… 失いつつある）→ 時代

創る　　　　　　　tsukuru　　　　　　make, create

p304
1 元老　　　　　　　genrō　　　　　　　elder statesman

勢力　　　　　　　seiryoku　　　　　　power, influence

3 （まだ十分確立しなかった）→ 政党政治

確立する　　　　　kakuritsu suru　　　establish

政党政治　　　　　seitō seiji　　　　　party politics

4 横暴　　　　　　　ōbō　　　　　　　　tyranny, oppression

5 失望　　　　　　　shitsubō　　　　　　disappointment

9 意思　　　　　　　ishi　　　　　　　　will

懲罰　　　　　　　chōbatsu　　　　　　chastisement, punishment

控える　　　　　　hikaeru　　　　　　have (in the background)

10 倫理的に　　　　　rinriteki ni　　　　ethically

根　　　　　　　　ne　　　　　　　　　root

11 超越者　　　　　　chōetsusha　　　　transcendental being

（超越者が定めた）→ 絶対的な基準

12 浅い　　　　　　　asai　　　　　　　　shallow

p305
3 乃木大将　　　　　Nogi taishō　　　　General Nogi (Nogi Maresuke, hero of the Russo-Japanese War, 1849-1910)

4 責める　　　　　　semeru　　　　　　reproach, censure

5 殺す　　　　　　　korosu　　　　　　kill

（明治天皇 …… よりどころとしていた）→ ようなところ

6 人倫関係　　　　　jinrin kankei　　　human relationships

p305

7	よりどころ	yoridokoro	foundation, ground
11	無	mu	nothingness
	空	kū	emptiness
12	結びつける	musubitsukeru	link, join
13	従属する	jūzoku suru	subordinate

p306

1	罰	batsu	punishment
	こわい	kowai	(be) afraid (of)
3	復活する	fukkatsu suru	be reborn, resurrected
	なる	naru	succeed, attain

(なるならざるは……天命を待つ)→という気持

	任せる	makaseru	leave to
4	人事	jinji	human affairs
	人事を尽す	jinji o tsukusu	do one's best (all that is humanly possible)
	天命	tenmei	Providence, fate
6	眞宗	shinshū	Shin sect of Buddhism (=Jōdo Shinshū, "True Pure Land sect")
	報恩	hōon	repayment of on
7	原理	genri	principle

Source: Abe Yoshishige 安倍能成, Karaki Junzō 唐木順三, Katsumoto Seiichirō 勝本清一郎, Takeyama Michio 竹山道雄, "Taishō no seishinshi" 大正の精神史, Jiyū 自由, Jiyūsha, October, 1961, pp. 100-101.

Abe Yoshishige (1883-1966), philosopher, was president of Gakushūin University. Karaki Junzō (1904-　) and Katsumoto Seiichirō (1899-　) are literary critics. Takeyama Michio (1903-　) was formerly professor of German literature at the University of Tokyo.

INDEX

This is an index to all vocabulary entries except notes and proper nouns. Numbers refer to the page and line numbers carried at the left side of the text pages. An asterisk preceding a number denotes a word introduced at this point in kana or in kanji with furigana. Thus, the entry eiga *17.3, 162.4 refers to an entry on page 22 of this volume (page 17, line 3 of Volume II, where the word is written えいが) and another on page 104 (page 162, line 4, where it is written 映画).

ā 38.13
abunai *76.13, 287.2
afureru 283.3
agaru 1.5, 43.9, 75.4, 197.5
ageru *50.12, 250.3, 255.12, 261.8, 262.1, 264.9, 279.8
ai 179.11, 191.5
aibiki 244.11
aichōteki 289.8
aijō 248.11
aimai 243.11
aisuru 191.5
ai-taisuru 283.6
aite 150.10
aji 237.1, -no aru bun 54.13
akari 19.3
akarui 63.11
akejikai 228.3
akeru *123.5, 228.3, 257.4, 283.13
aki 286.9
akiraka 195.8
akirameru 242.8
akireru *230.9
aku 228.9
akumu 293.6
akusento 20.6
akutō *223.4
amadera *118.8
amado 293.3
amanjiru 218.6
amari 25.9
ame *69.3, 87.5
-an *282.10
ana 288.2
anatagata 211.2
ani 291.10

ansatsu 230.6
anshin 85.3
antai 217.7
antei 183.13
anzenben 198.6
aokusai 268.10
apāto 70.11
appaku 220.5
arai 275.4
arasou 187.1
aratamaru 185.2
aratameru 132.1, 175.3
arata ni 47.1
arawareru 124.2, 185.11, 208.11
arawasu *50.4
arayuru 156.2
are kore 17.11
arigatai 245.6
arigatakunai 173.1
arigatasa 264.5
arigatō *43.2, -gozaimashita 85.2
arikata 234.12
ari-no-mama 188.2
arisama 126.4
aru 80.3
aru 125.2
arufabetto 93.3
aruiwa *112.5, 162.3, 166.13, 189.4
aruku *9.3, 70.10
asa 87.5
asai *287.12, 304.12
ashita 20.9
asobase kotoba 276.7
asobihanbun 174.8
asobu *17.5, *24.10, 163.1

asu 20.9
ataeru 151.12
atama 163.7, -ga warui 177.11
atarashii *11.10, 41.11
atarimae 236.5
ataru *49.12, 151.1, 223.3
atashi 274.11
atchikotch 228.9
ategau 226.5
ateru 280.2
ato *34.1, 39.13
atsui 156.5
atsui 170.7, 218.12
atsukau 206.5
atsumari 177.5
atsumaru *40.13, 106.6
atsumeru 230.4
atsuryoku 145.1
attōteki 195.8
au 26.4, 191.3
-au 167.4
awaseru 63.2, 225.7, 262.12
ayashii 75.7
ayumi 144.9
azana 167.4
azemichi 131.3
azen to suru *290.8
azukarishiru 230.6

ba 207.2
baai *67.11, 98.3
-bai 107.4
baidoku 291.10
baien 265.7
baishū 212.11
baka 220.8

bakabakashisa 245.9
bakageta 217.4
bakemono 170.10
bakuchiuchi *215.9
bakudan 269.9
bakufu *118.4, 137.5
bakusen to shita 255.10
bamen 205.13
-ban *19.13, 70.9
barabara 213.13
basha 229.7
basho 110.13
basu 161.2
batsu 306.1
beddo 64.7
bengi 232.5
benkyō *3.7, 66.2, -ni naru
  *9.4
benri *25.5, 75.1
beru 283.13
bessō 279.11
besuto serā 94.3, 162.3
betsu 170.10, 174.1, 271.5,
  -to shite 301.6
-betsu 198.9
betsugyō 284.8
bijutsu 126.7
bijutsuhin 128.2
bikkuri suru 287.4
bimyō 247.8
binbō 217.7
binbōburui 219.8
bīru 44.1
birudingu 191.10
bisei 264.5
biteki ken'o 191.4
biten 278.2
bitoku 277.13
bō 96.9
bō 252.13
bōkansha *223.8
boketsu 235.3
boku 172.1, -mitai ni 223.3
bokura *37.4
bōmei 229.12
bon 262.1
bonjin 207.12
bon'yari -suru 287.9, -to
  shita 189.2
bon'yō 303.12
boroboro 267.10
borogire 268.8
bōrupen 70.4
bōseki 200.10

bōsō 234.13
botchan 224.2
bōtō 182.3
boyakeru 294.7
bubun *51.8
bukimi 293.5
Bukkyō 258.2
būmu 94.2
bun 19.11
-bun 149.7
bungaku 82.4
bungakusha 229.12
bungakushi 203.3
bungakusho 162.4
bungeiran 215.2
bungo 150.7
bunka 69.11
bunkazai 267.1
bunken 292.1
bunmei 112.13
bunmō 176.13
-bun no 9.12
bunpō 236.12
bunrui 243.9
bunseki 260.4
bunshi 206.5
bunshō 173.7
buntai 241.6
burujowajī 147.9
bushi 186.7
bushu 96.8
busshiki 264.8
busshitsu 257.11
-butsu 195.6
butsudan 261.8
butsuzō 125.4
butten 289.6
byōdō 166.9
byōki 157.5
byōku 188.9
byōsha 270.6

chaji 285.3
chakai 290.12
chansu 202.9
chaseki 285.4
chi 167.6
chi -no tsunagatta 249.8
chichi 24.1
chichioya 149.5
chichiue 265.10
chigai nai 191.11
chigau 32.1

chihō 133.2, 159.3
chii 76.13
chiiki 144.13
chiisa na 19.5
chijin 46.6, 123.1
chijō 167.7
chikagoro 41.7
chikai *2.5, 40.1, 56.7
-chikaku 106.5
chikara 24.5, -ippai 293.1
  -o ireru 271.7
chikazuku 113.4
chikushō 283.10
chimei 92.1
chimeiteki 238.7
chimitsu 274.3
chinben 234.13
chingin 200.6
chinmoku 278.5
chinrōdō 200.2
chiri 105.1
chishikijin 138.3
chiteki 178.4
chitsujo 197.9
chizu 103.4, 105.8
chō 195.5
-chō 15.12
chōbatsu 304.9
chōchin *263.1
chōdo *17.6, 131.4, -ii
  *20.5
chōetsusha 304.11
chōhei kensa 176.13
chōhōkei 131.8
choichoi 182.3
chōjō 296.1
chōki 202.11
chokin 149.13
chōkoku *104.2
chōkoku 269.5
chokugo 268.12
chokusetsu ni 195.2, *233.
-chōme *40.4
chōnan 43.6
chōnanken 166.13
chōnin 31.5
chōsa hōkoku 176.5
chosakuken 192.6
chosuichi 202.4
chotto *27.1, 221.13
chū 20.4
-chū 203.3
chūgakkō *29.8, 51.13
chūi 211.8, -o okotaru

287.7
nūjitsu 205.1
nūki 302.10
nūkō 232.10
nūmon 93.10
nūmon 283.4
nūōshūken 144.4
nūsei 69.6
nūshakusho 204.1
nūshi 20.1
nūshin 262.9
nūshin 25.3
nūshinchi 110.13
nūshō kigyō 194.12
nūshoku *71.2
nūshōteki 189.9
nūto 224.4

aden 154.7
ai- 31.7
ai- 105.9
ai 20.4
ai 204.11
ai 285.6, 298.2
dai *229.7
aibu *13.9, 26.6
aibubun 105.9
aibutsu 118.3
ai chū shō 20.4
aidokoro 261.6
aigaku 25.3
aihyō 203.10
aiji *31.3, 42.10, -ni
  suru *24.6
aikoku 264.1
aimyō 185.3
aitai 41.2, 221.5
aizai 186.7
akara 92.12
ake 221.7
akkyaku 216.10
akuon 172.11
akuten 151.4
amaru 219.3
amasareyasui 244.8
amasu 183.12
ame *178.4, 219.7
an 218.1
andan 58.12
anjo 167.2
ankai 144.8
anmen 220.12
anpen 268.2

dansei 32.8
danshi 132.2
danson johi 250.1
dantai 216.8
dantai kōshō 198.13
danzetsu 234.2
daraku 206.5
dare 80.3
dasu 26.5, 41.7, 76.3,
  76.4, 119.6, 278.5, 285.1
-date 284.9
datte 226.9
deau 69.13
deiriguchi 139.4
dekakeru 228.11
dekasegi 200.1
dekaseginin 200.3
dekiagaru 51.9
dekigoto 165.2
dekireba 6.6
dekiru dake 192.11
dekishi *191.6
deku no bō 158.2
demokurashī 178.9
denbun 149.9
denki 300.1
denpō *52.9, -o utsu 149.6
densha 118.2
denshin 208.9
denshō 234.6
dentō 167.9
denwa -ga kakaru 20.8
denwachō 244.10
depāto 252.13
derikēto 247.1
deru 24.10, 69.4, 93.4,
  183.2
deshi 167.5
deshipurin 301.8
desukeredomo 5.9
detaramesa 242.10
do -ga sugiru 237.1
-do *11.13
dō- 20.6
dō 268.13
dobashi 287.10
dōbutsu 83.9, 258.5
dōchō 168.1
dōchū 80.11
dodai 246.2
dōgi 213.2
dōgu 236.7, 261.8
dōhai 173.10
dōji *21.10, 50.11

dojin 75.5
dōjin 215.9
dōjō 189.11
dōka 266.1
dokan 283.2
dōkan 187.10
dōki 188.6
doko 105.11, 222.6
dōkoku 243.12
dokoro ka 241.12
dokuji no 170.9
dōkun *20.6
dokuritsu *165.8, 272.5
dokusha 207.10
dokusho 52.2
dokushoyoku 161.12
dokusōteki 236.12
dokutoku 198.8
-domo 217.5
dō mo 225.12
donkan 241.13
dono 280.3
dōraku 285.3
dōro 266.2
doru 17.4
doryoku 209.6
dōsa 76.6
dōshite mata 173.3
dōshitemo 27.2
dōtoku ishiki 203.6
dōwa 262.5
dōyō 209.4
dōyō 237.4
doyōbi *17.2, 86.1
dozō 284.9

e -ni chikai 56.7, -ni
  kaku 56.8
eda *80.13
efekuto 233.5
egakidasu 205.6
egaku 186.11
egoizumu 298.7
ehagaki 263.8
ehon 262.5
ei 279.5
eibin 209.4
eiga *17.3, 162.4
eigakan 163.2
eigo *6.1, 49.8
eika 280.8
eikyō 113.1, 211.11
eikyū 267.3

eiri   197.13
eiyū   262.9
-eki   *10.6, 118.2
en   17.10
en   286.5
enerugī   303.10
engeki   262.7
enpitsu   *154.9
enpō   115.6
ensei   222.4
ensoku   263.6
erabu   281.11
erai   272.9
eru   138.4
-eru   145.6

fāsuto nēmu   167.4
fonetikku shisutemu   49.1
fu-   151.6
fū   *33.4, 56.9, 186.13, 274.4
fuan   189.2
fuannai   282.2
fuben   192.10
fubo   31.2
fubunritsu   300.9
fuchi   287.1
fūchō   208.5
fudan   150.6, -kara 185.5
fue   266.11
fūfu   240.5
fufuku   271.4
fuhenteki   234.11
fujin   137.2
fujin   278.3
fujiyū   224.1
fujun   270.12
fukai   31.2
fukameru   162.7
fukeiki   201.8
fukikomu   211.7
fukkatsu   306.3
fukō   *123.8, 212.5, -ni shite 220.11
fuku   *117.2
fuku   *283.7
fukujū   249.1
fukumu   195.3
fuku no kami   264.1
fukuzatsu   189.1
fukyū   177.2
fuman   303.5
fumi   152.9

fumuki   274.5
-fun   10.7
funa   *288.1
fune   *18.5, 75.3
fun'iki   243.13
furi   197.5
furigana   *54.4
furo   291.10
furoya   *128.5
furu   87.5
furu   295.1
furueru   191.10
furui   33.4, 131.9
furukusai   *225.13
furyōshōnendan   291.13
fusai   167.3
fusegu   216.11
fusei   166.8
fushigi   161.9
fushizen   233.11
fusoku   188.4
fusuma   286.2
futan   267.13
futari   1.4
futatabi   182.5
futatsu   3.13
futo   228.13
futoi   24.4
futoru   86.9
futsū   *51.12, 82.7
futsugō   239.10, -o hataraku 212.6
fuyo   211.12
fuyukai   206.8
fuyuyasumi   85.13
fuzai   242.11
fūzoku   289.8

gā   282.12
-gachi na   243.11
gai   242.13
-gai   297.11
gaibu   145.2
gaikei   208.10
gaikōkan   *71.11
gaikoku   40.13
gairaigo   52.8
gaisai   219.10
gaishutsu   27.1
gaisuru   243.9
gakkai   27.5
gakkari suru   291.6
gakki   69.13

gakkō   31.4, -ni agaru 43.9
gaku   284.2
-gaku   38.13
-gaku   195.4
gakumon   240.5, -teki 162.8
gakuryoku tesuto   29.6
gakusei   25.13
gakusha   40.13
gan   299.12
ganrai   218.2
garasu   52.7
gasshō   261.9
-gata   200.1
-gata   211.2
-gatai   298.4
gatatsuku   299.2
-gatsu   6.6
-gawa   *24.8, 96.12
gehin   277.11
geijutsu   *134.8, 207.3
geijutsuhin   271.11
gekkan zasshi   164.2
gekkyūbukuro   261.11
gemin   230.6
genan   173.13
genbutsu   170.10
gendai   93.7
gengogakusha   92.7
gen'in   111.11
genjitsu   169.1, -teki 181.8
genkan   284.1, 284.4
genki   *40.10, 85.2
genmai   156.10
genmetsu   209.4
gen ni   245.5
genri   306.7
genrō   304.1
gensaku   204.13
genshi bakudan   269.9
genshō   95.10, 165.6, 208.4
gensoku   99.1
genson   142.1, 260.5
genzai   91.13, -no tokoro 182.12
gesaku   230.3
gesui   14.10
geta   228.9
getsumatsu   149.4
getsuyōbi   *20.3
gibun   241.12
gifubo   249.3
gijutsu   177.10
gimu   211.3
gimu kyōiku   177.2

nkō 285.1
ri 186.10
ron 180.9
sei 244.5
;o *6.1, 48.7, 153.4
;o 178.8
;ō 156.10
ban *131.4
-chūi made ni 217.13
gaku 72.8, -teki ni 244.6
go *17.5, 39.7
han 261.9
i 237.4
i 279.3
isagi 282.9
ishi *131.6
jūnotō *128.4
jūon jun 92.9
kai 211.6
ku 225.13
makashi *218.3
makasu 222.5
raku 285.12
rannasai 173.1
ran ni naru 56.5
riteki 197.13
riyaku 263.11
rufu 163.1
shō 212.10
ten 286.4
oto 89.4
zen 39.5
-zonji *1.9, 56.3
ai -ga warui 255.1
nbi 180.4
nka 289.10
nshuku 181.6
urai 75.2
rūpu 64.11
taiteki 189.11
ā 293.4
aku 130.1, -ni iu to
  110.11
akusetsuteki 209.13
akutai 302.9
yō 19.7
yō 195.5
ogyō 194.10
ōjūzaga *301.4
okuseki konkō 234.1
oson 249.10

a 57.7

ha 286.7
-ha 210.1
habakaru 211.5
-haberu 279.2
habuku 275.13
hachigashira *100.11
haeru 80.13
hageshii 144.13
haha 29.6, 157.7
hahaoya 80.5
haigo 84.4, 212.12
haikei 208.4
haiken 270.4
hairu 5.2, 283.4
haisen 268.12
haishi 233.12
haisuru 208.2
haitai 220.11
haji *211.12
hajimaru *86.1, 173.1
hajime 11.7
hajimemashite 2.11
hajimeru 91.7, -o hajime
  161.4
hajimete 2.1
hakai 212.4
hakairyoku 209.10
hakamairi 262.2
hakaru 234.5
hakase 92.7
hakken 159.2, 188.10
hakki 299.5
hakkiri 17.13
hakkō ichiu 243.12
hakobu 283.6
hakuchi *233.13
hakujin 24.9
hakushi 92.7
hamaru 286.12
hamaya *264.7
hametsu 298.1
-han 39.5
hana 263.1
hana 291.9
hanabi 228.1
hanahada 274.5
hanahadashii 230.2
hanareru 170.9, 200.9
hanareya 285.5
hanashi 56.1, 169.2
hanashigoe 228.11
hanasu *3.9, *25.9, 56.2
hanasu 287.7
hanbun 173.1

handakuten 151.5
handan 171.5
handen *131.12
han'i 254.13
hankō 166.8
hanseiki 107.3
hansen 289.12
hansha 220.4
hansuru 32.10, -ni hanshite
  216.3
hantai *33.3, 58.5, 150.4,
  216.12
hantoshi 42.5
happyō 177.6
hara 220.3
harainokeru 126.3
hariageru 264.5
haru 220.2
haru 286.9
haruka 249.12
hashi 139.3
hashi 228.2
hashira 233.1
hashirimawaru 85.5
hashirimoto 284.6
hashiru 26.9
hassō 90.5
hassō 176.3
hatake 105.12
hataraku 195.2, 212.6
hatashite 180.6
hatasu 187.4
hatoba 266.8
hatsuden 106.9
hatsuka 42.13
hatsumei 48.10
hatsumōde 264.3
hatsumono 261.9
hatsuon 48.13
hattatsu 143.5
hatten 178.2, 211.9
hayai 18.2, 115.12
hayaru 25.1
hayashi 10.6
hazu wa nai 191.6
hē 222.6
hebi 126.4
heichi 108.6
heigai *213.2
heihō kiromētoru 107.5
heiki 180.4
heiki 218.6
heikō 105.3
heion 218.8

heiso   262.9, -kara 262.9
heitai   176.12
heiwa   170.2
heiwaron   179.1
heiya   106.11
hekikan   284.2
hekoobi   *287.5
hen   96.9
hen   174.9
-hen   *19.4, 211.8
henji   81.5
henka   238.3, 276.8
henkaku   131.11
heta   25.9
heya   *20.1, 284.4
hi   22.10
hi   63.11, -ga kureru   123.8
hibiki   266.11
hidari   63.5
hideri   157.13
hidoi   243.9
higan   262.1
higashi   45.12
higashi kaigan   105.3
higoto   89.4
hihan   203.7
hihyō   203.5
hijō ni   *49.2, 95.2, 105.9
hikaeru   221.13, 304.9
hikaku   143.13
hikari   139.6
hikidasu   239.13
hikinobasu   290.4
hikisageru   230.3
hikitsugu   261.7
hikitsuzuku   229.7
hikizuru   246.11
hikkosu   261.5
hikōki   18.1
hiku   92.8, 207.11, 285.4
hiku   230.4
hikui   113.10
hima   96.2, 243.8
himajin   223.7
himatsubushi   162.11
hin   224.2, -no yoi 224.2
hinagata   250.7
hinan   206.10
hin'i   230.2
hiningenteki   190.1
hinjaku   223.5
hinnō   200.7
hinto   290.10
hipparu   263.2

hiragana   *48.3, 92.8
hiraku   139.5
hirayazukuri   284.3
hirei   249.5
hirō   220.10
hirogari   254.8
hirogaru   138.9, 250.8
hirogeru   58.7
hiroi   111.12
hiroma   286.4
hiromaru   175.9
hirosa   131.4
hirou   293.2
hiru   20.9
hirumeshi   228.2
hirune   285.7
hirusugi   20.4
hisan   187.3
hisashiku   250.1
hisen   289.12
hisomu   213.10
hitei   182.13
hito   1.11, 211.12
hitobanjū   70.9
hitobito   31.3
hitoe ni   285.9
hitogashira   100.10
hitokoro   303.1
hitokuchi   -ni iu 5.5
hitome   56.7
hitori   1.3
hitoriaruki   170.11
hitoritabi   85.7
hitotamari mo naku   245.11
hitotsu-hitotsu   66.4, 250.3
hitotsu ni wa   138.10
hitsuyō   91.6
hiwadabuki   *283.7
hiyayaka   193.1
hō   131.12
hōben   225.6
hobo   197.11
hōbō   *9.2
hodo   120.9
hodō   *70.10
hoesakebu   266.11
hōfu   241.4
hōgen   20.6
hogo   267.1
hōhō   *18.7, 48.10
hoka   26.1, 163.5, 260.1
hōkai   301.12
hokanaranai   260.1
hōkensei   143.8

hōkenseido   143.1
hōkō   225.9
hōkō   249.6
hōkoku   176.5
hokutō   105.3
hōmen   220.1
homeru   158.3
hōmon   179.2
hon   10.5, -o dasu 41.7
-hon   10.1
hondō   208.3
hon'i   273.8
honki   180.6
honmono   87.8, 171.3
honnin   215.8
honno   253.4
honoka   278.5
honrai   236.6
honsaiyō   198.4
honshiki   280.12
honshitsu   201.3
honshoku   163.3
hontei   284.9
hontō   85.6
hon'ya   93.9
hon'yaku   *36.3, 204.9
hōon   306.6
horekomu   303.7
horinukiido   284.6
horisageru   287.13
hōritsu   118.12
horobiru   217.3
horu   235.3
hoshi   296.1
hōshi   255.8
hoshii   86.3
hōshin   231.4
hoshō   183.2
hoshu   170.2
hosoi   281.11
hosonagai   105.3
hossoku   231.3
hoteru   24.8
hotoke   262.6
hotondo   *10.11, 173.12
hotori   285.5
hototogisu   279.3
hozon   267.3
hyakka jiten   92.1
hyakunen   9.6
hyakushō   31.5
hyō   97.1
hyōgen   150.6
hyōgo   216.6

yōgu *280.10
yōhon 235.3
yōjun 218.5
yōka 166.6
yōkihō 178.1
yōmen 209.1
yōonka 231.4
yōron 204.4

i 109.5
chi 249.12
chiban *11.10, 183.3
chibu 209.11, 216.1
chidan 218.5
chidō 85.4
chigon 216.11
chigyō ichigyō 19.7
chiichi 3.13
chiin 162.7
chiji 201.12
chijirushii 241.2
chijiteki 111.8
chimen 190.1
chinichijū 6.8
chū 239.10
dai 257.8
deorogī 271.13
do *135.4, 284.6
e *24.9, 64.4
eie 228.4
gai 93.3
gai 276.6
gaku 138.1
go 107.3
i *17.3, 63.7, 92.3, 222.2
iarawasu *49.10
ifurasu 217.2
i kagen ni 267.10
imawashi 276.5
in 231.2
isugiru 170.12
ji 186.10
jō 70.9
jō no 93.7
ka 177.6
kaga 40.12
kanaru *259.11, 272.1
ka ni 228.13
karu 156.8
ke 283.2
ken 165.3, 166.3
kenai 224.1
iki -o tsugu 221.13

ikiiki 270.6
ikinobiru 178.2
ikiru 170.12
ikisugi 235.3
ikka 279.9
ikka shinjū 268.4
ikken 19.10, 176.5
ikkō 225.12
iku 17.3
ikuraka 166.3
ikutsu *43.7
ikutsuka no 203.11
imada ni 250.3
ima ga ima 217.10
ima ni 172.2
ima ni mo 175.5
imasara 237.10
imēji 169.1
imi 49.5
ina 230.7
inaka 149.5
ine no taba 157.8
inoru *87.12
inryōsui 155.11
insatsu 243.9
inshō 151.12
interi 178.3
inu 24.2
inui *284.9
inu no ko 24.3
iori *279.3
ippai 286.7, 293.10
ippan 213.3, 238.8
ippō -ni oite wa 143.3
irai 82.4
irassharu 1.2
ireru 105.12, 156.3, 192.3, 205.11, 271.7
irigashira 100.10
iriguchi 2.4
irimajiru 246.13
iroiro 9.5, 110.8
iryūjon 171.6
isan 192.5
ishi *191.3
ishi 229.2, 304.9
ishidatami *283.4
ishiki 203.6
ishikiteki 238.3
isho 186.5
ishoku 226.10
isogashii *29.9, *40.11, 93.9
isogu 151.12, 168.2

issai 150.6
issho *25.7, 85.6, 220.11
isshō 31.12
isshōkenmei *162.1
isshu no 162.10
issō 231.10
issō 267.4
itadaku 261.10
itai 26.10
itan 231.7
itanoma 284.5
itanshi -o ukeru 231.7
itaru 143.8, 188.12, 242.4, 289.7
itasu 85.3
itatte 282.6
itchi 169.5
ito 126.3
itonamu 177.9
itsu 38.9
itsudatsu 233.2
itsuka 20.3
itsuka 174.8, 289.10
itsu no ma ni ka 81.9
itsushika 263.10
itsu to naku 229.3
itsutsu 14.5
ittai 182.6
ittei 131.4, 169.3
itteikikan 200.9
ittōkoku 219.12
iu *5.5, 9.8, 49.8, -made mo nai 112.13, -ni iwarenai 229.1
iwaba 183.5
iwayuru 177.3
iya 175.4, 229.9, -de tamaranai 291.11
iya 164.13, 221.1
iyoiyo 239.1
izen 82.5, 263.9
izen to shite 221.5
izure ni shitemo 248.7

jā 39.7, 40.4
jakkan 236.13
jānarisuto 170.3
ji *2.12, 26.10
-ji *20.7, 39.5, 90.6
-ji 149.7
jibun 4.13
jibun 221.2
jibuntachi 76.9

jidai 69.8, 106.3
jidaiokure 216.8
jidōsha *26.8, 70.10
jifu 209.13
jiin 263.7
jijitsu 180.1, 215.10
jijitsujō 192.10
jijō 191.11
jijoden 207.3
-jikai 228.3
jikaku 263.10
jikan *9.3, *19.7, 31.7, 39.10, -o tsubusu 163.2
jiken 186.8
jikkō 181.6
jiko 248.2
jimu 243.9
jin 283.10
-jin 7.2
jinari 294.12
jinbutsu 290.10
jingū 263.7
jinja *134.8, 262.8
jinji -o tsukusu 306.4
jinkaku 212.12
jinkō 9.10, 194.8
jinkōteki 137.8
jinmei 92.1
jinmin 132.1
jinrikisha *11.11
jinrinkankei 305.6
jinruiai 179.11
jinsei 265.11
jinshin 209.10
jinshin kōgeki 215.3
jirei 218.2
jisannan 201.6
jisatsu 185.6
jisei 302.12
jishin 171.3
jishin 193.1
jisho 91.1
jisonshin 188.3
jissai 18.4
jisshi 232.1
jisshitsuteki 238.11
jisshō seishin 210.1
jitai 238.2
jitai 281.3
jiten 91.6, 91.9, 92.13, 104.11
jitensha 86.5
jitsu 179.8
jitsumei 280.1

jitsu ni 276.8
jitsu wa 96.5
jitsuzai 257.9, 291.3
jiyū 4.2, 10.2
jizoku 112.2
-jo 253.6
-jo 280.6
-jō 20.7, 192.10, 197.7
-jō *279.2
-jō 284.2
jōbu 156.6
jochū 38.2
jochūbeya 284.4
jō chū ge 19.12
jōen 291.5
jogakusei 277.3
jōge 4.8
jōhin 225.13
jojōsei *166.5
jōken 112.9
jōkyō 149.4
jōnetsu 297.4
josei 32.8
joshi 132.2
joshi gakusei 26.1
jōshiki 162.7
jōsōbu 178.3
jōtai 171.9
jōzu 25.9
-jū 6.8, 19.13, 70.9
jūatsu 302.10
jūbun 49.10, 258.7
jūdai 238.7
jūgyōin 197.4
jugyōjikan 244.5
jukyōteki 203.6
jun- 274.4
-jun 92.9
junbi 193.1
jūnendai 298.2
junjo 92.10
junpū bizoku *302.4
junsa *212.7
junshi 185.1
junsui 185.9
jūrin *217.3
jusha 257.2
jūyō 131.10
jūzei 268.4
jūzoku 305.13

-ka 2.7
-ka 69.1

-ka 69.9
-ka 110.13
kabe 295.9
kabuki 205.1
kachi 234.5
kachō 248.13
kādo 71.12
kādo bokkusu 70.5
kadojimen 284.9
kaerimichi 20.5
kaeru *9.5, 81.4
kaeru 220.3
kaeru 266.1
kaesu *69.11
kaette *185.11, 275.10
kagaku 137.13
kagami 223.9
kagayaku 220.12
kage 157.3
kageki 232.7
-kagetsu 192.13
kagiri 244.3
kagiru *168.1, 179.3, 189.6 197.10, 228.10, 241.2
-kai 19.1
-kai 231.2
-kai 284.9
kaichū 37.8
kaifuku 201.12
kaigai shokoku 137.5
kaigan 105.3
kaigi 209.4
kaihō 298.4
kaiimoji 63.12
kaijō *28.10
kaikoku 239.3
kaiketsu 181.9
kaiko 226.9
kaikoku 139.5
kaikyū 209.11
kaimono *70.4, 86.2
kaisetsu 264.5
kaisha 164.9, 197.4
kaishaku 203.11, 213.7
kaitōsha 253.10
kaiwa *1.1
kajō 201.5
kakaeru 226.2
kakaru 1.10
kakaru 17.11
kakaru 20.8
kakaru 283.8
kakawaru 255.3
kakedasu 228.9

kakehanareru 228.13
kakeru 63.13
kakeru 96.4
kakeru 101.7
kakeru 209.7
kakeru 175.4
kakiageru *42.5
kakiarawasu 48.9
kakikonasu 281.8
kako 90.8, 166.4
kakō 207.3
kakomu 131.3
kaku 49.6
kaku *56.8, 64.7
kaku 181.9
kaku 227.5
kaku 261.13, 301.7
kakuchi 264.4
kakujin 247.11
kakumei 167.11
kakuritsu 304.3
kakusu 81.8
kakusū 102.5
kamae *101.4
kamau 225.8
kamera 264.6
kami *36.8, 257.3
kami 125.7
kamidana 261.6
kamigata 274.1
kamijochū *284.12
kamikaze 117.1
kaminari -ga naru 125.9
kan 64.6
kan 96.9
-kan 116.4
-kan 282.4
kanaderu *285.9
kanagaki 233.5
kanai kōgyō 195.6
kanarazu *82.5, 93.2, 166.4
kanarazushimo 166.4
kanari 300.12
kanashii *80.8
kanashimu 163.9
kanazukai 231.5
kanben 267.10
kanbun 173.5
kanbyō 157.6
kanchō 197.10
kandō 186.2
kane 17.4
kane 261.9
kan'ei jiten 91.9

kanemōke 240.5
kangae 76.1
kangaedasu 57.13
kangaenaosu 203.9
kangaeru 5.1
kangeki 271.3
kango 243.5
kanji *3.5, 48.3, 281.13
kanji 84.3, 127.1
kanjin 283.6
kanjiru 146.7, 166.3
kanjō 156.13
kanjō 241.6
kankei *49.8, 69.9, 211.10, 305.6
kankyō 254.8
kanmuri 96.9
kannen 232.11
kanojo 191.5
kansei 204.10
kanshi 243.1
kanshin 76.7
kanshin 183.4
kanso 234.9
kansuru 69.11
kantan *50.11, 101.12
kanten 243.7
kanwa jiten 91.6
kanzen 196.1
kao *123.6, 223.9, -o dasu 285.1
karada 42.9
karā firumu 70.5
karakuri 233.2
karamiau 247.8
karasu 265.5
kare 75.9
kareru 288.1
kari 275.11
kariru *69.12, 205.11
kasen 106.8
kashin 185.5
kashin 208.5
kashira *100.8
kashiya 261.5
-kasho 287.13
kasuka 228.12
kata *1.9
-kata 18.7
-kata 200.1
katachi 56.8, 255.7, 285.7
katakana *48.3, 102.1
kataki 298.8
kataru 179.3, 206.11

katatoki mo 287.7
katazuku 273.6
kategorī 65.7
katei 162.5
katei 188.12
katō 206.5
katorikku 140.10
katorikkukyō 141.1
katsu *207.12, 257.7
katsu 249.4
katsudō 106.4
katsudōshashin 245.8
katsugu 263.3
katsute 215.2
katte 213.11
kattehōdai 301.11
kawa 9.9
kawairashii 24.9
kawari 70.2, 175.1
kawaru *9.6, 58.13
kawaru 209.6
kawashimo 19.4
kawatta 103.8
kaya 293.7
kayabuki *157.4
kayōbi *19.9
kayou 263.3
kazai dōgu 261.8
kazan 106.3
kaze 156.4
kazoedoshi 203.2
kazoeru *18.7, 243.7
kazokutachi 189.11
kazu 102.6
kazu sukunai 206.2
ke 85.5
-ke 132.1
keibo *279.9
keiei 194.5
keigen 269.1
keigo 173.11
keihō 197.7
keihōjō 197.7
keijū 268.11
keiken 120.11
keiki 198.6, -o tsukeru 221.3
keikō 162.12
keikoba 285.8
keiren *234.7
keiseimoji 64.9
keishiki 210.2
keishi sōkan 212.7
keiyaku 200.12

keizaiteki 137.11
kekka *165.3, 176.7
kekkō *39.12
kekkon 118.10
kekkonshiki 264.7
kekkyoku 247.4
kemuri 26.8
-ken 82.1
kenbun 229.8
ken'i 209.3
kenka 157.11
kenkyū *20.7
ken'o 191.4
kenpō 182.1
kenri 247.7
kenryoku 212.1
kenzen 221.5
keredomo 119.2
keshikaran 234.3
kesshite 156.8
ketsui 182.6
ketsuron 236.2
kettei 231.5
kezuru 220.1
ki 10.1
ki 257.11, -ga suru 230.1,
  -ga tsuku 80.12, 223.5,
  -ni iru 212.6, -ni kuwanai
  212.2, -ni naru 81.6,
  223.8, -o tsukeru 80.12,
  173.1
kibishii 178.2
kibō 244.9
kibun 245.7
kichaku 225.9
kichijōten 267.4
kichō 183.7
kien 303.9
kieru 189.6
kigenzen 167.6
kigyō 194.11, 197.13
kihaku 272.12
kihan 242.7
kihonteki 195.11
kī hōrudā 70.5
kii 281.13
kiji 188.9
kijun 237.6
kikai 169.6
kikan 197.10
kikan 200.9
kiken 213.6
kikidasu 291.7
kikiiru 285.9

kikinareru 174.11
kikoeru 47.3
kiku 42.12
kikyō *83.2
kimatte iru 175.5
kimeru *192.2, 246.6
kimi 71.6
kimochi 146.4, 185.13
kinben 177.13
kinchō *283.9
kindaika 69.9, 71.3
kindaishi 71.3
kindenhō *131.12
kinensai 228.6
kinen sutanpu 263.8
kinjo 39.13, -zukiai 255.1
kinkō 179.10
kinnen 41.5
kinō *23.3, *70.9, 167.12
kinō 201.9
kinō 232.5
kinryoku 212.1
kinshi 263.6
kin'yōbi *21.2
kirai *135.5
kirau 212.10
kire 125.7
kirei 10.13, 86.10
kirisutokyō 259.8
kiritsumeru 220.6
kiroku 133.5
kiromētoru 107.5
kiru 150.3
kisai 279.12
kisekidan 262.8
kisen 266.10
kisetsu 261.9
kishukusha 205.6
kiso 209.8
kisokutadashii 131.5
kissaten *163.2
kisshōten 267.4
kita 81.13
kitanai 11.1
kitto 24.4
kiwa *286.8
kiwadatsu 196.5
kiwamete 177.3
kiwami 187.5
kiyasui 169.3
kiyoi 283.10
kizuku 192.13
ko 24.3
kō 63.6

kōba 195.1, 198.5
kōbai *295.8
kobukai 286.9
kobun 215.8
kochira 76.1, 215.12
kochira koso 2.11
kodai 131.12
kōdan 262.7
kōdo 143.8
kōdō 171.5
kōdō 250.10
kodoku 229.4
kodomo *31.10, 63.8
koe 75.12, -o dasu 76.3
koeru 281.12
kōfuku *211.10, 232.12
kōgeki 215.3
kōgen 211.5
kōgi -ni deru 69.4
kogo 152.9
kōgo 151.1
kogoto *226.3
kōgyō 195.6
kōhan 119.10
kōhan 194.3
koi *288.1
koi 289.9
kōi 182.5, -ni deru 183.2
kojin *165.8, 185.9
kōjō 198.5
kōka 270.12
kōkei 257.6
kōkeiki 201.7
kōken 267.8
kokitsukau 220.7
kokka 110.3, 213.6
kokkai 250.3
kokki 228.4
kokko 268.3
kokkuba 284.6
kōkō *80.4, 248.10
kōkogaku 70.1
kōkōgyō 194.12
kōkoku 162.3
kokonoka 69.2
kokonotsu 14.8
kokoro 24.6
kokoromochi 193.2
-koku 106.6
kokuchi 295.3
kokudo 105.10
kokugai 229.12
kokugo jiten 91.6
kokuhaku 207.2

kokuji 231.4
kokumin 176.11
kokunai 138.10
kokuritsu 33.11
kokusaiteki 137.3
kokyō 208.13
kōkyō 112.10
komaka 260.4
komaru 18.12
kome 159.4
komoru 255.6
komu 162.9
komyunikeishon 177.9
kon- 19.13
kōnai 139.2
kō nari na togeta hito 267.8
konban 71.10, -jū ni 19.13
kondo *26.9, 33.12
kōnen 284.8
kongakki 69.13
kongetsu 3.7
kongo 267.8
konkyo 245.7
konnan 48.9
konnichi 108.2, 110.4
konnichi wa 1.2
kono 211.6
konoaida 10.13
konoha 294.3
konomae 42.1
konomu 172.13, 270.10
konpai 220.10
konponteki 143.7
konran 138.10
konshū 86.1
kontorōru 198.5
kon'ya *20.10
koppu 52.7
kōran *286.5
korasu 286.1
kore 221.8
kore-kore 287.2
korekushon 129.9
kōri 64.4
koritsu 145.2
koro *9.8, 19.3
korosu 305.5
kōryo 240.6
kōsai 137.12
kōsatsu 246.9
kosei 211.9
kōsei 231.12
koseki 263.7

koseki 279.12
kōsetsu 281.7
kōsha 101.5
kōshi 204.8
kōshido 228.5
kōshin 248.10
koshiraeru 219.8
kōshita 260.2
kōshō 198.13
kōsoku 233.1
kotaeru *18.1, 81.5
kotei 300.6
kōtei 297.9
koto 285.9
kotoba *31.9, *57.11, 85.7, 167.1, 274.2
kotobagaki 279.5
kotogotoku 220.6
kotogoto ni 212.11
koto koko ni itaru 242.4
kotonaru 143.4
koto ni 172.12
koto ni naru 9.12
koto ni shite iru 5.6
kotosara 229.3
kotoshi 9.2
kotowaru 125.9
kōtsū 106.9
kōun 202.9
kouri 195.1
kōwa 228.6
kowagaru 157.10
kowai 306.1
kowareru 242.5
koya 157.4
koyama 294.6
koyū 237.7
kōyū 131.13
kōzan 201.4
kōzangyō 195.5
kōzō 236.6
ku -ni suru *158.4, 192.7
kū 305.11
kubetsu *32.7, 170.10, -ga tsuku 280.5, -o tsukeru 276.3
kubunden 131.1
kuchi -e dasu 278.5, -ni suru 33.3
kudareru 303.7
kufū 192.12
kugi -o utsu *135.6
kuguru *284.1
kūhaku 234.6

kūki 266.7
kumazasa 287.1
kumiai 198.8
kumiawaseru 152.5
kumitoru 277.7
kumo 126.3
kumoru 228.3
kumu 281.3
kun 48.11
-kun *4.10, 43.6
kuni 32.3
kunigamae 101.5
kunigara 217.11
kuniguni 69.5
kunren 301.5
kunshu 232.12
kuōtēshon 275.12
kuraberu 106.2
kurai 295.9
-kurai 75.2
kurasu *80.5
kureru *123.8
kureru 149.10
kurikaesu 80.12
kurisuchan 90.8
kurisumasu 70.5
kurō -o suru 281.1
kurofune 208.9
kurosu refarensu 101.1
kuru 17.6
kuruma *22.6, 71.6
kurushii 191.13
kurushimu 191.2
kusa 57.7
kūsō 291.1
kutōten -o utsu 149.7
kutsu 86.3
kutsū 188.9
kuu 224.12
kuwashii *11.8, 208.12
kuwawaru 249.2
kyaku 96.9
kyaku 252.11, 285.2
kyakushōbai 263.13
kyakushoku 291.5
kyō 1.3, -ni kagitte 228.10
kyō 262.1
-kyō 141.1
kyōchū 230.8
kyōdai 167.5
kyōfu 295.2
kyōgen 237.12
kyōgū 189.5
kyōiku 177.2

kyōiku kanji *53.8
kyojū 137.9
kyoka *130.2
kyōkai 140.12, 263.4
kyōkasho 95.6, 262.5
kyōko *229.2
kyōkō 202.11
kyokubu 223.3
kyōmei 182.12
kyōmi *17.8, 120.7
kyomukan 265.12
kyonen 86.2
kyōryoku 111.10
kyōryoku 176.4
kyōsei 161.1
kyōshi 203.4
kyōsō 144.12
kyōtsū 171.1, 197.11
kyōyō 162.7
kyū 191.5, 238.12, 295.8
kyūdōsha 207.13
kyūgeki 144.7
kyūjitsu 42.6
kyūka 96.5
kyūkanji 91.10
kyūkei 234.4
kyūkutsu 221.13
kyūsoku 144.2
kyūyo 197.4

ma 284.1
ma 295.7
mā 215.9
machi 9.1
machigai *5.11, 150.1
machi kōba 195.1
mado *24.8, 139.5
madoguchi 265.1
maguchi 220.2
-mai *128.11, 131.4
maiasa 261.8
maigō 216.1
mainen 107.4
mainichi 85.5
mairu 10.9
majime 226.11
majiru 281.4
majutsu 209.1
makaseru 306.3
makazu 284.4
makeru *156.1, 161.7
makitsukeru 125.7
makki 143.13

makoto ni 284.10
makuramoto 293.2
mama 188.2
mamahaha 279.6
mamonaku 133.3
mamoru 181.8, 255.8
man 9.10
manabu 146.11, 176.2
mane 166.2
manekineko 264.1
maneku 285.2
maneru 173.6
manga 262.5
mangetsu 294.6
ma ni au 91.11
man'ichi 191.6
man'in densha 161.10
manten 177.1
Man'yōgana 281.3
manzen 216.13
manzoku *160.2, 180.1, 221.11
marude 224.13
maruta 283.4
masaka 269.9
masashiku 279.13
mashite 233.7
massugu 131.3
masui 234.6
masumasu 164.8, 196.4
mata 25.2
matchi 22.10, 154.9, 176.8
matsu 38.6
matsu 157.3
matsudai 230.5
matsuri 263.1
matsuru 262.8
mattaku *9.6, 42.7
mawari 105.6
mawaru 23.1, 220.7, 268.1
mayou 81.4
mazu 26.2, 174.10
mazui 226.3
mazushii 200.8
me 26.10, 131.4, 284.2, -ga mawaru 220.7, -ni tsuku 299.7, -no kataki ni suru 298.8, -o hanasu 287.7
-me. 15.11
mechakucha 218.4
medatsu 247.2
megurasu 286.5
meibutsu 254.2
meidai 224.10

meijiru 231.2
meirei -o dasu 76.4
meishi *104.12
meisho 263.7
meiyo 224.5
meiyoshin 186.10
men 66.4
menbā 301.13
me no kataki 298.8
menseki 106.2
meshita 3.11
meshitsukai 173.8
mētoru *25.4, 70.9, 107.5
metsubō 217.10
metta ni 277.3
meue 3.11
mezameru 209.12
mi 229.4
mibun 167.2
michi *19.4, 215.12
michisugara 229.6
midashi 93.5
midoriiro 131.5
mieru 38.10, 175.9
migi 63.4
migurushii 191.11
miidasu 242.8
mijika 262.9
mijikai 106.8
mikakeru 162.2
miki 293.5
mikka 9.2
mikoshi *263.2
mikawasu 161.2
mimi 174.12, -o sumasu 228.12
miminari 294.13
mina 166.9
minami 81.13
minasu 167.5
minato 137.3
minkan kigyō 197.13
minna 5.12
mi no ue 228.13
minpō 302.3
minshushugi 244.9
minshūteki 237.12
minzoku 110.3
miru 9.3
miryoku 239.8
mise 195.1
miseru 26.3
miso 156.11
-mitai 223.3

ite aruku 9.3
itomeru 120.12
itsudo *107.7
itsukaru 96.8
itsukeru 96.6
ittsu 4.1
iukeru 105.12
iwatasu 220.12
iya 262.10
iyamairi 262.10
izu 10.13
izukara 33.1
izuumi 106.10
ō 11.13
ochidasu 258.13
ochiiru 92.13
ochikaeru 264.7
ochikitaraseru 297.13
ochikusare 285.7
ochiron *10.7, 149.6
oderu 290.9
odoru 227.1
ohō 208.10
oji 37.4, 48.1, 56.9, 63.12
okka 234.11
okuhyō 183.7
okusuru 229.9
okuteki 125.4
okuyōbi *13.2
on 25.4
onban *123.5
ondai 71.4, -ni suru *32.5, -no 241.2
ongamae *101.5
onmō 176.13
ono *33.2, 38.4
ono 56.8
onogatari 290.13
onogokoro -ga tsuku 263.9
onogoto 274.3
onozuki 226.10
orau 268.3
ōretsu 224.13
oshi 272.9
ōshiageru 16.2
ōshikomu 141.7, 215.7
oshiku wa 226.5
oshi-moshi 38.2
ōshiwake nai 255.3
ōsu 2.9
otareru 286.8
oto 86.9, 170.8, -ni suru 48.5

motomeru 75.4, 192.1
motomoto 63.8
motozuku *32.11, 131.12
motsu *17.8, 31.4
motte iku 75.7
motte kuru 22.11
mottomo 91.13
mottomo 119.9
mottomo 215.10
mu 305.11
mube *286.7
mubō 233.12
muchi 241.13
muen 259.11
mugen 202.4
mugon 277.12
muhō 212.13
muika 24.2
muimi 186.13
mujun 242.12
mukaiau 246.4
mukashi *31.4, 48.2
mukashi nagara no 278.4
mukau 189.10
mukeru 293.11
mukō *76.5, 173.5
mukōgawa 24.8
mukōgishi 287.11
mukō sangen ryōdonari 254.11
muku 211.11
mura 80.7
mure 264.3
muri 114.2, -o suru *42.8
muron 207.11
musaboru 232.13
musekinin 238.13
mushi 65.8
mushi 180.2
mushiatsui 293.2
mushiro 195.2
mushūkyōsha 258.4
musū 170.10
musubi-tsukeru 123.3, 305.12
musubitsuku 200.4
musuko 261.10
musume 166.13, 291.9
muttsu 151.4
muzan 267.9
muzukashii *3.13, 52.5
myōban 71.6
myō na 222.4

na 98.1, 179.8
nā 226.13
-nado 137.2
nagai aida 31.3
nagame 131.2
nagameru 286.8
nagare 106.8, -o kumu 281.3
nagasu 157.13
nageru 293.11
nagori 246.11
nai 194.5
-nai 297.11
naibu 208.9
naibu seimeiron 297.8
naifu 191.9
naigenkan 284.4
-nai kagiri 189.5
naishi *178.8, 225.10
naishin 192.2
nai to wa kagiranai 168.1
naiyō 81.12
nakaba 47.1, 246.10
nakahodo 287.10
naka jochū *284.12
nakama 187.3
nakamairi 219.13
nakanaka 41.4, 281.2
nakigoe 293.4
naku 80.10, *279.3
nakunaru *124.4, 185.2, 243.4
nakunasu 233.3
nakusu 231.9
namae *2.12, -o tsukeru 43.3
namajii 220.2
namakemono 221.1
nami 294.10
-nami 284.6
namida -o nagasu 157.13, -o ukabete 261.12
namida moroi 245.6
-nan 188.9
-nan 201.6
nandaka 40.11, 215.8
nan de mo nai 41.10, 187.2
nando mo 80.12
nanige naku 261.2
nanigoto 206.10
nanihodo ka no 260.3
nanimono 257.2
naninani 275.13
naniwabushi *262.7
nani yori mo saki ni 191.8

nanka 223.10
nankun jiten 104.11
nanpa *75.3
nanra ka no katachi de 255.7
nansei 105.3
nante 221.12
nan to 161.12
nantoka 178.9
nan toka shite 138.4
nan to naku 229.13
nanuka 27.6
nao no koto 216.1
naosara 282.2
naosu 153.3
narabu 92.9
narasu *261.9, 295.7
narau 31.11
nareai 252.7
narenai 81.3
narikakeru 175.4
nariyuki 231.13
nariyuki makase 231.13
naru 125.9
naru 306.3
narubeku 20.10
naruhodo 161.6
nasakenai 253.9
nasaru 85.2
natsu 156.5
nattoku 211.3
na yori mo jitsu 179.8
naze 111.11
nazoraeru 250.13
nazukeru 69.8, 279.11
ne 304.10
negachibu 300.3
negatte yamanai *211.3
negau 180.8
-nen 9.6
nen'iri 270.6
nenmatsu 89.3
nennen 9.10
nenpai 253.5
nenrei 253.10
neru 20.10
nesshin 161.3
neuchi 284.3
nezumi 126.4
nezuyoi 254.3
nichijō 169.2
ni chinande *279.11
nichiyōbi *19.8
nigekomu *119.3

nigeru 126.2
nigoru 172.12
ni hanshite 216.3
Nihonken 24.3
Nihonshu 155.10
ni itaru made 143.8
ni kagirazu 197.10
nikkan 161.7
nikki *17.1
nikkunēmu 104.9
niku 272.2, 281.12
nikushin 167.8
nikutai 257.13
-nin 1.6
ningen 31.12
ningensei 32.10
ningenteki 190.1
ningyō 86.2
ninjō 248.12
ninshiki 138.3, 166.10
nintei 237.9
ni oite wa 194.5
ni ōjite 198.4
niru 100.8
nisan 99.5
nise 252.5
nishi 73.6, 105.6
ni shiku wa nai 230.3
ni shitagatte 170.8
ni shita tokoro de 291.3
nitchū 42.6
ni tsurete 202.2
niwa 85.5
niwashi 286.1
-ni watatte 250.7
nō *134.5
nō 201.10
nobanashi 239.1
nobasu 275.11, 287.5
noberu 114.4
noboru 13.2, 80.9
nochi 63.7, 204.7
nō-gakkō 159.6
nogareru 302.10
nōgyō 105.10
nohara 154.9, 157.3
nōhitsu 281.10
-no imi de 162.11
nōka 200.4
noki 263.1
nokinami 228.4
nokori 278.5
nokoru *33.8, 81.13, 280.10
nokosu *20.1, 194.3, 261.7

nomi 206.2
nōmin *108.10, 194.7
nominarazu 191.6
nomu *44.2, 149.11
no na no moto de 259.1
nonki 222.2
nōringyō 195.5
nōritsu 243.9
noronoro 70.10
noru *75.3, 161.2
noru 204.3
nōryoku 176.1
nosabaru 272.9
noseru 216.5
nōson 200.7
nōto 70.4, 204.5
nozokikomu 287.6
nozoku 210.4
nozoku 261.6
nozomu 273.9
nukedasu 205.6
nukeme no nai 226.6
nyō 101.7
nyōbō 228.10
nyū 101.7
nyūansu 166.12
nyūgaku 33.12, 35.5, 178.6
nyūgakugo 178.8
nyūsu 78.6

obake 262.6
ōbei 196.5
obieru 293.6
ōbō 304.4
oboe 225.13
oboeru *3.6, *17.13, 76.12
oboete oku 98.1
o-bōsan 120.10
ochiru 286.9
ochitsuita tokoro 162.6
ochitsuku 163.4
odoriko 291.1
odoroku *28.11, *125.10, 177.4
odoru 284.2
o-fuda 261.7
ogamu 262.12
ōgesa *219.7
ōgi *39.2
o-hairi kudasai 1.2
o-hatsu 261.9
ōhi 203.5
oi 167.12

i 9.10
ikakeru 287.4
-inari-san *264.2
i ni 223.3
-inori mōshiageru *87.11
ioi 279.8
isogi 168.2
itamaeru 266.4
-iwai 262.11
jiru 198.4
jōsan 290.12
kage *241.3, 255.6
-kage-sama de *40.11
-kane 17.4
kāsan 27.3
kashii 290.7
kashisa 192.8
kasu 197.8, 240.1
kaze 117.4
kidasu 293.2
kina 9.10, 82.5
konau 132.7
koru 131.11
koru 215.6
kosu 127.1
kotaru 287.7
ku 195.5
ku 283.4, 286.3
ku 106.11
kufukai 286.2
kureru *116.10, 194.3
kurigana 235.2
kuru *26.12, 87.12, 119.4
kuyukashii 274.4
kuyuki *220.1
-kyō -o ageru 262.1
mae 37.4, 81.3
-mairi 264.12
-mamori 264.7
-medetō *43.1
-me ni kakaru 1.10
-me ni kakeru 63.13
-meshimono 277.4
-mi-ashi 277.4
moidasu 24.11
moiokosu 232.11
moitatsu 230.9
moki o oku 218.9
mo ni 48.3
monzuru 250.10
moshiroi *17.7, 63.13
motedōri 228.8
mote genkan 286.2
motte ninjiru 219.13

omou 24.5
omoya *284.4
ōmune 260.7
on 31.1
on 48.11, -o nigoru 172.12
on'ai 248.10
onaji 18.9
onajiku 201.2
o-negai 97.2
o-nēsan 232.4
ongaeshi 256.3
o-nīchan 232.4
onjō 252.8
onjōshugi 197.9
onkeikan 198.3
onna 239.10
onna ippan 239.13
onna no ko 24.10
onsen 291.7
oputimizumu 303.3
ōrai 221.2
ore 212.2
ori 229.9
oriori 229.7
oriru 15.11, 89.7
orooro 158.1
oru 80.13
oru 247.12
osaeru *272.8, 287.5
osamaru 295.9
osameru 132.6
oseji -o tsukau 222.1
oshaberi 274.6
oshi 293.8
oshieru *31.7, 52.1
oshihiromeru 213.3
oshimageru 232.12
oshimai 227.5
oshitsukeru 182.3
oshiuri 233.11
sohiyoseru 264.4
ōshū 228.6
osoi *116.3
osonae 261.10
osoraku *208.4, 274.13
osore 166.1
osoreōi 230.7
osoreru 126.2
osoroshii 182.7
osorubeki 233.2
osowareru 295.2
ossharu 275.13
osu 263.9, 283.13
o-tagai 167.4

o-taku *38.3
oto 228.2
otoko 33.10, -o ageru 250.3
otoko no ko 42.13
otona *252.2, 281.4
otōsan 24.4
otosu 283.3
otōto 174.10
otto 118.11
ou 157.8
ōwarai 155.9
owari *82.6, 93.6, 144.7
oya 80.2
oyabun 252.2
oyagokoro 252.8
oyobosu 209.10
oyobu *113.12, 242.13
oyoso 241.13
ōyoso 172.6
ōyuki 70.8
ōzappa 247.4
ōzei 161.10

pāmanento enpuroimento 197.1
pan 224.6
pāsento 64.10
pātī 71.7
pēji 19.6
pēpābakku 95.2
peten ni kakeru 218.4
pisutoru 191.9
pon 228.2
puran 11.3
purezento 87.11
puroretaria 270.9

-ra *37.4, 191.11
raigetsu 18.11, -sōsō 22.12
rainen 43.9
raishinshi 149.6
rajio 262.7
raku 241.8
rakugo 262.7
ran 286.8
rankan 286.5
ran'yō 173.10, 212.4
rasshu awā 161.10
rei -o ageru 50.12
reigai 200.7
reigen 249.5
reinen 87.4
reiraku 265.5

reisei 186.11
reizoku 185.7
rekishi *56.2
rekishi *191.8
rekishi jidai 106.3
rekishimono 262.8
ren *283.8
ren'ai 206.5
renchū 83.3, 215.6
renjū 83.3, 215.6
renraku 229.5
rensai 290.5
retsu 105.3
riaritī 171.3
riarizumu 203.11
riaru 171.9
rieki 232.13
rigaku 146.11
rihi 213.9
rikai 179.12
rikoshugi 256.2
rikuriēshon 162.11
rikutsu -no tatanai 216.13,
  -nuki ni 248.8
rimen 213.10
ringyō 194.10
rinji 198.4
rinkaku 294.7
rinriteki 304.10
rinsen 284.3
rippa *126.5, 213.8
rirē 116.8
rirekisho *176.9
riron 204.6
risōteki 179.11
ritsu 177.3
riyō 94.7, 105.11
riyū 118.10
rōbashin 273.9
rōdōsha 198.7
rōhi 245.11
rōjin 76.8
rojiura 228.4
rōka 294.9
rokujūyosai 230.11
roku na 220.6
rōmaji 93.5
romanchishizumu 299.9
romanha *210.1
-ron 179.1
rongo 167.6
ronjisaru 245.3
ronrigaku 224.10
ronshō 258.8

rōryoku 224.6
rui 241.12
ruiji 260.8
ryakushite 245.8
ryakusu 275.6
-ryō *109.5, 249.4
ryōgawa 283.5
ryōkin 149.7
ryokō *21.5, *25.8, 85.2,
  263.6, 264.11
ryōrinin 225.13
ryōriya 284.6
ryōsha 209.5
ryōshin *82.6, 262.10
ryōshin 209.4
-ryū 226.5
-ryū 281.8
ryūdōsei 198.9
ryūgaku 186.3
ryūkōka 289.10
ryūnyū 202.2
ryūshutsu 201.5

sa 236.8
sabishii 213.10
sadamaru 246.3
sadameru 132.3
saegiru 224.4
sagasu 244.10
sageru 230.4
sagi *218.3
sagi *282.11
-sai 18.8, 230.11
saibansho 229.7
saichū 298.12
saidai 183.5
saifu 265.13
saigo 124.7, 126.5
saijō 226.4
saikin 91.7
saishin 176.6
saisho 125.6
saishūkan 282.4
saiyō 131.13, 197.6, 198.4
saizen 238.7
sakai 297.4
sakana 65.10
sakan na 299.7
sakan ni 241.4
sakazuki 222.8
sake 149.12
sakebu 228.12
sakeru 192.10

sakeru 220.3
saki 25.6, 191.8, 193.2
sakizaki 264.11
sakka 272.2
sakki 24.9
sakoku *137.5
sakuhin 120.12
sakuin 97.13
sakuji 57.11
sakumotsu 109.2
sakura 293.5
sakusha 126.9
sama *27.8
samatageru 207.9
samui *26.6, 64.6
samuke 295.3
samurai 32.1
samusa no natsu 158.1
sanbutsu 273.5
sangaidate 284.9
sangyōbetsu daikumiai 198.9
sanka 182.5
sankeisha 264.3
sankōsho 205.11
sanmenkiji 188.9
sanpai 263.12
sanpatsuteki 297.3
sanpo 19.4
sanrin 10.2
sansei 222.3
santa maria 141.9
sara ni 246.3
sararīman 161.4
sasaeru 237.8
sasayaka 283.5
sashikakeru 286.6
sashikomu 139.6
sashitsukae *211.12, 225.12
sassoku 93.9
sasuga 278.3
sate 237.7
satosu 253.3
-satsu *19.12, 290.6
satsuei 264.6
sawagimawaru 217.11
sawagu 228.10
sayō 209.1
sayonara 40.6
sayū 66.1
sazukaru 263.11
sazukeru 132.6
se 287.13
segare 261.11
sei 35.8

-sei 32.10
-sei 43.8
seibo 279.9
seichō 298.4
seichū 225.10
seido 132.3
seifu 125.12
seigen 241.2
seigi 229.11
seihi 180.13
seihō 113.2
seihōkei 131.7
seiji 110.13, 304.3
seijin 259.1
seijitsu 179.5
seijō 257.6
seika 299.5
seikaku 176.10
seikaku 200.4
seikatsu 30.13, 108.6,
  -o okuru 119.4
seikatsunan 188.9
seiken 183.13
seiki *48.4, 82.4
seikō 191.6
seimei 207.2
seimon 283.4
seiri 268.2
seiritsu 198.10
seiryoku 304.1
seisaku 137.5
seisan 194.10
seisanbutsu 195.6
seisangaku 195.4
seiseki 181.7
seishi 273.4
seishin 197.9
seishinteki 188.9
seisho 257.4
seisuru 286.13
seito 263.7
seitō seiji 304.3
seiyō *32.3, 69.6
seizei 236.13
sejō 229.8
sekai 106.4
seken 228.13
sekentei 248.4
sekijūji 289.11
sekinin 238.13
sekijō 283.6
sekkaku *76.11, 285.6
sekkyokuteki 263.12
semai 105.8

semeru 305.4
semi 293.5
seminā 39.5
sen *129.1
sen -ni sotte 231.6
senaka 80.11
senchimentarizumu 289.9
senchō 75.6
sengen 119.7
sengetsu 42.13
sengo *95.4, 182.2
sen'in 75.4
senjutsu 232.9, 233.12
senkusha 297.6
senkyo *33.13
senman 9.11
senmon 164.3
senmonteki 162.6
sennen 179.2
sensei 26.3, -o suru 26.3
sensei 232.12
senseshon 206.3
senshū *38.11
sensō 111.10
sentaku 238.2
senzen *95.5, 177.6
senzo 255.9
seou *80.9
serifu 205.1
seron 253.5
sēru 86.1
sesekomashii 252.7
seseragi 286.10
sesshoku 221.11
sessuru 284.6
sētā 1.13
setsu 268.13
setsubō 211.2
setsubun 264.3
setsumei *18.12, 48.13
setsumon 253.11
setsuwa 81.12
settei 259.2
sewa 300.8
-sha 92.7
shagamu 293.3
shakai 162.6, 221.4
shakkin 219.8
shaku 222.9
shamisen 230.4
shashin 26.12
shi 189.10
shi 237.2
-shi 26.3

-shi 69.4
-shi 228.6
shian 230.3
shibai 237.12
shibaraku *45.2, *71.2,
  286.10
shibashiba 150.2
shichi -ni ireru 205.11
shichō 208.7
shida 294.9
shidai ni 204.5
shidōsha 183.12
shigeki 221.7
shigeru 286.7
shigo 159.2, 185.5
shigo 295.3
shigo nin 9.2
shigoto *41.8, 162.13
shihai 195.9
shihō 220.13
shihonkateki 194.5
shihonshugi 194.2
shiite ieba 187.5
shijimoji *57.13
shijin 166.7
shijū 92.5, 226.5
shikai 167.5
shikaku 281.7
shikamo 105.8, 176.2
shikari 232.4
shikaru 226.4
shikaru ni 274.12
shikashi 221.8
shikata ga nai *80.9, 163.5
shiken *19.9, 203.4
shiki -o ageru 264.9
shiki 295.3
-shiki 245.4
shikiishi 266.2
shikiri ni *271.6, 286.13
shikishi 280.6
shikkari 27.3
shikō 208.8
shima 75.4
shimaguni 105.2
shimai 174.9
shimatsu 269.5
shimeppoi 294.6
shimeru 200.6
shimesu 58.7
shimetsu 233.9
shimijimi 189.8
shimikomu 263.11
shimin 254.10

shimojochū *284.12
shinayaka 281.11
shinbun 38.13
shinbutsu 262.8
shingi 231.2
shingikai 231.2
shinja 141.4, 259.8
shinjiru 31.13, 257.3
shinjitai 54.8
shinjō 257.1
shinjū 268.4
shinkeishitsu 274.10
shinkeisuijaku 220.7
shinkō 259.9
shinkonryokō 264.11
shinpai 166.3
shinpen 290.9
shinpo 138.4
shinrai 185.10
shinri 123.10
shinri 188.2
shinrigaku 38.13
shinrui 248.6
shinsei *224.6
shinshiki 264.8
shinshisōka 206.9
shinshū 306.6
shintai 220.10
shinu 121.1
shinzuru 257.3
shippai 191.10
shirabe 107.3
shiraberu 96.6
shirase 186.4
shirauo *10.13
shirazushirazu 229.4
shirewataru *81.9
shiriai 205.10
shiritsu 25.13
shiroi 1.13
shirōtokangae 281.10
shiru 40.6
shirushi 58.5
shirusu 280.6
shisai 279.7
shiseikatsu 207.2
shishi 83.8
shishōsetsu 207.5
shisō 31.3
shita 8.3
shitabataraki 215.7
shitagatte *151.2, 170.8,
  217.8
shitagau 200.4

shitai 192.11
shitamachi 10.10
shitashimi 186.3
shitashimu 262.3
shitauke kōba 198.5
shitsubō 304.5
shitsugyōsha 201.13
shitsuke 302.8
shitsukeru 262.13
shitsumon *17.11, 96.2
shitsurei nagara 216.7
shiyō 95.1
shiyōnin 173.7
shiyū 131.13
shizen 131.9
shizuka *9.9, 228.8
shīzun 117.7
sho 283.11
shō 20.4
shō 175.7
shō 241.11
shōdo 233.12
shōdō 217.4
shōdo senjutsu 233.12
shōgakkō *29.7, 43.8
shō ga nai 221.1
shōgatsu 147.6
shōgyō 194.12
shōhin 270.3
shōjiki 289.2
shōjiru 242.12
shōkeimoji 56.9
shoki 143.8
shōkin 268.12
shokku 206.8
shōko 258.13
shokoku 137.5
shoku 201.8
shokuba 201.9
shokudō *71.2
shokugyō 200.11
shōkyū 198.3
shomin 232.12
shomotsu 162.6
shonen 126.13
shōnibyō 271.2
shōnin 252.11
shōrai 93.2
shori 238.8
shosaku 237.13
shōsan 257.13
shosei 174.1
shoseiron 268.10
shōsetsu 120.11

shōshō 20.2
shōsoku 280.2
shōsū 297.2
shotai 281.13
shotchū 289.13
shōtotsu shiau 297.12
shōwindō 89.8
shoyūbutsu 236.9
shu 250.8
-shu 279.5
-shū 105.5
-shū 116.4
shūchi 230.2
shuchō 125.13
shūchō 75.7
shūchū 268.9
shudan 169.7
shūdan 250.12
shufu 200.13
shūgaku ryokō 263.6
shugi 194.2, 197.9, 234.4,
  244.9
shūgōtai 250.9
shugyō 119.4
shūgyō jindō 194.8
shuhō 280.12
shūi 242.5
shūjaku 235.3
shujin 185.9
shūjin 229.7
shujinkō 188.7
shujinmochi 270.10
shūju 131.12
shūka 282.3
shūkaidō *286.9
shūkan 80.3
-shūkan 116.4
shūkan zasshi 161.3
shuken 183.4
shūkyō 259.9
shunga *230.8
shunkan 230.8
shunpon *230.8
shuppan 204.11
shuppan 266.10
shuppatsu 260.8
shūrai *145.2
shurui *48.2, 150.1
shuryū 207.8
shūsen 268.12
shushō 179.2
shūshū 297.13
shusshin 206.5
shūtoku 177.6

shūtome 249.3
shu to shite 52.8
sō 170.7
soba 19.4
sōchō 89.5
sodateru 63.8
sodatsu *159.5, 302.12
sofu 282.10
sōgi *124.4
sōgo 259.12
soitsu 223.3
sōkaku 102.5
sō ka to itte 105.13
sokkuri 268.13
soko 182.12
soko 212.5
sokode 149.11
sokojikara 294.12
sokudo 143.5
son 197.12
sonaeru 261.9
sonawaru 278.2
sonkei 173.8
sono hen wa 211.8
sonomono 182.10
sonota 152.2
sono uchi 6.10
sonshō 253.1
sonzai 138.13
sōō 249.6
sora 265.7
sore mitamae 225.6
soretomo 238.4
sore wa sō to 42.11
sorezore 65.6
sōritsu 204.7
soroi 263.1
sōrō to shite *266.7
sorotte 220.7
sōryō 300.7
soshiki 197.11
sōshiki 185.3
soshikidateru 209.8
soshikika 144.3
soshite 106.11
soshō 157.11
sōsho *51.8
sōsō 22.12
sosogu 285.9
sō suru to 4.8
soto 29.12
sōtō 151.13
sotsugyō 203.3
sotsugyōsei 177.5

sotto 77.3
sou 231.6
sozō 267.4
sōzō 56.11
sū- 192.13
-sū 102.5
subarashii 257.7
subete 98.6
sudare 228.4
sude ni 231.3
sue 58.6
sugata 186.11
sugi 283.4
-sugi 90.6
sugikawa 283.7
sugiru 89.11, 237.1, 274.6
sugisaru 145.7
sugosu 85.4
sugu *65.13, 149.2
sugureru 277.9
suiei 191.6
suijaku 220.7
suijun 178.4
suiki 295.8
suiron 183.9
suiryō 277.7
suiryoku hatsuden 106.9
suiso 269.9
suisoku 234.8
suiyōbi *20.9
suji 290.2
sūji 253.13
sūkagetsu 192.13
sukanai 212.2
sukete mieru 296.1
suketogutsu 86.3
suki 63.7
sukī 71.6
sukikirai 237.3
sukima 277.8
sukkari 26.7
sukoburu 226.3
sukoshi 19.4
sukunai 10.2
sukunakutomo 166.12
sukuu 268.9
sumashite 230.8
sumasu 228.12
sumi 264.2
sumimasen 211.8
suminagashi 280.13
sumu *33.12, *123.7, 140.10, 151.8
sumu 139.2

-sun 220.13
sunawachi *48.2, 174.6
superingu 54.10
supōtsu 161.3
sura 150.4
surikireru 265.6
suru to 215.5
sushi 83.8
suso 293.7
susu 83.8
susumeru *18.3, 231.6
susumu 137.13
susunde 221.11
sutairu 95.5
sutareru *144.2, 175.9
suteru *80.3, 180.4
suzushii 228.3

ta 131.4
ta 145.6, 211.11
taba 157.8
tabako 22.10
tabakoire 230.4
taberu *83.10, 156.11, 301.5
tabi 161.12
tabitabi 179.8
tabō 95.11
tabun 86.6
tabun ni 253.11
-tachi 76.9, 189.11
tachiba 186.11
tachimachi 144.7
tachiyoru 263.8
tachiyuku 217.2
tada *91.9, 173.10
tada hitotsu 69.6
tadaima 220.9
tadashi *180.13, 279.5
tadashii 131.5
tadayou 278.5
taeru 230.1
taezu 228.3
tagai ni *144.12, 167.4
tagui 241.12
tahō 143.4
tai 219.7
taiboku 10.4
taidasei 221.7
taido 167.11
taigensōgo 241.9
taigun 113.3
taihen *9.4, 56.4

taijinteki 254.7
taikei 209.6
taiken 205.12
taiko 263.2
tainai 257.12
taipuraitā 70.5
tairiku 105.3
tairō 230.6
taisen *33.12
taisetsu 236.7
taishita 119.12
taishō 170.13
taishō 185.3
taishū 270.13
taisuru 139.5, 211.7
taitei *102.7, 188.11
takai 31.2
takami 293.11
takara -no mochikusare
285.7
takasugiru 86.4
take 283.5
taki 286.9
takigi *128.5
takumi ni 205.2
takusan *19.5, 70.2, 281.4
tamae 220.5
-tamaeru *266.4
tamagogata 295.10
tamaranai 291.11
tame *9.13, 133.5
tameike *131.6
tameru 149.12
tamotsu 179.10
tan- 145.6
-tan 132.2
tana 286.6
tanen 198.2
tango 277.1
tan'i 301.13
tanin 211.12
tanjōbi *18.8
tankikan ni 145.6
tankōbon 162.1
tankyū 260.9
tan ni 208.2, 212.6
tannin suru *215.2
tanomu *75.7, 149.5
tanoshii 163.6
tanoshimu 263.3
tansei 286.1
tappuri 281.12
tare *101.6
tariru 149.5, 175.11

tarumi 303.11
tashika 17.13
tashikameru 169.6
tashika na 49.4
tashō 11.11
tassuru 191.6
tasū 174.13, 194.12
tasuke -o motomeru 75.4
tasukeru *33.2, 200.8
tatakau 111.7
tatakinaosu 299.4
tatakitsukeru 266.2
tatande shimau *212.2
tatemae 246.10
tatemasu 284.9
tateru 29.13, 285.5, 295.10
tatoe 197.6
tatoeba *18.10, 49.6
tatsu 25.5, 76.11, 216.3
tatsu 234.6
tatsumi *285.5
tatta 215.5
tayoru 201.12
tazuneru 81.3, 125.3
tazusawaru 270.11
te 24.3, -ni ireru 192.3,
-o awaseru 262.11, -o
hirogeru 58.7, -o toriau
126.6
tegami *24.1, 71.12, -o
dasu 26.5
tegotae 293.11
teido 123.13, 143.10, 194.8
teigi 245.11
teikokushugi 234.4
teikyū 218.5
teinei *19.7, 276.5
teinen 197.4
teisei 275.1
tekisuru 221.10
tekisuto 79.2
tekitō 197.7
temae 255.1
ten 32.5
ten 106.6, 203.8
tenarai 285.7
ten'in 253.3
te-ni-o-ha 274.9
tenjō *83.10
tenkeiteki 196.2
tenki 69.4
tenmei 306.4
tennō 111.4
tennōke 132.1

tenrankai 241.13
tenshi-sama 303.13
tentō *234.5
teppai 180.4
tera 31.5
terakoya *31.6
terebi 86.13, 165.3
terefonbukku 154.8
tesuto 29.6
tetsudō 208.9
tetteiteki 269.8
to 123.5
-tō 186.10
tōan 203.7
tobi *284.2
tobidasu 286.13
tobikomu 293.7
tobioriru 191.11
tobu 282.9
tōbun *69.3
tochi 108.2, 132.1
tochi no ki *284.1
tochū *69.12, 125.10
todoku 149.9
togameru 189.7
togeru 143.10
tōgyo 238.3
tōhashin *213.9
Tōhō 260.8
toi 256.1
tōi *75.13, 112.11
tōitsu kokka 110.3
to iu no wa 216.2
tōji 119.2
tojikomeru 250.3
tōjitsu 228.6
tōka 2.7, 3.7
tokai 106.11
tokaku no koto 281.7
tokei -o susumeru 18.3
tōkei 253.6
tokidoki *22.1, 102.4
toki ni wa 66.3
tokoro 40.2
tokoro de 4.3
tokorodokoro 131.6
tokoro ga 49.12
tokoya 167.11
toku 258.3
tōku 294.2
tokubetsu 137.9
tokuchō 106.3, 238.8
tokugi 212.9
tokugishin 218.3

tokuhon 52.1
toku ni 145.4
tokushoku 110.2
tokushu 282.1
tokutei 237.5
tomaru *24.8, 205.10, 293.7
tomeru 22.6, 141.2, 258.1
tomodachi *9.2, 277.3
tomokaku 272.3
tomonau 220.11, 279.5
tomo ni 107.7
tonari *2.1, 284.9
tonikaku *163.3, 193.1
tōraimono 261.10
toreru 10.13
tori 57.7
tōri *24.8
toriageru 261.3
toriatsukau 186.12
toriau 126.6
toridasu 264.6
toridori 254.9
toriireru 135.11, 168.2
tōrikakaru 295.7
torikeshi 215.7
torimaku 212.7
tori mo naosazu 211.13
tōri ni 48.13
torinokeru 126.3
toriyoseru 280.12
toru *26.13, *71.12, *80.5, *109.2, *126.6, 149.7, 216.13
tōru 123.7, 131.3
toshi 18.7, 185.3, 277.4, -o toru 80.5
-toshi 42.5
toshokan *69.10
tōsō 297.13
tōsu 113.2
tōkei 191.6
totemo 5.9, 163.4
tōtō 227.5
totsugu *279.13
otsuzen *224.4
tou 180.6
oyakaku 230.7
tōyō 277.13
tōyō kanji *53.9, 92.4
tōza 239.6
ozasu 283.8
tōzen 178.10
tsubo 192.5
tsubureru 217.10

tsubusu 163.2
tsubuyaku 293.8
tsuchi 267.11
tsuchi-hen 103.13
tsugeru 144.7
tsugi *50.12, 99.1
tsugitsugi 186.8
tsugō *39.10, -ga ii 66.2, ga warui *1.4
tsugu *221.13
tsui 166.10
tsuide nagara 275.6
tsui ni *123.6, 216.9
tsuitachi 18.9
tsuite iku 86.2
tsuizui 231.13
tsūjiru 75.12
tsukaeru 185.6
tsukaiwake 274.9
tsukamaru 293.13
tsukamu 293.8
tsukareru *20.2, 85.9
tsukau 48.2, 222.1
tsukekuwaeru 223.13
tsukeru 4.5, 43.3, 221.3, 276.3
tsuki 45.3, 63.11
-tsuki 6.7
tsukiai 255.1, 285.1
tsukideru 139.2
tsūkin 229.6
tsukiyama 287.1
tsukiyo 293.3
tsuku 19.3
tsuku 75.6
tsuku 223.5, 263.9, 280.5
tsukuri 98.7
tsukuridasu 171.8
tsukurinaosu 233.10
tsukuritsuke 261.6
tsukuru *11.4, 56.3, 303.13
tsukusu *159.6, 306.4
tsukuzuku 268.1
tsuma 118.13
tsumabiraka *279.8
tsumaranai 157.12
tsumari 57.8
tsumetai *87.5
tsumi 197.8
tsunagari 246.4
tsunagaru 249.8
tsūnen 206.6
tsune ni 111.4
tsureru 80.3, 202.2

tsuriai 247.1
tsurukame *154.9
tsutaeru 76.2, 179.4, 206.11
tsutawaru 278.6, 280.9
tsūyō 278.3
tsuyoi 24.5
tsuyosugiru 113.8
tsuyu 228.3
tsuzukeru 113.1
tsuzuku *69.4, 110.5

uba *280.11, 284.12
ubau 244.6
uchi *9.4, 85.6
uchi 19.10, 167.5
uchi *274.13
uchikatsu 221.7
ue 126.10
uetsukeru 252.7
ugokasu 72.4, 184.1, 210.3
ugoki *57.10
uguisujō 264.5
ujigami 262.10
ujiko 262.13
ukaberu 261.12
ukeru 113.1, 290.6
uketoru *24.2, 182.6
uketsugu 300.8
ukime *217.10
ukiyoe *128.10, 230.4
ukiyoeshi 230.5
uma *116.6
umai 189.10
umarekawaru 299.5
umareochiru 167.6
umareru 24.3
umi 31.2
umidasu 237.1
umi-no-haha 279.5
umu 208.9
undō 170.2
unmei 265.6
uo 284.2
urayama 295.12
urazuke 247.7
ureru *147.7, 161.8
uru *94.8
uru 138.4
-uru 145.6
ushi 220.3
ushinau *108.2, 191.6
ushiro 45.3, 101.13

usuppera 272.11
usuwarai *223.12
uta 189.6, 280.5
utagau 176.8
utsu 135.6, 149.6, 149.7
utsukushii *10.6, 127.2
utsuru 120.10
utsushikaeru 205.2
uwaru 283.5
uyauyashii 280.10
uzumeru *139.1

wadai *62.3, 71.5
waei jiten 92.13
waga kuni 173.4
wagamama *213.4
wagaya 228.5
waka 282.2
wakai *33.1
wakamono 80.5
wakareru 110.4, 118.11
wakarewakare 187.4
wakaru 4.4
wake 280.5
wakeataeru 132.3
wake ni ikanai 216.10
wakeru 8.6, 66.1
waraibanashi 150.1
warau 156.9
ware 213.11
wareme *64.4
ware nagara 229.1
wareware 125.12
-wari 253.10
waribiki 253.13
warui *1.4, 170.5, 177.11,
   255.1
warukuchi 215.3
wasei 241.7
wasshi 275.10
wasureru 118.4
watakushi 18.2, -domo 217.5
watarioetaru 279.4
watasu 75.5
waza to 286.6

yaban 185.8
yaburu 197.12
yaeyamabuki 286.9
yagate 126.5
yahari 19.1
yakamashii 218.2

yaki 294.6
yaku -ni tatanai 76.11
yaku 107.3
yakudateru 234.7
yakuhin 191.12
yakume -ni mawaru 268.1
yakusoku 244.11, 247.4
yakuwari 202.5
yama 9.8
yamamichi 80.11
yamanobori 163.1
yama-no-te 131.2
yameru 17.4, 197.8
yamu 295.2
yamu o enu 270.11
yane *64.2
yarihajimeru 76.13
yaru 221.6, 226.10
yasai 156.11
yasashii 2.13
yashiki 282.10
yashinau 302.4
yashoku 295.8
yasui 86.4
-yasui 244.8
yasumeru 42.9
yasumi 71.8
yasumu 42.10
yato *294.10
yatou 197.7
yatsu 212.2
yatte iku 145.3
yatte kuru 76.8
yatte shimau 148.6
yattsu 8.3, 43.8
yattsukeru 212.3
yaya 259.9
yo 229.12
-yo 280.11
yō 222.4
yō 223.8
yōbi *13.2, 17.2, 86.1
yobinarawasu 282.10
yobiyoseru 77.3
yobu 75.9
yochi *223.4
yōchi 234.10
yōchien 263.3
yōdō 279.9
yōgo 95.5, 245.11
yōhō 151.1
yohodo 218.5
yoi 63.7, 92.3, 224.2
yōi 144.11

yokka 19.8
yoko 283.13
yokomuke 294.2
yoku 156.7
-yoku 161.12
yokubō 189.12
yoku irasshaimashita 1.2
yokujitsu 76.7
yokunen 205.5
yokuseiteki 298.1
yōkyū 245.11
yome 249.3
yomeiri 200.9
yomiasaru 204.4
yomikata 48.11
yomikudasu 281.2
yomioeru 282.4
yomiowari haberite 279.2
yomu *3.1, 232.3
yo no naka 219.6
yoridokoro 305.7
yorokobu 126.6
yoroshiku 2.9
yoru *23.3, 80.10
yoru 110.3, 280.12
yoru 287.1
yoseru 286.8
yōshi *70.5
yoshiashi 237.5
yoshi de aru 8.10, 20.8
yōshu 155.10
yōso 247.3
yōsō 264.9
yosu 155.8, 291.6
yōsu 125.2
yōsuru ni 208.12
yotei 203.2
yotsuyu 294.3
yottsu 14.5
you *210.1
yowai 270.12
yowami 271.1
yowamushi 223.5
yōyaku 228.3
yōyō 25.1
yoyū *220.5, 269.3
yūbinkyoku 265.1
yūdōteki 253.12
yue 172.9
yūgata 19.3
yuiitsu 238.2
yuiitsu muni 183.7
yuisho 285.4
yūi tabō 221.3

yūjin 167.5
yūjō 185.10
yukai 268.12
yūkaku 205.6
yukata 263.1
yuki *26.7, 87.5
yūki 241.10
yukkuri 44.3
yūmei *41.1, 82.1
yunyū *48.5, 113.2
yūran 264.4
yurushi 125.12
yurusu *118.12
yūryo 299.3
yūshoku 90.13
yūshū 178.3
yushutsu-nyū 140.6
yusō 115.6
yūsui 286.2
yuttari 284.13
yūutsu *266.8, 267.3
yuzuru 284.8

zadankai 297.1
zai 290.9
zaiaku 233.8
zaigakuchū 203.3
zaisan 167.1
zangyaku 273.4
zankin 83.2
zanson 242.11
-zaru o enai 180.10
zashiki 286.3
zasshi *52.2, 161.3, 164.2
zatto 231.2
zehi *39.2, 86.11
zehitomo 284.10
zen- 176.11
zen- 194.3
Zen 118.7
zen'aku 203.6
zenbu 92.11
zenbun 182.3
zen'i 258.5
zenkoku 40.13
zenkokumin 176.11
zenmen 295.8
zennen 204.7
zenpan 209.10
zenryoku 268.9
zensha 101.5
Zen-shū *124.4
zentai 41.4

zentaishugi 302.11
zentei 169.3
zenzen 75.13
zettai 118.13
-zō 126.7, 169.3
zōen 285.13
zōgen 254.1
zōka 249.5
zokujin 213.5
zoku ni 241.11
zokusuru *165.6, 236.10
zonjiru *2.4
zonjō suru 280.11
-zu 56.5
zubon 20.4
zuibun *222.2
zushi 58.13
zutto 25.8, 41.8